Intuitive Being

Intuitive Being

Connect with Spirit, Find Your Center, and Choose an Intentional Life

JILL WILLARD

HARPER**ELIXIR**

An Imprint of HarperCollins*Publishers*

HARPER**ELIXIR**

HarperCollins books may be purchased for educational, business,
or sales promotional use. For information, please email the Special
Markets Department at SPsales@harpercollins.com.

FIRST EDITION

Designed by Janet M. Evans

Library of Congress Cataloging-in-Publication Data is available
upon request.

ISBN 978–0–06–243654–2

16 17 18 19 20   RRD   10 9 8 7 6 5 4 3 2 1

To All.

CONTENTS

INTRODUCTION

As a broadcaster, my husband loves to share a good story. One of his favorites to tell is the story of our four-month ultrasound appointment during my second pregnancy. We were seeing a doctor in a posh, state-of-the-art office in Beverly Hills, California, where we would "officially" find out the gender of our nugget, who we had already named Ella James. "Your baby is not cooperating!" the doctor joked as he moved the ultrasound wand over my round belly while staring at a screen. He pressed down a little firmer, then exclaimed, "*Ah*! Looks like you are having another boy!"

My husband looked at me very, very surprised. He knew I had intuited we were having a girl and that the information that came through to me intuitively was simply never wrong. When intuition spoke, it spoke . . . and, by that point in my life, I had learned to listen. This moment was like many before, when my poor husband looked at me as I sat quietly, smiling lightly while I waited for the truth to reveal itself.

Maybe it was because of the quiet that had settled over the room, but for whatever reason (maybe *his* intuition), the doctor continued to probe and search, despite the fact that he had already "determined" the gender of our baby. "*Ah*!" he said again a few seconds later. "Nope . . . you are having a girl!"

I have been in touch with my intuition for as long as I can remember. When I was a very young child, my family lived overseas in Europe. Many of my earliest memories involved looking up and listening to conversations that adults were having while we walked on century-old cobblestone streets. Despite the fact that we were living abroad, I spoke English, and I did not verbally understand the German and French conversations the adults were having at first. What I began to understand was that I was able to derive information about these strangers despite our lack of verbal communication. I somehow knew what had happened, what was happening, and at times what was about to happen as well as how they were feeling and doing. As a child, I interpreted this as the sky or cobblestones around us talking to me, giving me information. As an adult, I understand that my intuition has been engaged since a young age, and it's made life more rewarding (and understandable) ever since.

Intuition is a knowing. A deep, clear one. Some call it wisdom in truth, and some call it divinity at its finest. Intuition is simultaneously completely magical and exceptionally practical. It is both not of this world and yet centered completely within each and every one of us. Intuition *empowers* us to know ourselves and our body like no one else can. It empowers us to know others. Being intuitive can be one of the greatest joys in life; it keeps life rich and unexpected. It keeps us completely in the now.

In the pages that follow, we will walk through a step-by-step process that will help you hone your intuition and make it easier for you to hear, listen, understand, and connect with. We will look at how and why intuition works, based both on my own lifelong experience with it and through information that I have been given in the decade I have officially been doing intuitive readings for clients. Yet, at the same time, part of the magic of intuition is that it's not completely tangible or explainable. It's just something that *is*. And a stellar trusted relationship can be born once we personally experience this. I feel this is one of the most beautiful parts of our intuitive experience.

We have lived in a research-based world for a long time, one where many people pooh-pooh ideas that cannot be proven empirically (yet). But, the true fact is, even the most scientific and logical person has experienced intuition at work, even if it's something she or he is completely unable to explain. Intuition comes in both big and small ways. I would guess that you have at least one wondrous example of intuition in your own life already. There are also many small, regular occurrences of intuition that occur on a daily basis, which we are often not even aware of. Intuition is at work in those little moments like when we call a friend to check in, only to find out they were in need of a little love, or when we get a tug that we should leave for work a bit earlier than usual, only to find there's a traffic delay and we actually needed that extra time.

Although the intention of this book is to provide you with tools to wrangle your intuition and make it easier to access, it's also important to understand that you are already intuitive. We all are. It's something that's built into each and every one of us. We might think of our intuition like our biceps. We all have them, and we all use them on a regular day-to-day basis. Some of us just spend more time stretching and strengthening them.

Strengthening your intuition will change your life. Our intuition is that part of us that already has the answers. When we listen to it, intuition will guide us along the life path that will be the most fulfilling and increasingly joyful. The positive ways in which intuition can transform our life are endless—physically, relationally, financially, intellectually, and even professionally. Not only does intuition help unlock all these doors, but also, as we walk through the process that will lead to this enhanced intuition, we will inherently enrich our life physically, intellectually, emotionally, and spiritually. The whole process is one of the strongest examples of the beautiful, positive design of this universe we live in.

To let our intuition ring through more clearly, we often must first shed the emotional and old layers of our life that cover (not covet) this voice of knowing. Bettering our intuition also inherently fine-tunes and increases the levels of health and harmony in our life. Activating our intuition allows us to understand why we hold on to certain memories while it simultaneously adds more richness and meaning to our current life experience. This combination offers both personal and collective healing—healing that can better our life and even influence our DNA.

It's a big promise, I know. But that's the beauty of intuition—once you unlock it, everything becomes possible.

1

WHAT IS INTUITION?

Let's start at the very beginning. What is intuition? Put in its simplest terms, intuition is a knowing. But it's a different kind of knowing than the purely physical or mental, academic knowledge we tend to focus on in the Western world. Intuition also draws upon the creative side of the mind— that part of the mind that is connected to all of creation. This is also known as the feminine or being side (or aspect) of our intellect. Unlike the more linear, logical part of the mind, intuition sees the wholeness of a situation or moment in time rather than one side or analytical perspective of it. Intuition is a knowing and wisdom that flows through us. It is an inner voice that, in order to hear it, we must quiet the mind.

In my experience, one of the biggest hurdles to accessing our intuition is *believing* that it exists and giving credence to those little nudges, signs, and insights that seem to come without logical explanation. Once we accept intuition as fact and begin to use it as a compass to guide us through life, its existence and its power are inescapable. And we gain astounding facts to prove its worth.

Intuition comes in many forms—it can roar in like a tornado (like when you have a strong and sudden feeling that you shouldn't follow through with plans for no apparent reason, only to find out that you avoided a negative or dangerous situation) or arrive as a slight whisper (like when a friend you've lost contact with pops into your head, then calls later that same day). These can be classified as the loud or quiet knocks. Intuition may involve synchronicity—when we see some sign that echoes a thought we were just having or speaks clearly to an issue at hand. It can even involve mediumship, which is essentially being attuned to the presence of those who have passed. Whether the repercussions are big or small, intuition can serve as a homing device through life that makes it easier for us to stay on a positive or north-bound path. It ensures that we're always moving forward. We can even think of it as a fun (yes, fun) walkie-talkie with the universe.

Depending upon how we look at the world, we may believe that intuition comes from an outside source that is larger than us—that it is a sort of universal knowing or guidance system. Or we may believe that it comes from within us, from a quiet, center space that remains strong, stable, and untouched even in the midst of the chaos of our daily lives. It can be both of these things. Another possible way to look at intuition is as the integration of what is within us and what is outside of us—that we are all connected in one and the same energy, a form of being within and without at once.

Intuition merges tangible seeing (or the overly trained masculine or linear side of us) with subtle being (the under-recognized feminine or more circular side of us that is open to receiving the subtle information that exists within and emanates from everyone and everything around us) in the present moment. Intuition can be visualized as the personification of a single entity of energy that comprises and includes everything and everyone. Or it can be visualized as the space or air between two trees. To connect with our intuition, it is wise to align ourselves with and listen to the collective, to nature, or, as some may call it, the universe.

Intuition can do much more than bring benefits to any of us, although it certainly does that. The journey to connecting with our intuition can reap just as many, if not more, rewards as the final destination of attunement. When we are in touch with our intuitive nature, we are flowing with (and within) the world and our own lives as they are, in their most natural and fruitful state. Intuition connects all beings, and it works for the good of us all when used with this intention. The more people on this earth who are aligned with intuition, the better off we can become. If we lived in a world where everyone wholly listened to, trusted, and bravely followed through with intuition, there would be absolutely no war or violence. We would be out of the fight-or-flight part of our mind that so dominates our actions today. If we paired an open intuition with an open heart, dishonesty and cheating would be replaced with honesty, bravery, and consciousness. We would be out of our overly used warrior or competitor part of the mind. The concept of lack or not being enough would have an opportunity to vanish.

Acting in the interest of ourselves as individuals and in the interest of the collective can dovetail into the same notion when a trust is formed with our intuition, our deep inherent wisdom. Understanding wholly that there is *enough* and what is lacking is what we are not bringing forth could help unmute the part of the mind (and life experience) that suffers from feelings of loneliness and isolation. Our intuition allows us to tap into a higher form of intelligence and guidance that is always at work in the background (where most of us keep it), doing its very best to steer us in the right (or forward) direction—in the direction that is the most connective and compassionate, that works in wholeness.

Before we veer into the ethereal, though, it is important to understand that, ultimately, intuition is a grounding device. Listening to our intuition does not suggest that we throw all rational thought into the wind. Intuition is, at its core, very logical. It leads to good and fruitful decisions, decisions that forward our life, enhance our well-being, and steer us toward the happiest and most fulfilled versions of ourselves . . . only it does so by calling upon information that is not readily seen when we rely only on the analytical side of our mind. Essentially, intuition calls upon a collective body of information and provides us with a plan of action.

Intuition is often referred to as the sixth sense. Think, for a moment, about how our other senses (sight, smell, sound, touch, and taste) guide us through information collection and decision making. Our eyesight and earshot let us know when our surroundings may be unsafe, providing us with the opportunity to choose a beneficial decision to move in a different direction. Our sense of smell allows us to recognize if something is pleasant and good for us or off and unsafe to eat, guiding us to a decision that is most healthy. Our touch allows us to feel our way through a situation and to indulge in pleasure. Our taste helps us to nourish ourselves with what we need in the moment and to savor and enjoy healthy nourishment. Intuition works in much the same way as the five more tactile senses. It helps us maximize our enjoyment of life and keeps us safe, healthy, and out of danger. Intuition is like a large flashlight in a dark New York City alley at 3:00 A.M. It illuminates the dark corners and lets us know when something is or is not right. We just need to learn to trust intuition in the same way we trust the illumination that physical sources of light provide—they're all the same thing in different forms.

Intuition is more than a sixth sense, though—it also encompasses a seventh sense. If the sixth sense tells us that *something* is or is not right—for instance, if you have the feeling that your brother is in trouble and you should give him a call—the seventh sense tells us *what* is not right. The seventh sense, then, would tell you that your brother has a flat tire and needs your help. The difference between these two senses is specificity and accessible, distinct details. The more we work on attuning our sixth sense, the better we will become at tapping into our seventh sense.

Moreover, it is a very holistic process. Intuition is not just a decision we make in our mind—it is also something we feel in our bones. Specifically, it's something that we simultaneously process through our mind, heart, lungs, joints, and gut. We'll discuss all of this in depth as we move through the pages of this book. But for now, remember that intuition has a lot to do with being in the moment, because it is in the moment that we receive all of this sensory information. One of the easiest, most accessible, and commonly recognized ways of being in the moment is through meditation and stillness, and we'll be practicing that as a tool for enhancing our intuition throughout the pages that follow as well.

Before we move on to the nuts and bolts of intuition, there is one final concept that is crucial to understand: *intuition is never wrong*. Stop and think about that for a moment. Even the most rational thinking can at times lead us astray. We can interpret intuition wrongly, but what intuition shows is never wrong. Acting from an emotional space can often cloud our perception and judgment or misguide our actions. Neither of these two modes of decision making or taking action is foolproof. Intuition, on the other hand, will never lead us off course. How powerful is this? How much safety can we derive from this fact? We may not always decode or understand our intuition correctly, but intuition itself is always on point. It is the heart of all things harmonious and healthy. It is of the highest intelligence known to humankind. Together, we will go through a series of pragmatic steps that will arm us with the tools we need to ensure that we are able to best decode and understand the information that intuition provides us.

What Does Intuition Feel Like?

Some people experience intuition by seeing things. Some experience it by hearing things. Some might experience it as a download into their brain—it's not clear how the information got there; it just *is*. Some might see numbers, colors, or words. All of this is intuition. I'm often asked how it feels when intuition comes in. The best way I've found to describe it is that it's information that presents itself visually, almost like a clear, recent memory—only it's often a memory of something that hasn't happened yet or that can't be rationally processed.

Take a minute to conjure up a vivid memory. Notice what it feels like to see that memory in your mind's eye. You can "see" it, but can you physically see it? It is there in the air in front of you (or you stare to a point like it's there), but really you are connecting to a part of the mind that is projecting the memory into the air or line of sight. Now think about a conversation you've had in the past day or even longer. Can you hear it in your mind even though you're not audibly hearing it? You "hear" it, but do you really hear it in what we would call the now? That's what intuition is like for me, and for many. Unlike with memory, however, the experience of intuition is never emotional in its moment of speaking. Sometimes I find myself *having* emotion afterward or *reacting to* information with emotion, and this difference is important to understand so we know what we are seeing is fact and not emotion (nonfactual)—after all, we *are* human. But the intuitive information itself arrives without emotion. Information can be light or heavy (for example, if I intuit that a friend has cancer), but as soon as that emotion comes in, I realize I am immediately snapped out of my intuition and it becomes something else. I begin acting from a different part of the brain than the center or front, where the third eye, or "higher" eye, is believed to be. This is important to understand.

As we grow our intuition and our intuitive part of the mind, we must understand if what we are "reading" is factual or coming from the emotional space of our mind (or heart). This will make more sense as you test your intuition out. When something comes—like you sense that a friend is about to call and she does—you will know you are taking steps to strengthen your intuition. If it is something more, perhaps something deeper in emotional weight such as cancer coming in, I recommend (and I still do this) to ask for more signs. We will discuss this later in the book, as it's so important to pair our inner guidance system with a higher guidance system (such as universal energy, angels, source, spirit, God, or your preferred term). Intuition never acts alone and is not for one person alone, so if you are feeling overwhelmed with what is coming in, it's time to take a step back. Get help or go back to doing breath work and taking time alone to hone the aspect of intuition without fear or emotion. We will discuss this throughout the book.

Fate Versus Free Will

Aside from delivering information about what is currently happening, intuition may also offer information about what is *going* to happen or about things that have already occurred. The ability to access information about the future raises important questions about fate versus free will. My own guidances and the experience of the readings I've done have helped me understand the dynamic between fate and free will. In this life, there is definitely a higher *chance* for certain things to happen—this seems best described as fate or destiny. Fate can also be contained in our DNA or heredity (in other words, based on the things our ancestors did), or in our collective karma—the specific things an individual soul came in to accomplish in this lifetime based on things that came before, almost like a rebalance under a cosmic order.

Free will, on the other hand, is what we do with all of that in the moment. We make choices, and those choices affect the chance that various outcomes will or will not come to fruition. Here is an example of that in practice. I may meet with someone and know that if they continue smoking for two more years, their fate carries the potential for them to get cancer. However, I also know or "see" that if they *choose* to quit smoking within the next two years, they can avoid that dire fate. That is where their free will kicks in. Intuition is information—nothing more and nothing less. As humans, we can choose what to do with that information. So it is ultimately not a matter of fate *versus* free will; our life is a combination of *both* fate and free will. When we're tuned in, intuition can be used within that structure to assist us in making educated decisions that will guide us along the most positive and beneficial life path possible.

Even though we are fated to do some things, I believe there is choice in all human matters. This is why I do not believe everything happens for a reason, as some say, or better stated, for a good reason. We have a role in each thing we do, by our choice, and even with fate, there is room for options. The responsibility in our adulthood to realign ourselves or our past decisions will help our own karma as well as the collective choices of a group, nation, or globe. Taking responsibility is key for understanding higher wisdom within ourselves as well as connecting to higher wisdom outside of ourselves. This is becoming an *intuitive being*. I feel we humans have lost the connection to taking responsibility for *ourselves*. This is a key element in truly understanding fate and free will as well as in turning old unknowing into new action.

It is because we are creatures that operate on both fate and free will that balancing out our energy centers is so crucial. If we're centered too much in our lower three energy centers, we're ego focused and weighted too much toward choice. If we're floating around in our upper four energy centers without being rooted down to earth, we run the risk of leaving too much up to fate, chance, or destiny, to the point where we are not active in our own life experience. We want to strike that perfect balance that will allow fate and free will to dance gracefully together throughout our life.

What I see through intuition has already formed; it has just not dropped into present life yet. Many people who have had near-death experiences come out of a coma or brush with death to say the same thing. They went *somewhere* (Heaven? The future? Who knows?) and saw things being built, made, or experienced that later came to be here on earth. Some parts of how all of this works are still a mystery to me at this point. I only know that it occurs, that it's real and fascinating, and that insights happen more often as our intuition grows.

Mediumship

Another aspect of intuition about which people have a lot of questions is mediumship—communicating with those who have passed on. I find that my friends and clients are alternately fascinated and terrified by the idea. Just to be clear, communicating with the souls of those who have departed does not need to be a *ghostly* experience. You don't have to have a séance, and it's not scary at all. In fact, it can become one of the most comforting experiences you could ever hope to have, for two very kind reasons. First of all, there is no greater source of peace or comfort than knowing that your loved ones are *never* gone. They are *always* with you, whether they are in this world or the next. Second—and I absolutely cherish this—in my experience, regardless of what kind of lives they lived here on earth, those who have passed are always the highest, kindest, most peaceful, and true versions of themselves. When we die, we let go of ego-based thinking and doing, anger, aggression, grudges, pettiness, and the sorrows that plague us in life. Most are peaceful souls, rooted in kindness and in love. In other words, they have returned to a natural state of consciousness, of feeling one with everything and everyone.

Mediumship often comes through to me as a spirit or energy in the room—whether it's audible, visual, or just generally sensory. Sometimes I see a figure or form, but I generally ask not to (faces still scare even me . . .). Interestingly, when I am doing a reading for someone and the soul of a loved one who has passed away comes in, the energy or imagery shows up behind and above the person the reading is for. It is still fascinating, even for me.

My first experience communicating with someone who had passed happened at the most peaceful time possible . . . while I was driving (without kids in the car)! I was in my moving vehicle, running simple errands before a trip to visit my dear friend Erin. As I was driving, I heard a voice speaking into my left ear. Since I was alone and the radio was off, this made absolutely no sense to me. A voice claiming to be my dear friend's father who had passed away over a decade ago was speaking to me (it felt similar to answering a phone call: "This is Mr. Branning here, and I'd like to speak with you"). After a few long seconds, I realized what was happening and understood that this was real, in real time, and it was Erin's deceased father who was talking to me. I must admit I felt scared, then angered, then calm, all in the flash of a second or two. But deep down in my soul I knew it was important and I was meant to surrender . . . and listen. As much as I was unclear about quite how to act next (Pull over? Take him to the store with me?), he continued speaking, touching on a lot of facts about what his daughter was doing (unbeknownst to me), and making it clear that he was concerned about a few of her choices.

I was confused by the entire conversation because Erin and I were very close and I was completely unaware of everything that he said was going on in her life. True story (as this all is): I actually argued with this disembodied floating voice because I didn't believe what he was saying. I had not intuited the things he was saying, as I had learned many years ago not to see things about friends, family, or anyone not asking to be seen (we will share how to do this later in chapter 8). Nevertheless, I shared my experience with Erin when we were face-to-face a day later, she asked for a reading, and it was perfect (maybe fate knew that before I did). To my complete surprise, she confirmed that everything her dad had said was true. Erin and I both began tearing up because of the clear truth and healing that it had brought.

If you are scared by the idea of mediumship, I want to say a few things here. One, I had been doing readings professionally for a bit of time before this happened. Second, I was running errands *to* go see Erin, which *connected me to her*. And third, Erin's dad had played on that very land where I was driving (I know again . . . spooky), which I did not cognitively know because we grew up together in a different town. The whole experience was eerie and yet at the same time, very explainable, rational.

Another form of mediumship that is more commonly known (whether it's believed in or not) is the sensation you get when you're in an old building or staying at a very old hotel—that feeling or knowing (sixth sense) that someone else is somehow there in spirit or was there at one time. This can look or feel like chills or a seemingly random thought coming to you that turns out to be true (for example, *I know this used to have yellow tiles on the wall*, or *An old man who wore slippers lived here*). These moments, the thought that you're surrounded by energy you can't quite see, can startle anyone.

This experience of picking up on a vague kind of energy compared with the example with Erin's dad is another example of sixth versus seventh sense. In the former case, you feel spooked ("What was that?"), but you don't know why. With the seventh sense, you know exactly whose energy you're picking up and what they're trying to communicate.

I cannot express enough how comforting the experience of mediumship is and how extremely enlightening and informative it is. In all of my experiences with the realm of the departed, the souls have come through with facts about their relationships with their loved one. And, most of all, they have come through with nothing short of beautiful, healing energy. They have dropped their ego along with their physical body, and any altercations, misunderstandings, or arguments that existed in their prior lives are completely meaningless. They understand their role in events and interactions from this lifetime. They often come in apologetic and wanting to clear energy. They come in to help their loved ones drop any guilt—which often holds us back—and they are *always* here to assist. If you take nothing else away from this book, remember this: *those we love never leave us.*

Signs and Synchronicity

One of the clearest indicators that your intuition has kicked into gear is when you start noticing signs and synchronicity scattered throughout your life. Signs are those little guideposts or moments that come in to point the way forward. They don't have to be big moments, just moments that stick out as a little wink of wisdom. As far as I can tell, the universe has a sense of humor and great timing, and it seems as though it often expresses that through clear, surprising signs.

Here's one of my most recent favorite examples: As we were just beginning to write this book, a cowriter, Nikki, and I were strolling down a beach in Santa Barbara. She asked me a pretty complex question about the workings of the universe and, for reasons completely beyond me, I answered her by drawing a correlation between what we were talking about and the character Sue Sylvester from the television show *Glee. And I had never seen the show.* I laughed as soon as I finished answering the question because I had never even watched *Glee;* I had no idea where that answer came from. No more than two minutes later, Nikki and I looked up to see Jane Lynch (who plays Sue Sylvester's character) walking past us in the opposite direction. Jane even paused for a moment and gave us a kind, intrigued glance. It was such a strange, unexplainable series of events and "coincidences" that Nikki and I *knew* it was a sign that we were on the right path with this book. And the signs did not cease or lessen after that—that is not how this well of information works. You do not use up your tickets, unless you begin to fear it happening or overthink it.

This example pertains to you as well because the odds fall in your favor when you open your third eye! When you begin to feel braver and start to calm your senses, your brain and your body open for new *wow* to happen before your eyes. This can happen when you drop your children off at school and look up to see a person you were just thinking of, or you turn on the radio and hear the song you were humming that is decades old. This can happen when you are strolling with a loved one and a subject (or someone) you were just speaking of, famous or not, walks right by. These are signs—I call them winks—that you are on the fun or welcoming track of adding your sixth and seventh senses to your beautiful main five senses. Ahhh, does life become more intriguing and worthwhile.

Because signs can be subtle, and because believing in signs—intentional messages from the universe meant to convey a truth to you personally—is not in accord with a rational, empirical worldview, we often dismiss them as mere coincidences, missing their simple perfection and guidance. But make no mistake: signs are a very real phenomenon. They can be sent to us from our higher self, our angels, our guides, or universal energy. Many feel they are a product of thoughts, actions, or metaphysics. Where they come from, however, is ultimately unimportant; what *is* important first is that we pay attention to and do not dismiss them. Then we must ask ourselves (this might feel funny or clunky at first): Was that a sign or just a neutral piece of information or happenstance? This is an important distinction. Signs will act like magnetism to you. After your third eye is more open or strengthened, signs will have a glow to them (no, I am not teaching you hallucination). The power of your intuition is that, over time, if you are reading signs wrong, your gut, your body, and your mind will show you. Things will feel more messy or uncomfortable. This is not the grace or assistance of a sign. Again . . . take time to breathe, center (can be done in three minutes), and act, or ask to draw signs and wisdom from this cool, calm space. The brain is proving its power in a part of the mind that sees and knows things that are coming from a higher sight plane. This is the intuitive plane or connection not wanting to lead us astray but rather trying to heighten our sight. Do not overthink this. The overthinking clouds the ability both to see signs and to understand their meaning. A funny push-pull, I know.

Trust that a sign will *never* lead you astray—this is the deal for clarity and more belief in yourself—even if it might seem to do that in the moment.

Again, signs are infinite in numbers and are waiting for you at all times. Take your time looking around. Or try to be calm within and be more of a peaceful magnet. Then begin to trust yourself. (You will see that balancing energy centers will help with this trust.) *Bring signs forward* by asking for signs for a specific situation, especially after meditation or prayer. You will be more centered in the part of the mind that will radiate the calling. Patience will sometimes be key. Breath, again, is key. Always, to the best of your being, wait to let the bigger picture play out, and then you can marvel at how signs were guiding you all along.

Signs will always come in the form of a white flag . . . even when they might feel like a red flag. There is nothing to be afraid of. Remember, your body and your mind will find signs comforting (before the thinking mind sets in and worries) by letting yourself be in your being or receiving state. Ask yourself: Am I in this state? Was I in this state when I saw what I think were signs? Here, as throughout this book, awareness of self, how we are doing in a moment, and what state we are in (Tired? Agitated? Dehydrated? Critical? Annoyed? Full of sugar?) play a role in our clarity of being. I cannot state this enough.

Signs are also a primary mode for communication with our deceased loved ones, if we so choose. Or often *they* choose to try to communicate with us, whether we are aware or not. Many times clients have exclaimed that they've left a reading in which we've discussed a passed loved one only to get in their car, look up, and see their deceased loved one's favorite bird or insect flying by (and there are no others in sight or they're odd for that location). Or—and this happens often—they turn on the radio on the way home and find that their deceased loved one's favorite song is playing. The next morning, they might go into a coffee shop and hear their loved one's name being called out. I promise you, none of this is an accident. It's simply an alternative form of language that closes the gap between this world and another. It is becoming known as a form of quantum physics or the law of allowing the attraction.

When you're aware of signs, not only do you notice them more, but you also receive them more often. Here's a simple exercise that will help you to better understand the guidance and majesty of signs, and to help manifest more of them in your life. Keep a little journal or make a note on your smartphone every time you see a sign. Write down what you think it's telling you and how you took action. (And by the way, taking action may be nothing more than a simple thank-you to acknowledge the sign.) Read back over your notes in a few months' time, and you might be surprised at the results.

Synchronicity is when signs pointing forward or toward healing come together. This means we are carrying on to be more in the present or to notice our current moment with more accuracy and emotional intelligence (versus denial or stuffing away unfelt emotion). We can think of a sign as a single note while synchronicity is a symphony. Being in the right place at the right time is synchronicity. Manifesting your destiny is synchronicity. Have you ever met a person in line and oddly felt as though you'd met him or her before? Have you ever followed a seemingly random gut feeling to go somewhere that you hadn't planned on going or that didn't make sense, only to follow through and have something wonderful happen while you were there? All of this is synchronicity. Here is how you can recognize synchronicity in current time: It's those moments or situations when everything seems to come together seamlessly in a clear harmony to an nth degree, a factor beyond measure. This can be more of life. This is what intuition can help offer. When you can't believe how wonderful a moment was and it leaves you feeling lighter and more full of belief—that, dear heart, is synchronicity. And this starts with knowing we have a choice of what we choose to believe in, to cocreate, and with remembering that thoughts can sabotage how things become outward experience, including how synchronicities occur.

Four Aspects of Being

To understand how intuition works, we have to first understand how *we* as human beings work. One powerful way to break this down is to look at the self as being composed of four main parts (or bodies or aspects, as I—and readings—like to call them). We will stick to the term *aspects of being* for helpful visualization. These are:

Physical being

Emotional being

Intellectual being

Spiritual being

In this model, each of these four aspects of being ideally constitutes 25 percent of our wholeness or whole being. In reality, though, most of us tend to rely most heavily on one or two of these aspects. For example, those of us who are grounded in the material and logical aspects of life are often most in touch with the physical and intellectual beings. The more creative, free-spirited dreamers among us, on the other hand, are often most in touch with the emotional and spiritual beings. Each aspect is very important and of value, but it is by acknowledging and (hopefully!) balancing all four that health and intuition prosper. Each of the four aspects of being serves an exceptional and distinct purpose. If we are a bit too reliant on our rational mind and our intellectual (mental) being over-fires at the cost of the other three, we may lack in emotional intelligence and seeing others with clarity, which are extremely important, not only to our relationships and connections with others but also in pragmatic ways, such as making savvy and astute business decisions. This affects our trust of others, and our intuition has a tougher time being seen or heard. If, on the other hand, we are unbalanced with an emphasis on the spiritual or ethereal aspect of being, we may live life in an untethered way that lacks grounding and does not manifest the tools we need to physically survive and thrive when it comes to the logistical decisions in life that serve us. Our connection to our intuition can suffer because we do not believe what we see is real or comes in tangible ways.

Each of these aspects of being is either masculine or feminine in nature, regardless of our gender. We each have a masculine and a feminine side, like we discussed in parts of the mind, as well as the capacity for healthy, balanced masculine and feminine aspects. Masculine aspects represent doing and accomplishing—the yang and linear parts of our life experience. Our feminine aspects are what synthesize our experience—it is that yin part of ourselves that integrates our experiences and helps us to practice creating new openness and being in the moment.

This is a state of being I love to call a new now. Finding balance is key, as is understanding how each of these four aspects of ourselves serves us and works in tandem with the others in a given moment. Like all relationships, there must be space for equal worth and weight distribution. The understanding that the four aspects are better together helps intuition be seen, heard, and listened to.

The Physical Being

The physical being is often the only being we think of as real—it is our biological being, the bones, skin, muscles, and everything in between that comprise our physical existence. It is our home, our temple, and where our self and soul reside or center. The space near the breastbone reminds me a lot of the center of the bull's-eye because our physical body is at the intersection of all human experience. We are living this life in human form, and it is our physicality that makes us human—our body is a beautiful thing. Our physical body is how we present ourselves to the world in aesthetic form. This aspect of being is associated with the masculine and finite aspect of our self.

Our physicality has a lot to do with things that are material, tactile, and in existence. Our physicality ties us to this earth and makes us both a part of and one with the earth. Think of all the pleasure we are able to derive and experience from pure physicality: the feeling of sand or dewy grass underneath our feet; light wind and sun on our skin; touching and being touched by someone we love; savoring a favorite meal. It is important that we take care of our physical being—which is the foundation and beacon for the other three aspects of being—by making healthy decisions and fostering strength through activity, movement, and nutrition. A healthy physical body sharpens our mental processes, moderates our emotions, and tethers us so that we can experience spiritual connection in a balanced and even way. We can think of the physical body literally as the mecca in which our mind and soul live—we want to keep it strong, soulful, and supportive. Not to mention that a good-looking, supported structure requires us to pay attention to and love and nurture ourselves.

When we become overly focused on the physical, however, we run the risk of becoming too concerned with the material and those things that are seen only with our eyes and thinking brain, prioritizing power to an unhealthy degree, polarizing and limiting creative thought, and having difficulty seeing the larger world or worldview outside of ourselves.

Being out of touch with our physical being is like keeping the eyelid of our third eye shut tight. We are constantly receiving physical pings from our intuition—they may arrive in the form of chills or a gut feeling. When we are not in our being, we simply don't have the ability to attune ourselves to what intuition is telling and showing us.

The Emotional Being

Ah, emotions. While our physical being is what makes us human, it is our emotions that add the juice to our life. Our energy in motion: e-motion. Joy, happiness, love, sadness, anger, and loneliness are part of the human experience. These energies in motion are the vehicles through which we can direct, grow, and evolve—to have the experiences that often take us where we need to go. While we may think of emotions as a more ethereal part of our being, they also play a large role in how we make important logistical decisions. They deeply affect our brain and our heart. Our "thinking." Our action.

Emotional intelligence allows us to gauge situations and understand with greater depth the people and scenarios around us. This is an important link to intuition and our connection to what we see and know. For example, our partner may tell us that he or she is not stressed about a situation at hand, but our emotional intelligence allows us to read between the lines, to have a greater understanding of what he or she is *really* feeling as opposed to what's being said, and to act accordingly. In addition to adding depth to our intellectual body in this manner, a balanced emotional being helps us sense and experience the spiritual aspect of ourselves, our fellow humans, and the world around us.

A balanced emotional being is a key component of our physical health as well. When we feel emotionally healthy (or have the tools to know that we *don't* feel emotionally well and need help to move toward wellness), our physical well-being is inherently enhanced. So is our intuition. How? We have more awareness of information coming from the heart. We also understand that if we are experiencing strong emotions within, we may not be hearing our intuition clearly, as the mind is not in an intuitive space but is instead in fight-or-flight or competitor mode. Clear, balanced communication does not often come from this space.

Our emotions represent the feminine aspect of our human beingness and bond us to ourselves, those in our life, and the world around us. Emotions allow us to create connections and to have a deeper, more fulfilled life experience. And, yes, emotions can be an experience. Far from *just* being feelings, our emotions are intricately tied to our nervous system and deeply affect our hormones, hydration, insulin, cortisol, and adrenals. They are also tied to water, both literally and figuratively—we can hold on to water weight when our emotions are turbulent, and they also often show up as water in dreams. We can feel emotionally flooded from emotions as well.

Like every other one of the four aspects of being, the emotional being can also be over-triggered to our detriment. When we are too tapped into emotion or on emotional overload, our sense of logic may be impeded. We may begin to feel out of control, like a tree whipping in the wind that's been bent too far or like once-calm water that has been stirred up into a tidal wave. Intuition relies deeply on emotions staying in check (or, at least, in harmony) because we must disconnect from emotional influence when tapping into our intuitive space.

The Intellectual or Mental Being

The intellectual or mental being represents our rational and logical processes. It is the part of us that observes the world and people around us and makes judgments and analyses in a more linear way. Clearly, we would be unable to survive or to live a safe, secure, and independent life without the intellectual being. It plays a huge role in decision making and in letting us know what pragmatic and objective moves will serve our best interests, whether those decisions pertain to health, business, domestic life, finance, or even our relationships. Without a properly functioning intellectual being, we are unable to thrive in life in any sort of structured way. Our intellectual being supports us physically by helping us to make good decisions that keep us safe and healthy. It also acts as a sort of centering for our emotional and spiritual beings by keeping us grounded in day-to-day life and matters of a practical nature so that we don't float away in a sea of emotions or let our thoughts get overly creative or remain unmanifested. This being is associated with the masculine aspect of our self.

As with the other aspects of being, a balanced intellectual being is very important to our overall well-being. Of course, there should be a rational, logical component to most of the decisions we make in life. *But* when we consider life from a purely intellectual place, our emotional intelligence is stymied, if not altogether neglected. Chances are that a life dictated by the intellectual being will be more black and white than Technicolor. We may understand the black-and-white outline of a situation, but we will not likely be able to see the rich colors that fill it in. And those colors tell us a *lot*. In the Western world, we tend to overemphasize the physical and the mental or intellectual—learning to balance these masculine aspects with the feminine emotional and spiritual aspects of being is one of the first keys to tapping into intuition and fostering more colorful, connected, and fulfilled lives.

The Spiritual Being

The spiritual being offers great bliss and intuitive access, and actually has little to do with believing in organized religion. In fact, religion can very often limit our spiritual aspect because, at times, it has the tendency to divide and create a learned judgment of "us against them"—even if in subtle and unintentional ways (such as, *I believe this and you believe that,* or *This is right and that is wrong,* or *This is your God and this is my God*). When we are in touch with our spiritual being, we are not only connected with that sense of being part of a greater whole, but we also become more aware that man-made law has only some to do with whole spiritual or universal law. We understand that there is something greater than us that cares for us all evenly, and we know that we are all in this together. That knowledge supersedes *all* "insights" that punish, classify, or organize humans in a linear status. In short, our spiritual being gives us a sense of oneness. This knows no colors or labels. It allows us the freedom and strength of knowing that even when the waters are at their roughest, we are not riding the ship without a first mate or compass. When we are tapped into our spiritual being, we are often inviting our intuition in. The spiritual aspect of being is associated with the feminine view of inclusion.

Some people may understandably wonder what use this spiritual being *really* serves in modern life as we know it. Actually, it helps us a lot—and perhaps more now than ever. In this world where physical and mental aspects count for so much—and where we are so interconnected yet, ironically, so isolated behind our screens, our labels, and our walls—our spiritual being infuses our life with a sense of greater meaning and belonging. It supports our emotions and allows us to experience the more magical sides of existence rather than an existence where we just plod along from point A to point B. It allows us to let go of our need to control. And, finally, it acts as armor for protection and clarity from the mental, emotional, and physical imagery and energy coming at us more and more often.

It has been said that we are spiritual beings living a human life. A whole, functioning spiritual aspect of being—which many of us are lacking today—is critical to the human experience. It provides greater depth and meaning to *everything* we experience, "good" and "bad." But note that in this equation, just as important as existing as spiritual beings is *living a human life*. Life is rich but at times might not feel so, beautiful but at times might not feel so, and more highly (sometimes *comically*) meaningful when we are tapped into our spiritual aspect—and this aspect greatly relies on energy that is much more unifying and open than most of us are in this moment. It is important to balance our inherent spiritual nature with the grounding in the here and now that comes with our physical and intellectual aspects of being. With this, we will be able to enjoy a higher, more expansive, and magical life experience while still savoring all of the lessons and human connections it has to offer. All of this is important to furthering the journey of our soul, which ultimately brings us home to that center space within each and every one of us that is infinite and connects us as one.

Check In: The Four Aspects of Being

The vast majority of us tend to naturally lean more heavily toward relying and believing in one or two of the aspects over the others. Imbalances can switch over time and during certain phases of life. These shifts may be very obvious, or they might sneak in under our radar. Checking in on a regular basis—and even just knowing these elements exist—can help us find easier alignment and more fully experience all that life has to offer in its various facets. This chart breaks down each of the four aspects of being and provides a bit of guidance in terms of what you might be experiencing currently and which aspects might need a bit of attention and love to come into full balance.

	Physical	Emotional	Intellectual	Spiritual
Feminine/ masculine:	Masculine	Feminine	Masculine	Feminine
What it is:	The biological, physical body.	Energy charge or feeling the quality of our thoughts in motion; state of our nervous system and hormones. Emotion.	Thoughts, attitudes, and discernment. Judgment thoughts could turn into prejudices. How we perceive our own worth and value. Equated knowledge.	High, forgiving connection to all living things, including all energy seen and unseen, to organic *chi* energy or life force, to our vibrations and the earth's vibration, and to nature and consciousness. Always creative and all-inclusive. Always acknowledging partnership of higher guidance or creator with creative. Air.
What it represents:	Our physical experience in the world, physiology, and the ability to heal. Physical growth and manifestation in form.	Bridge between the physical and intellectual where our experience of the world is synthesized and interpreted. Our feelings and relationship to all things and occurrences.	Intellect, analytical thought, information processing; how we learn and how we use our words; creating contribution and uniqueness. Focus, clarity, direction, and contributions.	The unity of all living things and the union of our soul, life experience, and destiny. Cocreating a better life and awareness as well as a clear vibration for all. Experiencing heaven on earth. Living richly and without suffering or alienation. Connection and oneness. Divine creation. Giving without lacking.
Balanced qualities:	An open, flexible, healthy body free of pain, toxicity, and acidity. All vitamins, minerals, hormones, and blood pH are balanced.	Inclusive, empathetic, open, honest, and nonjudgmental; ability to give without expectation. Hormones (cortisol, insulin, estrogen, and so on) are balanced. The heartbeat is even and slow, blood pressure is balanced, and body is neither de- nor overly hydrated.	Abilities to problem solve, communicate concisely, innovate, and solve emotional and physical issues. Little waste or nonsense. Conclusion.	Calm, fearless, highly creative, and able to operate without limits. Feeling youthful, energetic, and supported. Experience great *joie de vivre*. The synthesis and balance of the other three aspects of being, to merge with all that is.

Under-balanced:	Body ages rapidly and breaks down easily. Organs do not function optimally, and body feels tight, heavy, and stressed. Posture is unaligned and fascia hardens. Lack of physical support, including food, shelter, safety, and security.	Lack of emotional intelligence, trust, and ability to read people. Fear and neuroses as well as emphasis on the self with little empathy for others. Self-doubt, projection, and loss of sleep. Dehydration, bloating, inflexibility, and joint stiffness. Bleeding heart. Not enough boundary.	Confusion, brain fog, lack of purpose, lethargy, neuroses, doubt, low self-esteem. Lack of menstrual period and poor self-care. Judging others from a place of lack; "armchair quarter-backing." Judging without maturing. Controlling situations without true action.	Disconnected from feeling of oneness with others and the world around us. Feeling that we are victims of our own fate. Disconnection from instincts and intuition. Feeling of being left out. Overreliance on doing and controlling the external. Celibacy and/or keeping spiritual "highs" at bay.
Over-balanced:	Overemphasis on strength, youth, and outer beauty. Doubting that the body can heal itself and reliance on outside sources such as surgeries and drugs. Bypassing natural remedies in favor of fast fixes. Excess weight gain or significant weight loss. Inability to share resources.	Vacillating between passive and aggressive. Obsessive, irrational, easily irritated, depressed, anxious, and hopeless in terms of relationships and situations. Can manifest as weight gain or weight loss. Feeling of a heavy heart, heavy menstrual cycle, and throat closing. Chest tightness. Closed heart. Too much boundary.	Egocentric, excessively driven, sociopathic, exclusionary, number one, narcissistic. Lack of empathy. Doing too much and being on overdrive; adrenal overdrive and racing thoughts. Can physically manifest as headaches, jaw aches, and stomach lining issues. Thoughts become things, often too rapidly, and in an uncontrolled manner. Controlling situations aggressively without pause.	Head in the clouds, inability to turn thoughts into reality, false god complex, lack of interpersonal responsibilities. General feeling of entitlement. Gluttony or hoarding resources, including spiritual works or insights.
Tools to bring into balance:	Simple movements and slow, balanced, repetitive sequences. Meditation, walking, massage, yoga, stretching, weight-bearing exercises. Deep breath work.	Anything that releases emotion, tension, stress, and anxiety. Meditation, dance, cardio, laughing, and breathing techniques. Restorative yoga, sauna, light detox, or fasting. Practicing clearing old memory triggers and replacing them with feelings of forgiveness.	Diaphragmatic breath, Kundalini-type breath work, twists, yin yoga to calm thinking mind and remove energy from jaw and joints, moderate cardio, talk therapy, getting in touch with and releasing emotions. Teamwork in spiritual quests. Mental release, which can come from listening and giving or receiving emotional support. Group talk therapies.	Meditation, breath work, generosity, and paying it forward. Forgiveness, healing, and asking for help. Connecting personal gain with universal oneness. Gratitude and creative expression are an endless well.

Energy Centers

Energy centers and their described space and presence began to come into readings long before I truly knew what they were, so I sure understand if this term is foreign to you. An *energy center,* in English expression—or *chakra,* in Indian expression—is a center of "spiritual power in the human body" by Google's clean definition, and a vibration of light energy and color. We will use the term *energy center* in this book simply to make it easy to understand the language of this possibly newer concept.

The energy and power that radiate in and around every human being is fascinating to me, and you might begin to think so as well. Throughout my intuitive life, I would wonder how I knew what I knew, how I saw it. Interestingly, I found that energy centers were largely the reason why. The information within an energy center is clear, precise, and astounding. Energy centers offer information on our health (and lack of), our love (and lack of), and our sense of worth or agency (or lack of). And when you begin to tap into your intuition, you might not see color, but you might easily begin to read what is happening within you—and within and between other people. And this can offer great radiance and health to you and those around you. This ability to read and support human beings in reaching their highest heights is what I believe intuition is meant for.

Let's take a second to talk about energy and what it is made of. It can be called life force, chi, oxygen, movement, watercolor, essence, *prana,* or universal flow. The important part is that, whatever we believe it to be, we call upon this energy as often as possible to help us thrive, grow, and have a positive and balanced life experience.

Our energy is housed in and channeled through our energy centers, which are spread throughout, around, and above and below our physical body. You can think of them as holding clusters or legions of information, energy, maturity, and experience that we carry within ourselves—our life experience is, in a way, etched into them. It is through our energy centers that we act or react in our relationships and life experience and that we assimilate input. This input can include anything from thoughts to food to encounters with others. Intuition is very much a form of input, so it is through our energy centers that we process the information life and intuition provide us with. Each energy center receives intuitive input in a distinct way, and also works in tandem to help us receive the entire intuitive picture and our life experience in the most whole and efficient way possible.

Our energy centers move through and fuel the four aspects of being. This means that to be physically, emotionally, mentally, and spiritually balanced, our energy centers must be balanced. When we balance our energy centers, we create a more solid foundation through which to get in touch with our intuition, and the energy centers have a healthier representation in each of our four aspects of being.

When energy centers are balanced, our mind and body are balanced. Our health is balanced. What will that *feel* like? Light, clear, blissful. Life is manageable. This means that when all seven main energy centers are in balance (many, including myself, believe there are more, smaller, portals of energy in and around the body that are affected as well), then we feel complete clarity and centering in our mind, our body including our metabolism and lymphatic system is working very efficiently, and we have a peaceful, happy disposition—no matter what our outside circumstances.

How do we use intuition in connection with our energy centers? That is the basis for this book. As we mentioned, energy centers radiate our health and life experience in any present moment, and they offer a lot of information about our state of mind, our state of being. *Becoming an intuitive being is knowing more than meets the eye.* Intuition and energy centers offer this more tangible way to hear our inner voice and see what the universe is trying to show us. This is an irreplaceable body-soul-mind-spirit guidance system. When we understand energy centers, we begin to understand one another better. We begin to understand what our body and emotions are telling us. This offers freedom to serve and assist healing.

I know this can feel like an esoteric idea, so let's talk about some real-world ways we can determine whether or not our energy centers are balanced. Our energy centers may become unbalanced when there's too much or too little energy present.

Some signs that you may be experiencing an imbalance in one or more of your energy centers include:

Increased sense of living in the past

Increased anger

Consuming too much of one food or food group

Increased toxicity in the body

Increased disease and increased dis-ease (or a general lack of ease in life)

Increased negative experience with love, loved ones, or loss

Another sign of imbalance is finding yourself in the same situation over and over again. Examples of this include: repeating similar patterns in different relationships, repeated stagnation at work, repetitive financial troubles, and making the same negative choices time and time again.

Negative *déjà vu* situations such as these often occur for clear reasons. Our energy centers are a direct reflection of how we feel, how healthy we are, and our state of mind. As such, they will attract those things, people, and situations that represent the state of the relevant energy center at any given time. This is by design, to help us evolve and clear blockages. We can often fool both others and ourselves about how we feel about ourselves, life, pain, and relationships, but there is no way around the truth that our energy centers hold and attract.

We each have numerous energy centers, but here we will discuss the seven main ones that are located along the spine from our tailbone to our head. These are known as the larger ones with more force or primary function. It is these energy centers that we will focus on in the context of intuition throughout this book.

Each of these energy centers is associated with a specific aspect of and function in our life, a particular life phase, and a color. These colors can be seen in our aura (the emanation of energy that surrounds each of us—and all living things). Ideally, we do not want any one color to be too light or too dark. This can indicate an imbalance in the energy center—in other words, either too little or too much energy surrounding that space in and around the body. A light shade of a color often indicates that we are not fully or healthily functioning in the associated energy center; a heavy color often indicates that we are overemphasizing, overusing, or relying too much on that energy center . . . most likely to the detriment of other energy centers. We are ultimately aiming for the perfect balance.

Energy Center	Location (in Body)	Aspect Represented	Ideally Come into Fruition	Color
First	Sits bones, base of spine down through the legs, and feet	Our roots, sense of safety, security, first memories	Age: 0–7 years old	Red
Second	Pubic bone area, sexual and reproductive organs	Our relationships to pleasure, ourselves, others, and all things; creativity	Age: 7–13/14 years	Orange
Third	Gut/Stomach	Our power, worth, self-worth, and assertion	Age: 14–21 years	Yellow
Fourth	Heart	Love and our connection to and compassion for all living things; understanding we are all one	Opportunity to fully mature: 21–28 years	Green
Fifth	Throat	Purification and using our voice, speaking the truth	Opportunity to fully mature: 28–35 years	Royal blue
Sixth	Third Eye	Our intuition, wisdom, understanding, knowledge, and high creativity	Opportunity to fully mature: 35–42 years	Bright purple
Seventh	Crown of head	Our connection with higher energy, light or spirit, trusted guidance support, universal law, the divine source, knowing heaven within and all around us	Opportunity to fully mature and be of wise use: 41/42+	White

One of the most important things to understand about energy centers is that they build upon, interact with, and balance one another. We can visualize the seven energy centers as forming a tree, with the first energy center serving as the roots and the seventh energy center being the birds flying above the tree. In order for the tree to stand tall and flourish, to bear fruit and withstand strong winds, its roots have to be strong and deep. Its trunk has to be stable and healthy, and its branches have to achieve a powerful balance of strength and flexibility.

Although we may continue to learn lessons involved with each of these energy centers throughout our entire lifetime, each center has the potential and capacity to come to full maturation during a specific life phase. For example, the foundation of our first energy center is built and deeply influenced during our formative years, from birth to about age seven. This energy center involves our roots, meeting our basic needs, and very often, it dictates what we need to feel safe and secure throughout life. It makes sense that our ideas and primary experiences here would play a large role throughout our life because during these earliest years, we are completely dependent upon others to provide security and simple basic life necessities for us. If we do not develop a strong system of roots in the first energy center during childhood, it can be difficult to breed a healthy second energy center.

The second energy center helps determine how we cultivate pleasurable relationships of all varieties (with ourselves, with others, with our body, with food, and so on). As we move into the second energy center between ages seven and fourteen, our world concurrently greatly expands beyond just our primary caregivers to our peers, neighborhood, teachers, coaches, and so on. It is through these relationships that we acquire our mature sense of self and other. Because our ideas and experiences of safety and security have already been at least somewhat developed in the first energy center, that experience will serve as the foundation for the relationships we form while moving into the second energy center in our preteen years (and beyond). For example, if we built a strong sense of safety and security in the first energy center, we may very well gravitate to relationships in the larger world that also make us feel safe and secure—in other words, healthy relationships. If we feel less stable in our first energy center, we may have the tendency to find ourselves in relationships that reflect our inherent feeling of instability and insecurity.

And so it continues as we move up to maturing a new energy center approximately every seven years, with each energy center building upon the ones that came before it. Just as a tree cannot stand tall and be vibrant and healthy with rotting or shallow roots, we have fewer chances to live a stable, healthy life if our energy centers are not balanced or healed when necessary.

If, for example, we have an imbalanced first energy center and feel unstable in our roots—likely because our needs weren't met as a child—we will continue to draw situations to us that make us feel unstable and unsafe until we go back and resolve that imbalance. This is for our health, not for our suffering. Remember, nature, our body, and our cells are always turning over new leaves—but first we must shed the old ones. Stagnation and repetitive patterns happen when we become stuck in an energy rut that inhibits growth.

Once we learn how to clear and rebalance our energy centers (a topic we'll cover thoroughly and specifically in the pages to come), this no longer happens. *Freedom!* Intuition is free to flourish and bring with it much added joy and experience, and to support great opportunities in our life. Despite the fact that the expansion of each energy center is associated with a particular age, we can—at *any* time—go back to clear and strengthen any and all of our energy centers.

To bring all of this back to intuition, intuition is often seen as seated in what is called the sixth energy center, thought to be found in our third or "higher" eye, through the brow space, in (or near) the center of the mind. It can reach its fullest potential about age forty, yet reliance on our intuition, I believe, is introduced to us before our first breath. And just as our lungs bring us oxygen and our heart pumps blood and nutrients through our system from the very first moment of life, so too does our intuition immediately start providing us with information from the first instant we believe life begins.

Intuition is an inherently ethereal quality. If we are not rooted down to earth and physical life by our lower energy centers, we can become untethered by intuition, essentially losing our footing in the world; likewise, if we are not emotionally well-balanced, the voice of our intuition becomes muddled in a flood of emotion and fear. When we balance our energy centers, we are opening a clear pathway for intuition to flow through us in a way that will truly benefit not only our own lives, but also those of all of our loved ones and the situations around us.

How It All Works

We now understand the four aspects of being we will use to create "whole" being experience—our physical, emotional, intellectual, and spiritual beings. And that each of the seven main energy centers that run through those aspects represent an important facet of our life—our roots, our relationships, our power, our connection to the world, our voice, our intuition, and our support from something beyond our thinking mind. We cannot hone and deploy our intuition without healthfully balanced bodies and energy centers.

In the chapters that follow, we will take an in-depth look at each of our energy centers, beginning with the foundational energy center that represents our roots and childhood experiences, and moving all the way up to our connection with our highest guidance system. We'll examine how balanced each of these energy centers is by taking a look at how they are currently manifesting themselves in our physical, emotional, intellectual, and spiritual lives. In some cases we will find that these energy centers are perfectly well-balanced. In other cases, we will find that there is some work to be done to balance out specific energy centers.

Learning how to use our intuition is as much about recognizing our intuition exists as it is letting the outside world interact with this fun, fruitful opening we've created within ourselves. Intuition offers knowledge, assistance, and graceful new ways of being. Using our intuition does not need to feel scary or overwhelming. If we are coming to learn about our intuition as grown adults, it might require us to open some parts of the mind long left untouched. This is okay. If it does feel emotional or overwhelming, the understanding of energy centers and the tools in balancing our energy centers and past life experiences should greatly help. Remember, your intuition is here to help not hinder.

So *how* will intuition change your life? You might begin to notice the nudges in your body, in your gut, or in your joints. You might stop ignoring the knocks and signs that come almost comically at times (we hope to catch the signs before they come dangerously). You might begin to open your heart energy center just enough to bring yourself to write a letter you *know* needs to be written. You might extend a hand, versus judgment, to a neighbor or foe. These are all aspects of our intuition. And the rewards are tenfold. Again, a win-win action, that involves a new way to look at winning. All of these examples are using your deep wisdom to cocreate a shift in consciousness. Activating a new space in the mind. Your own mind . . . and possibly others'.

That our everyday *being* offers us a lot of information to work with even when we do not necessarily cognitively understand this concept might feel strange at first. Trust. It may be that you have been taught (or choose unconsciously) to look at life through using only the analytical side of your mind. In these pages you will find tools to work other parts of your mind and intellect, already in place and ready to be activated, or remembered.

Your intuition will work with the information around you. You have a say in what you "see" intuitively. The more you see clearly, the more life changing intuition might feel. Your life might change in the first moment you pick up this book, or you might find a defining moment later, when you read a passage that offers the key to unlock a new piece of knowledge. The journey is yours. If intuition offers you simply an awareness of how deeply you are breathing and how much deeper breath offers to balancing your mind (and life), then that is a life-changing step on its own.

One of my most eye-opening realizations as an intuitive is learning how connected we are to this world we live in. I found this both comforting and mind-boggling, until I realized how my breath alone changed my body, emotions, and thoughts almost instantly. Breath also greatly helps when I find myself in awe of the power of intuition and how it can change situations instantaneously. This realization changed my life. By understanding both your intuition and what blocks intuition, you will find changes in your life you never thought attainable. Some simple and some profound. Opening our intuition balances weight, aging, hormones, and even fear. This is quite life changing. We will see by balancing energy centers that the work we need to do to hone our intuition simultaneously enhances every aspect of our life and helps us to live and love more happily, more fully, and more vibrantly.

Remember, you're already intuitive. We all are. It's something that's built into each and every one of us. We have all been given this gift to use on an everyday basis. Let's unwrap it and put it to work! Think of this book as your owner's manual so that you can experience the entire intuitive package.

2

THE FIRST ENERGY CENTER: THE ROOTS

Our Basic Needs

Now that we know what an energy center is, let's connect this knowledge more deeply to intuition. The first energy center helps our intuition show up in a grounded, secure, and manageable way. This grounding also assists us to take the information that comes in and turn it into useful, practical tools or instruction. For example, if we want to build a shelf, intuition can assist our analytical side in choosing what store to buy the materials from, what style we personally prefer, and also where to find the tools we need for the job. Sometimes we'll even hit the sale without knowing. Creatively, intuition will let us feel secure in our choice of the type, or "look," of the shelf. Once you get better at listening to your intuition from a secure place, the intuitive information gets more practical and magical at the same time. My family teases me that I rarely use the paper instructions to put things together anymore! And I pick out furniture quickly and surely. This energy center literally helps intuition come in more tactile and practical ways.

Using our intuition, we are making room in our life for new experiences, for new ideas and relationships to plant. We want this new to feel good and healthy, and to offer security to our entire being. We also want there to be room in our life for the new, so sometimes housekeeping is needed in the physical body or physical home. This is tied to our first energy center and what we create in our life to feel secure and surrounded by comfort. Cleaning house to hear our inner voice better . . . there is just nothing like this act. When we feel grounded and clear of the past, our first energy center will help us feel more capable, smart, and in control of our life experience. Intuition helps the past clear for a healthy and safe present.

If we are not feeling secure, we may be in our fight-or-flight, or warrior-competitor, part of the brain more often than not, and this is not wholly where intuition resides. Intuition can often be turned on and off by this feeling of a lack of security or completely ignored because we find no safety in it. This could be an old lock and key. If our parents or home life felt threatening in any way in childhood and we have not done the work to clear up this pain (this can be emotional or psychological, not just physical) then our roots and stability may still be suffering. As well, if our family's view of intuition equated it to the devil or witchcraft, this also can be held in our root.

We need a grounded approach to handle and discern what we see and hear through our intuition. Physical changes may literally begin to occur in our body, like weight loss in the hips or thighs. Joints like knees and ankles may become less swollen. When we begin to let go of the past and grow stronger roots, our brain steps out of fight-or-flight mode more often and we do not release as much cortisol, which helps us to stay more centered and present in a calmer, peaceful state. We might find we do not eat emotionally as often because we are feeling more secure, more seen, more heard, and this will lower blood sugar and the release of insulin. Not to mention we might crave more rooted vegetables and foods from the earth, because we are more in touch with our adrenals and a healthy gut. This can begin clearing our past experiences of feeling unsafe and strengthening our security. We then show up, take up more healthy space in our environments, and trust intuition as more of a guide.

When I was five years old, my parents moved our family from Europe back to Northern California. From the outside, our life was pretty idyllic. And in many ways, it was. I loved being outside and creating projects from the earth, which the beautiful California landscape offered in abundance. Yet, in those early years, I also carried a certain unease within me, deep down in my roots. My nature was a bit different than my nurture, and I often didn't feel seen or heard, though I loved and adored my family. I valued emotions as energy in motion from a very young age, and my parents didn't seem to see or experience life in a similar way. They did not openly understand intuition, which came more naturally to me. They showed less emotion; where I, on the other hand, was more a bleeding heart. Had I been armed with the agency to make my own decisions as a child, I probably would have made different choices than those my parents did, such as talking more about our feelings and addressing the old pain that lingered in our household. My family offered physical stability, but I longed for a more peaceful and nourishing environment. For me, *this* was nourishment. Instinctively, I began to trust and rely on my inner voice.

This is childhood as we have known it for generations. Decisions are usually made for us by our primary caregivers, and we are dependent on others to provide our basic needs. Our sense of safety, security, and the meeting of our basic needs are completely in the hands of those who raise us. Some of us feel like we have a voice in this, even from a young age; others of us do not. Like many, I fell into the latter category.

Even though I was different from my parents, I still sought their approval and the sense of safety that comes from that. It was usually through managing my outer appearance, excelling in outer accomplishment, or staying quiet that I got that approval. Often, I felt that very few authority figures in my childhood mirrored back to me who I really was—I felt like most adults saw me as who they *wanted* me to be and to become rather than as the little person I actually *was*. Because of this, despite the fact that my basic needs (safety, physical security, and shelter) were technically met, I felt a basic mistrust of the outside world's maturing ability to mirror my needs and provide steady, reliable roots, as my parents and home pretty much *were* my world.

In addition to the physical traits we all carry in our DNA, we also carry with us the history of our ancestors—and, of course, we are all greatly influenced by how we ourselves were nurtured. Just as I did not have a complete feeling of safety, security, and being seen instilled in me as a child, neither had my parents: And because they hadn't received this, they didn't quite know how to provide it. Clearing out our roots helps clear these cycles.

For me, the combination of all of these factors resulted in me feeling a bit unprotected and unsure that my needs would be met, both in my childhood and in my early adulthood. As a result, I tended to forego my own needs for the sake of others, and I gave more than I received. These early experiences resulted in me forming weaker roots—something that I was faced with resolving later in life. I still must revisit this energy center ritually.

Perhaps some elements of my own experience sound familiar to you.

All of the issues I experienced have to do with the first energy center, which is also known as the root energy center and is energetically associated with the color red. If you think of the energy centers as a pyramid, the first is at the very base. As the foundation of the pyramid, the strength and integrity of the first energy center is essential for supporting all six of the others above it. It is the primary building block upon which everything else is based.

We begin creating our roots (and our first sense of security) from the moment we come into this world and through the age of six or seven. This is an important step in trusting our intuition, *feeling secure* within. As children, our sense of security and safety comes from having our basic needs met, from our relationships with the people who meet them, and from feeling grounded in our sense of self. The conditioning that results from that early relationship with our primary caregivers continues to be impactful throughout our life. These are the people who are responsible (until we hit adulthood) for forming our ideas about what it means to feel safe and secure—or, unfortunately in some cases, what it means to *not* feel safe and secure. These are also the people who play a large role in our self-perception. If we do not feel seen and heard by our primary caregivers, we will most likely take this feeling with us throughout life until we do something to change it.

As our grounding force, this first energy center is very connected to earth and ground, and it governs these most basic elements of our life. This includes all of the things we need to survive and feel safe and hold agency: food, shelter, and protection from unmanageable hurt, all of which likely are provided by a parent, by family, or by a primary caregiver. Intuition requires survival and agency to see and trust our intuition as real. As the energy center that forms during our earliest years, the root energy center governs our feelings of safety and security, and the belief that our most basic needs will be met. Figuratively, it is these things that nourish and grow our roots. Think of the roots of a tree: they dig deep into the earth and provide water, nutrients, and minerals for the entire tree. Our roots do basically the same thing—they ground us so that our footing is stable and provide us with physical nurturing. Also like the roots of a tree, our roots allow us to eliminate and release waste in order to remain healthy. In this case we can think of waste as old thoughts, toxic life experiences, and unhealthy memories.

As we move our way up through the energy centers of the body, we find that the higher we get, the more light and esoteric they become. It is for precisely this reason that we need to have strong roots that draw us down so that the earth can support us and keep us nourished and grounded. *This grounding allows our intuition to expand without carrying us away like leaves in a blowing wind.* So, although these lower energy centers may seem a bit more dense and unrelated to intuition, they are absolutely *essential* to the intuitive process. We must have this balance of grounded and winged energy to simultaneously stay connected and be free to experience the many rich facets of intuitive being. The root energy center lets us use our intuition without getting blown over by what we see and know. Our roots also act as a flushing system to help eliminate what we see and know through intuition. This is important because if we do not let go, we will ultimately carry around too much of our own past or other people's stories with us.

Do you feel grounded in your life? Are you secure in what and who you are? Are you confident that you have everything you need to survive? If you cannot answer yes to these questions, it is challenging to feel free and safe in the world and in relationships, to feel as if you have say over your own life. Intuition will help here, and perhaps you are beginning to see why this first energy center is essential for our intuition to begin to be more noticed. Without it, we can feel unstable—in our sense of self, our sense of well-being, our trust in the world, and our safety in our relationships—because of our looser footing within our own life experience.

One of my favorite things about the root energy center is that it's cut-and-dried when it comes to determining whether or not it is in balance. We can't *pretend* our basic needs are met—it is a question with a yes-or-no answer. *Do I feel safe and supported, physically, emotionally, mentally, and spiritually? If not, why am I feeling unsafe? Am I providing myself with my basic physical, emotional, intellectual, and spiritual needs? Are those who I am closest to and who I depend upon in life providing for or supporting me in these ways? If not, what do I need that I don't have?* Answering these questions is helpful in determining what work we need to do to make sure that all of our needs are being met. What might feel tricky is how far back the insecurity goes. Not all falls on our parents. Society, neighborhoods, and DNA play a role in our rooted energy too.

Here is the good news: *no matter how unstable our own roots may feel, at any point in our life, we have the choice to go back and give ourselves those things that our primary caretakers may not have been able to.* You can provide your own roots and that essential feeling of safety and grounding. We will discuss specifically how in the next two chapters on relationships and worth. As adults, we can learn how to wholeheartedly take care of our own basic needs and, with that, we can clear out our roots that are broken or uncomfortable, replacing them with new roots that are deeply grounded in safety and security. This process means that we have to acknowledge what we were missing in our earliest years, which, for some of us, can be painful. This does not mean that we should (or *will*) forget our life to date or rewrite history; rather, it means that we learn to forgive and begin to take care of our needs fully and responsibly. This idea of healing goes for all of the energy centers, but it is particularly important to keep in mind with the primary ones because we really have little or no power over how those roots are initially planted.

The First Energy Center and the Physical Being: Rooting into the Earth

Some of the first things I see when I meet with clients are any physical ailments, misalignments, or imbalances they may carry. Since the first energy center is situated in the lower region of the body—including the sits bones, seat, hips, legs, knees, ankles, and feet—issues in these areas are a clear indication that a person usually has some sort of imbalance in their first energy center. Furthermore, in adulthood the higher roots we carry in our body, such as the teeth, are also related to the first energy center.

The first energy center also governs our joints. Why? We carry old emotion there. As the hips are the biggest joint in the human body, many of us hold memories, old pain, or discomfort in that area—in particular, pain that reminds us of parental patterning. Tightness (or lack of openness) is often another telltale sign that a person is experiencing first energy center imbalances. This is probably not new information to you yogis or meditators out there who have likely either heard about the connection between hips and emotions in classwork or have had the experience of hip work suddenly bringing up a rash of emotion—often out of the blue and when you least expect it. Our hips do not lie. Intuition helps bring these truths out of our hip closets. Actually, that is a pun in itself, as we may dress a certain way to hide old pain or insecurities.

Our body is so amazingly simple and complex that the physical cues it provides us with are even more specific than this. The left side of our body (right side of our mind or brain) governs the feminine and, as a result of this, reflects the nature of our relationship with our mother (or the primary feminine caregiver in our life). The right side (and left side of the brain) represents the masculine and our father (or patriarchal influence). Through readings, I've found that we carry unresolved emotions about the mother or feminine element in our hips—if we feel stiff or "stuck" in the hips, we are likely carrying old or negative energy about a feminine figure or something repressed from our roots. Extra energy surrounding the hips can also represent trauma in the sits bone region or anger toward feminine elements or weakness. If our hips are fluid and open, that energy is likely neutral, empathetic, or a positive indicator of a healthy, productive relationship, either to the mother figure herself or to the truth of that relationship or about how we view "feminine" aspects such as emotion or spiritual nature. Readings have shown me that the energy from our relationship with our father or our own relationship with our secure masculine side is often carried in our thighs. Again, soreness and extra weight or bulk often represent an imbalanced or negative relationship with our paternal figures or idea of ourselves as secure authorities of our self; svelte, fluid thighs (of all sizes) are indicative of a healthy, resolved relationship or ownership of getting our own physical needs met. These are for all body types. It's about feeling free, secure, and clear in the physical sense—your best self in this current moment.

With all of this in mind, take a moment to be quiet, concentrating on your breath, and tuning in to your own body. Remember, breath is key to moving old energy out and fresh new energy into our personal space (or aura). Intuition loves this type of moment—to be heard, with stillness. Take special note of the areas we just discussed and notice your physical state. Does it provide any relevant information about those primary caregiving relationships or gender roles in your own life?

To see how all of this works in practice, I'd like to share a story about one of my first clients, a lovely and charismatic young woman named Jamie. When I first met Jamie, she was experiencing chronic lower back and joint pain, swelling in her feet, and extra weight in the lower part of her body—all classic physical manifestations of root energy center imbalances. She was floating through life, feeling ungrounded and literally uprooting her life circumstances all of the time. She was constantly moving homes, changing her furniture around, and transitioning relationships, and she couldn't seem to keep monetary debt at bay (a common sign of a feeling of lack of worth and security). As if all of that wasn't difficult enough, Jamie was insecure and angry.

Through our reading, we were able to determine that Jamie's anger and insecurity linked back to the very earliest years of her life, before her memory even kicked in. It turned out that Jamie's mother held a lot of resentment and anger from her own upbringing, which was ultimately transferred over to how she mothered Jamie. Both subconsciously (during her youngest years) and consciously, Jamie picked up on this and, like a lot of us, the anger and resentment she felt toward her mother added weight to both her life experience and to her hips, which resulted in poor leg circulation. As Jamie aged, this, at times, exacerbated her joint issues and produced swelling in her feet. All of this was compounded by the fact that Jamie's father had been moved around a lot during his own childhood and thus had an extremely difficult time laying down his own roots. The anger Jamie's father carried was passed down to her and showed up as blocked energy, which often manifests as weight and tightness, in her thighs.

It was almost as if Jamie's body was bearing down and widening to offer the grounding she'd never had. This made Jamie's everyday experience both unhealthy and tiring. By going back and unearthing some of Jamie's forgotten past during our reading, we were able to help her clear some of that negative energy she'd been holding on to.

I saw Jamie again three months after our second reading and was amazed at her transformation. Her health had greatly improved, the swelling in her body had gone down significantly, and she generally felt much more comfortable in her own skin. She was involved in a new, more stable romantic relationship, and she was moving toward being more financially secure. Although she was already lovely the first time I met her, Jamie's entire essence was happier and healthier as she took ownership of her past and immersed herself in her present experience. A lot of this was a result of the fact that Jamie was able to start talking with her parents about their own past experiences, which had, in turn, been passed down to her without pause. In doing this, she helped clear the energy that had been blocking her root energy center for so long. I love Jamie's story because it demonstrates the power of awareness and how it can heal us on a physical level. It's not always easy to do, but once we accomplish it, the entire composition of our life (and body) can change for the better by clearing out the old roots and making room for the new.

Jamie essentially rerooted herself. She acknowledged her childhood insecurities and those times when she felt as though she had not been seen or heard. She began to routinely journal as a way of expunging her feelings and, in the process, realized that some of her old memories were nothing more than perceptions and old projections, and that she was currently projecting some of her old fears about insecurity and doubt into her present relationships, including her relationship with her now-aging parents. She accepted her parents as they are and were.

Jamie also took the reading's insight and addressed the physical issues that were manifesting in her root energy center by doing strong standing yoga poses like tree and mountain pose. She began to walk barefoot regularly—on grass, sand, and soil—using that sensation of her feet merging with the earth as a literal grounding and releasing device. She also began to add colorful seasonal vegetables with deep roots to her diet. Food is, as we know, a key building block to all that we are—in the literal sense, what we eat is what we become and how we sustain ourselves. If we do not feel rooted, physically ingesting roots into our body offers support to an old experience that is missing.

What Jamie essentially learned in the time between our first two visits and subsequent visits was that she had the power to strengthen her roots. At any time. It just took focus and honoring her situation for what it was. Doing this provided Jamie with greater stability in her current and future relationships, a topic we'll really delve into in the next chapter.

The First Energy Center and the Emotional Being:
Finding Our Roots in Forgiveness

Those of us who had happy, healthy childhoods that provided us with a sense of well-being and feeling outwardly seen and loved generally develop strong, deep, and stable roots. Like a lotus flower, the further our roots implant themselves into the muddy earth, the more we are able to cultivate beautiful blossoms. Those of us who do not or did not have the benefit of this sort of upbringing may have more shallow roots. When we do not have the foundation of mirrored love, safety, and being seen, it becomes much easier for the world around us—including our relationships and the events in our life—to make us feel ungrounded, voiceless, and easily swayed.

A person's sense of security in the world and in life begins in the womb and with the energy experienced there. At every stage in babies' lives, it is important that safe, calm, and grounded behavior is displayed to them so that they can soak up and mirror that energy. They then know it is okay for them to take up space energetically. Their systems are intuitive and instinctual sponges, as were yours at this age.

Despite our parents' and caregivers' best intentions, we are often taught to share or give too early in our childhood, which can negatively affect our roots in terms of emotional balance and self-regulation. The ages of two or three, right around the period when children first encounter situations in which they decide whether or not to share, is also a period crucial to our understanding of security and ownership of self. Our intuition literally knows to claim ownership of our security, or self for healthy growth at this stage of self-development. When children learn they must share something before the concept of ownership is understood, it is harder for them to feel seen and understood, to have a sense of ownership, and to experience emotional grounding. Rather than openly sharing because ownership is understood, children learn to give disproportionately. (How many adults *still* have a hard time sharing their possessions?) Women and girls are especially susceptible to being taught to give away energy more quickly. This actually has a negative effect of intuition for us all as we lose the ability to trust the feminine side of our mind, including "women's intuition." All children are affected by a mother who does not trust herself fully.

Children are more willing to share their things and trust themselves once they learn they are secure, are seen and heard, have ownership, and can hold on to the item as long as they need to—in other words, they have *choice* in the matter. Our lessons in sharing affect our sense of security and agency down the line: how we grow into adulthood, re-create roots, and find security in the self. Many of us *had* to share for the purpose of well-intended politeness. When we are taught to share after the point where we understand that we are provided for with physical and emotional space and physical resources, we are freed up to give to others without experiencing anger, negative emotion, or a sense of lack. When we feel like we don't have anything that is ours alone, it becomes difficult to give to others without experiencing a lack or depletion. I've noticed this with males who covet numerous cars (that they don't allow anyone to drive or touch) and women who hoard dolls, shoes, and clothing finding it hard to share until they decide they are done with the item, the physical worth being gone. This is also common in sexuality and relationships, as we will discuss in the next chapter.

This sense of taking up space and security ultimately has little to do with material goods once our need for shelter, food, and attention are met in adulthood. Children who are from poor families and do not have a lot of toys, but who are raised with love and a sense of protection and provision, will likely still be generous with their few belongings because they can remain confident that their needs will be met. We'll come back to this idea of taking up space in much more detail later, when we discuss the third energy center, which is largely about our personal power, self-worth, and showing the world our internal fire.

But, of course, we're not all lucky enough to receive this feeling during our earliest years. So how do we rectify this when we become older? The answer is simultaneously simple and difficult: we must forgive those in our life (including our own older self) who have played a role in causing us to feel this lack of safety and security. It sounds almost overly simplistic, but true forgiveness can be difficult. It's like searching out and pulling up all of those weeds that have grown inside of us for years and years and tilling the soil so that they can't grow back again once we've eradicated them.

Forgiveness looks different for each of us. For some of us, it might involve a conversation with an individual or a group. For others of us, it might be a matter of journaling or meditating and offering up a form of internal forgiveness. An important element of this, though, is not a *gesture* of forgiveness but a true *feeling* of forgiveness. Sometimes it might take a while to get to this clear space . . . and that's okay. However long it takes, it is deeply worth getting to that blank slate that allows us to create fresh, fertile soil in which to plant sturdy fresh roots. Intuition rooted in this fresh energy brings fresh new ideas. It's the same kind of energy match as the way we describe manifesting our dreams and desires.

Another way we can create this feeling of security and stability that may not have been provided to us during childhood is to provide roots to children or youths in our care. They can be family or in our community. This work can help us connect to our own inner child or basic needs left unmet.

This can be done intuitively versus going into the fear-based part of the mind. How? With focus on the moment at hand or by writing emotions that come up to be processed and released in a timely fashion, *away* from the children. By focusing on breath and keeping the nervous system (and our internal fear) calm, we are accessing our intuition . . . our stillness. From here new ways of finding our security can form. This will probably require outside help. Professional help is recommended, as it ensures you are not going to loved ones who have unhealthy roots of their own and possibly helped create yours. Working with children to provide healthy roots for both them and you is for those of you who did *not* suffer deep childhood trauma that is not yet resolved. For those who have had severe trauma is their childhood it is important to have consistent help and support, talk therapy, and belonging in a group of caring individuals or joint cause, to stay grounded in any present moment. Working alone with children is not advised as incidents can trigger deep emotions still not realized within.

To provide roots to children, no matter how young they might be, pay attention to who they are. From a place of awareness, do everything possible to make sure their basic needs are met and they have the security and safety that you might have been missing out on as a child yourself. The action of providing strong roots for others helps to stabilize our own as we gain strength and ability in the process of doing so for others. Again, watch what feelings come up to be processed, and do so with capable adults. In giving to others, we also learn to give to ourselves. We begin to see our instinct to nurture and connect rise up to consciousness, and we give a new chance for old pain to heal. If we come to quickly realize we are not comfortable being with children or helping youth thrive in a healthy manner, this too is a sign to get help expressing your feelings in a safe, wise environment.

The First Energy Center and the Intellectual Being:
Sowing Our Own Roots

Once we've done the work of forgiving painful or hurtful experiences and people (and it may feel like *work*), we can really delve into building our own roots. Not only is this process extremely empowering, but it also allows us to be the architect of our own lives. No one knows what exactly we need to feel safe and secure better than we do. For some of us, these needs might be fulfilled in a new relationship with ourselves or others. Or it may be found in material possessions or wealth. For others, it may be in a new or secure home, location, or job. Only you can know.

Identifying what we need to feel safe and secure in life in this moment is the first part of the process of establishing healthy and stable roots. We want to begin moving forward by, first, going back and clearing the past. A simple meditation or breathing exercise can work wonders for doing this. First, grab a pen or pencil and a piece of paper. Then find a quiet, comfortable place to sit. With your mouth open or closed, inhale the air all the way down to your diaphragm; on the exhale, push all of the air back out through your mouth. To bring yourself into the moment and silence the thoughts swirling through your mind, as you breathe in, silently recite, *I am breathing in*. As you exhale, silently recite, *I am breathing out*. Now close your mouth, and try to breathe in and out through your nose. Continue this breath for one to three minutes (and as long as you'd like). When you've finished, ask your now quieter mind: What do I need to clear out from my past? What do I need to let go of? Write down whatever comes to you, no matter how nonsensical or irrelevant it may seem. You might surprise yourself with what you learn and know.

Another method is to ask a trusted loved one or close confidant what you tend to focus on when you discuss your upbringing or the first years of your life. It's amazing how we often have the answers we need right there but sometimes need a second party to point them out to us. A kind mirror helps us heal.

A third option I like is to ask the universe for some help. Let intuition begin to shine through with the power of the magnificent energy of a more open universe and possibly what we call the miraculous. Begin your day by setting an intention to clear out whatever no longer serves you from your past and adding open-mindedness toward help from something bigger or more than self—then see what the day presents. The universe has a way of showing us what we need to clear out through the signs or inexplicable coincidences that pop up once we give voice to our intention.

Finally, do some *literal* clearing. Clean out your cupboards, closets, garage, piles, or storage areas—anywhere that you have a tendency to tuck things away so you can deal with them later or put things out of sight. This, too, is a powerful way of clearing out your roots and physical foundation. This gives your mind and body more room to move. Intuitive information is a form of movement.

Once we clear out the past, we make way for the new. We can move past those voices of others or previous versions of ourselves that may be giving us an outmoded notion of what we need to feel safe and secure in the world. With those voices quieted, we can be in the present moment to understand what we need *now*.

In some cases, this may be a difficult process because to determine what we *need* as individuals, we must first shave away the conditioning of what we were *taught* we need. It's like peeling back the layers of an onion. Perhaps our parents believed that a good, safe, and stable life consisted of owning a home. Without thinking too much about this, we worked toward home ownership only to find that it was ultimately not fulfilling . . . or currently possible. Often, when we desire something from an inauthentic place, it becomes difficult, challenging, or painful to draw into our life. Maybe a feeling of security comes from exploring the world—in which case following our parents' pattern of purchasing a home simply will not provide us with the same sense of stability and rootedness it provides them. Our roots are within and go with us everywhere we are. So for those with strong roots, remaining in one place is not always important or necessary for a feeling of stability and "home." For others, it is. The important part here is to know what *you* need.

Once we've determined what we personally need to feel most rooted and secure in life (preferably beginning with our nonphysical needs), we can begin to follow that path of working toward grounding our wishes and establishing our own sense of security. This security will help our intuition come alive, the way the mind loves organization and foundation. Even if it takes a while to acquire what you are seeking, there's often a great sense of safety even in knowing that you are doing the work that needs to be done to take care of *you* and your own specific needs. To move your life forward. This forward flow adds an intuitive feeling of accomplishment and confidence, which flows back to clearing fear around intuition. Another tool that has been hugely helpful for both clients and myself is bolstering this work with intention—stating wants and needs to the world and allowing the universe to do its work in opening up the right pathways. Perhaps you ultimately find that what you need to feel grounded is a bit more elusive—that it's not one specific thing you need or are lacking, but the *feeling* itself. In this case, try regularly reciting a simple mantra such as: *I am safe. I am provided for.* This is yet another form of an intention . . . and a highly effective one!

Let's take a look at how adopting the patterning of our families can manifest in root issues—and how intuition is no longer felt or heard. I met my client Eric when he was in his early thirties. By this young age, he had already worked in the stock market for more than a decade and was burning out quickly. In the past several months, he had discovered that all of the status symbols, professional accolades, and beautiful possessions that he had always believed would make him feel secure and as though he belonged weren't really doing that at all. Essentially, Eric felt empty—as though he had a huge hole to fill. He was working harder than he ever had before but making less money. He was beginning to feel suffocated by the pressure of paying a high mortgage for his Manhattan apartment and supporting his wife and child. Eric was no longer passionate about his job; he had gone into his profession only for financial security and as a means of supporting his family's needs. By the time he came to me for a reading, Eric was at his wit's end—he felt like he had worked very hard for all these years and deserved more than he was getting. His stress was exacerbated by the fact that, until this point, he had always used working out as a means of blowing off steam. Now even that outlet wasn't available to him because he had become too stiff to exercise.

When I first spoke to Eric on the phone, he was frantic, ungrounded, and compensating for his insecurities by presenting himself as overly confident. He talked about enjoying the fruits of his labor, but it was clear that he was doing this as a means of proving that he had agency over his own life. His intuition was very closed down. He did not see all the pain this chase has caused. My reading revealed that Eric did not, in fact, have agency over his life, as his relationships were crumbled and no external monetary gain could help him feel secure. In that moment, Eric felt completely unable to emotionally recalibrate and take care of himself or his family in the way that he wanted. This confusion and lack of complete control was ego shattering for him. It was from Eric that I was reminded that we cannot root easily if we do not trust the ground we're planted upon.

During my reading with Eric, we came to realize that not only was he overstimulated and overtaxed by his drive to meet exterior needs, but he had also lost his sense of reality. He was making stock market decisions that were gutsy but unrealistic. He was snapping quickly at his wife and child due to the stress and pressure he felt, and he got to the point where he required stiffer drinks after work each day as a means of slowing himself down. Eric was like a kite that didn't have anyone holding its string—he was floating away.

Through Eric's reading, it became apparent that this was all a result of the fact that, with good intentions, he had built a life that fulfilled not *his* needs but those exterior needs that his father and peers thought (and thus taught Eric) were so important. It was about acquiring exterior, material goods— extra cars, the "right" labels and memberships, gluttonous food, high bar tabs, and so on. Once Eric realized that the dream he was chasing and the needs he was trying to fulfill were not his own but, rather, those that had been passed down to him in his upbringing, he understood that he needed to re-direct his efforts and start working toward those things that *he* needed to feel safe, secure, and grounded in *his* present moment, not in someone else's past.

The reading gave Eric a plan to start grounding himself. Yes, he *did* need to get back to working out for his own sanity, but first he had to flush out the excess cortisol (stress hormone) and insulin his body was holding on to. I guided him in sitting meditation every day and concentrate on the feeling of his tush supported by the ground beneath him, all the while visualizing the stress, expectation, and need for labels flushing down, out of him and into the earth. (The earth can support all of the energy we no longer need; it's a form of recycling.)

It also came in that he needed to add more minerals, multivitamins, and water (all earth elements) into his body and to eat cherries and pomegranate seeds, take Himalayan salt baths, and drink more mineral-based water in order to draw more minerals and vitamins into his body (which, again, is exactly what roots do). These elements all both detoxify and promote absorption, and they are tools that often come in handy for someone who lacks deep rooting. Beyond all of this, I advised Eric to admit to himself in no uncertain terms that those things that somewhat fulfilled his lineage did not fulfill him. And beyond *that,* the intuition I received advised Eric to figure out what he *did* need to feel safe, secure, and grounded in life today. Again, this may sound easy, but it often isn't. It can be extremely difficult and confusing to redirect our thinking and learning to tune in to ourselves and our own wants and needs when we've been living our life according to the patterning of others. It can be surprising painful . . . as if we are literally sprouting new limbs.

Eric was up for the challenge, though. Within a few weeks of practicing the program that came through in his reading, Eric had already returned to the gym and was able to stretch more. He began to set new rules in his house that were not a reflection of the rules and priorities in the house he grew up in but, rather, that reflected what worked for Eric, his wife, and their growing family. Eric felt more present and stimulated by his surroundings. He let go of the need to compete and always be in motion. He decided to go to talk therapy to clear out the frustrations he'd held on to from his own upbringing. Releasing the burdens he'd been unconsciously carrying around for all these years almost immediately resulted in an improvement in Eric's health and sleep patterns. Most of all, Eric came to the realization that his life was his own to take responsibility for, and he ventured out on his own to create a new company. Eric felt renewed and replenished. So can you.

The First Energy Center and the Spiritual Being:
The Forest

So far in this chapter, we've focused on how the root energy center affects us on a personal level. It's also important to understand how the state of our root energy center extends outward to affect our communities and society as a whole on a global level. When we experience an abundance of root issues, so too do our loved ones, and when we as a collective experience them, so does the world at large. Just as the root energy center affects our personal ideas of basic needs and security, it also affects these issues on a broader scale. The more instability we feel with these issues in our personal lives, the more this is reflected in society.

Prime examples of societal root energy center institutions include the housing and stock markets, the health care system, politics, education, and the prison and justice systems. When we see these systems breaking down and the population experiences a general sense of lack and unease toward them, it is a sure sign of an abundance of broken roots within a society. We begin to try to root in unhealthy and controlling ways, such as creating more borders or feeling that resources are lacking. We may not offer security and stabilization to our neighbors.

Societal institutions are greatly associated with the root energy center. They provide a feeling of safety in numbers and security in community that harkens back to our more primal days. Imbalances in the root can lead to fight-or-flight responses—even when we are not actually in danger—that often cause us to seek bigger, "safe" structures to offer grounding or a sense of inclusion. This reliance on group mentality occurs more often when our own roots aren't stable. Some forms of organized religion are a prime example of this.

Organized religion may be used to fill what's lacking in one's root with rules, a security structure, and protocols or conditions to follow to avoid fear. When these are followed, practitioners are provided with certain assurances. This is not a negative thing in and of itself, but as with all aspects of life, balance, moderation, and an open mind are important. Roots should be established through a healthy balance of maternal and paternal energy. The feminine aspects of inclusion and equality are often not completely represented in religion.

Some who have not experienced solid roots may turn to organized religion for a sense of safety. If we cling to this and become fanatical as a response to internal fear or insecurity, then this structure can become more exclusionary and less rooting. On a global level, this can potentially become destructive. Pick up the newspaper on any given day and see where this sort of over-attachment and religious labeling can lead. It is uprooting.

It is so crucial that we remember we are part of a greater whole and that each of our lives and states of being matter—not only on a microcosmic level but also on a macrocosmic one. It can sometimes be difficult to snap out of the status quo and do the work it takes to make our life better and fulfilling. If you find yourself in this stuck mind-set, remember that what you do in your own life and how healthy and balanced you are have a *profound* effect on the environment around you. Each of us plays a role in building security and safety that children, children's children, and so on, will live with. We may be able to see in our own lives how difficult it can be to change patterning that is passed on from the older generations of our family. The best thing we can do is to try to alleviate these issues and imbalances so that those who come after us can start with a clearer and more solid foundation.

Intuition is deeply affected by our roots and our basic human needs being met. We are all physical beings—we cannot forget this fact. To hear our inner voice from a strongly rooted place should feel grounding and supportive like a barefoot walk on warm, fine sand or cool, fresh dirt. When we access our intuition from a secure place, while feeling safe and seen, intuition will offer wisdom without fail. From here our relationship with intuition begins to become quite reliable. We will discuss this further in the next chapter.

We do need silence and quiet time to hone this connection between intuition and our current moment in time. This is a form of intimacy that might feel new. Stay with this new feeling. Intuition will guide you. New situations and offerings of security will present themselves, often quickly.

Let's do a simple meditation to expand our roots, deepen our feelings of grounding, and strengthen our secure connection to our intuition.

Root Energy Center Meditation

Meditation is a key for clearing out our roots, our lodged memories, and our past. It also paves the way to a more secure future. Through meditation, we can open pathways for a new, rooted experience. We can ground and offer our first energy center a foundation that will allow our needs to be met in an easy, flowing fashion. Meditation greatly assists in this process of letting go of the old and drawing in the new through our feet and sits bones.

Mantras, or sayings, are a simple way of retraining our thoughts and our brain to come into a more present and relaxed mind. This assists in repatterning and breaking old habits in both action and thought. Before you begin your meditation, reflect on which of these mantras most resonates with you (or, if you'd like, create one of your own, beginning with the phrase *I am*):

I am rooted.
I am grounded.
I am safe.
I am secure.

Once you've selected your saying or mantra, find a comfortable spot to sit on the floor. Lengthen your spine upward and feel your seat connect to the ground. Whether you are inside or outside, become aware of the ground beneath you, supporting you. This helps you connect to the feeling of being supported and safe while meditating.

Your eyes may be closed or slightly open, whatever feels more comfortable or natural to you. If eyes are open, it can help to look down at a small angle, keeping your gaze on a spot on the floor in front of you.

As you begin to settle in, connect to your breath. If this doesn't come naturally to you, try repeating the following sentence in your head: *I am breathing in. I am breathing out.* The slower and more evenly you repeat this, the better. Begin to notice your inhale and your exhale.

Once your breath is slow and even, connect your grounding *I Am* saying with your breath. As you breathe in, silently recite, *I am.* As you breathe out, silently recite the affirmation part of your saying. Continue this breath-and-recitation pattern until your brain begins to calm and your mind can become a blank slate. This might take time, so be patient. The key is to perform this focused practice with a calm, open heart. This powerful *I Am* thought will center both your breath and your mind, and it will get you out of the pattern of fight-or-flight mode and analytical thinking. It will provide a way for your mind to relax and take ownership of the current moment and your intention. It will help you release current tension, mind wandering behavior, old thoughts, emotional and physical toxins, and blockages from your roots.

After connecting your thoughts with your breath, it can help to simply notice your chest and stomach rising and falling. When you are ready to finish, you may think of an internal dam, or root lock, at the base of your spine for the root energy to feel contained and connected. To create a root lock, contract the organs in your pelvis—for women this is a bit like a Kegel exercise yet a little deeper and higher—and visualize your breath reaching all the way down to your seat and exiting down through your legs, helping the circulation and elimination of old energy. Visualize new energy drawing up the feet, legs, hips, and sits bones, flushing and replenishing rooted energy. This visualization and practice can help energy feel directed and absorbed.

Continue breathing in new energy and life force, exhaling out old thoughts or energy. Give yourself between three and ten minutes per day for this practice, perhaps increasing the time by thirty seconds to a minute per week. Repeat this practice for five to seven days for a few weeks in a row. Begin to feel roots, feet, and legs become more energized.

The Root Guide

Ages:	0–7 years old
Color:	Red
In balance:	Feeling safe, secure, and provided for. Possessing a strong sense of grounding.
Imbalanced:	Joint pain or tightness (especially in the hips or knees); carrying weight in the hips or thighs; lower back pain; swollen feet; feelings of insecurity, not being safe, and unmet basic needs. Flighty personality that has a difficult time staying in one place, situation, or relationship for a long amount of time.

Supportive foods:	Bright red foods from the earth (check sugar content if appropriate), including red apple and cranberry, foods with roots such as radishes, red potatoes, beets; red beans and lentils. Red fruits, including watermelon, pomegranate, cherries, all red berries; food grown with deep tree roots or on a vine. Red herbal teas such as rooibos or hibiscus. Harvest grains and other deeply rooted grains and proteins. Earthly mineral stews and broths.
Beneficial practices:	Grounding down to earth by walking barefoot on soil, sand, or grass; doing strong, grounded yoga poses, such as tree and mountain. Eating rooted vegetables with an emphasis on those that are red or red-orange in color. Reestablishing roots by learning to forgive those mistakes or transgressions committed by caregivers in early childhood and learning to provide those things that instill a feeling of safety, security, and basic needs being met on a daily basis. Taking ownership of old story.
Sayings:	*I am rooted.* *I am grounded.* *I am safe.* *I am secure.*

3

THE SECOND ENERGY CENTER: THE SACRUM

Relationships

The second energy center is where it's all at. The second energy center governs our relationships with people and things, which is where so much of our attention goes. The second energy center is also all about forms of *pleasure*. In spiritual or energetic terms, we can relate this space in our body, around our sacrum (or sexual organs), to our relationship with people, things, joy, resources, attention, and creating (or creativity). The strong roots and grounded environment we create in the first energy center give us the foundation to enjoy pleasure, cocreating new ideas, and our loved ones in safe and secure ways.

Intuition can sometimes seem to stir up relationships because it gives us new information that can help us recognize when certain dynamics need to be flushed out. Bear in mind that ultimately this stirring (like the water element that represents this energy center) can bring contentment and more joy to everyone involved. This energy center affects intuition by supporting healthy relationships and bringing in joy. Healthy relationships in life beget a healthy relationship to our intuition. This energy center also tries its best to infuse health and to rebalance when our body lacks creative energy, isn't properly eliminating the old, or is damming forward flow. When unleashed to its full potential, this space in our body can deliver a lot of pleasure to our life through easier, more joyous relationships with stimuli, including sexual expression and orgasm. It also can bring new creation, new ideas, new relationships, and abundance. Doesn't this sound healthful and enriching? It is.

When you think of intuition, relationships probably aren't the first thing that comes to mind. That might be because when we think about relationships, often our mind jumps to thoughts of romantic partners, friends, or family. But our relationships actually extend out to encompass much more than that—they include our relationship with ourselves, our relationship with our community or outer world, and our relationship with everything *in* the world, both animate and inanimate. Intuition gauges all relationships as they pertain both to the pleasure they bring to our own lives, and the pleasure they bring to others. When intuition nudges us to let us know that this pleasure does not exist or has not reached its maximum potential, it encourages action.

Intuition can bring in great creativity, which is important for our own enjoyment and also for the collective experience. This means that when we ignore our intuition, we are actually ignoring our surroundings (including the Earth as a whole), our offspring, and fresh new ideas. This energy center offers new life in the literal sense as well as new ways of *being*. When we are in tune with intuition, birthing an idea, a child, or a new relationship becomes not only easier but also more enjoyable! We become more in tune with our emotional and creative nature, and this creates a beautiful cycle wherein our intuition becomes even *more* unmuted and unbridled.

Often the first inklings of independent creativity show up in grade school and junior high. During this period, the importance of our relationships with and focus on our peers, teachers, and hormones also increase. With the incorporation of all of these influences, we also become increasingly aware of how others see us. Our culture can become obsessed with this stage of growth, and some never completely mature past this age. Intuition helps us learn attachment and then un-attachment when we listen and understand that our creations (including the relationships we create) are never owned or meant to be kept only for the self. When we hear our intuition, our pleasure grows, as does our confidence to share ourselves in a creative and joyous way.

The second energy center affects our intuition by supporting healthy relationships that allow us to act with whole and pleasurable action rather than reaction. It can seem that what I do as an intuitive has the capacity to stir up relationships by bringing in information that encourages people to take action to alter them—and sometimes it *does* do that—but what intuition is really working toward is our destiny with more pleasure and enjoyment, the clearing of emotion for serenity. And so it can be inclusive of more joy. This is the type of relationship we want to cultivate with ourselves, our thoughts, our setbacks, and our mistakes. When we experience this in our own lives, we begin more easily to wish for the same compassion, empathy, and enjoyment for others as well. Intuition teaches us this when we listen to its wisdom. This approach to our relationships can also be cultivated on our own through parental influence by the time we are seven or eight years old, especially if it was mirrored to us during our young childhood.

Now, let's come back to the idea that the information intuition provides is always for the pleasure or good of all. In other words, what we create and enjoy is meant to be shared. When it's healthy, our relationship with intuition will feel like a gleeful squeal or hallelujah. It points us in the right direction to be braver and try new relationships as well as new ways of looking at relationships. Intuition creates those little nudges in us that seem to randomly encourage us to take a new class or pick up an old hobby we used to love. These creative endeavors—even when they seem little—get us back in touch with our creative and "being" side, and they help us to hear intuition even more clearly. On the other hand, if we quell our expressions of joy and pleasure, pleasure and new experiences becomes more limited as we age, and it can become more difficult to obtain that relaxed state we require to open a clear connection to intuition.

When our relationships with ourselves, others, or the world at large are out of whack, it becomes all too easy to unconsciously skew the information that intuition is providing, adding our own twist to it. We lack that clear connection that joy facilitates. When we do this, we are not acting as a clear conduit through which intuition's valuable information flows into or through us. (In fact, we may feel downright *repressed*.) This can happen in any number of ways, but a few primary examples of how our relationships affect our intuition and expression are: when we repress sexual pleasure, when we intuit information that we consider bad for someone we love and attach emotion or grief to it before deciding how to best honor the information, or when we receive information about our own lives that doesn't fit in with our worldview (or our *relationship* with the world) and thus do not heed it. Or we have a creative urge or desire that we do not bring to fruition.

Another major reason the second energy center affects our intuition is because it is here that creativity is biologically governed. Higher intuition (the information that comes from the divine energy within and around us) is inherently creative because it is a life force or life-enhancing energy—it comes from the source that actually *created* all that is. We want our second energy center to be clear and balanced because it allows our own individual creativity to connect with the greater creativity of the universe. And this is where magic happens. You can think of this connection between the second energy center and higher intuition as that of two people with a glimmer in their eyes having a conversation. They are in flow as their ideas and expressions move fluidly back and forth. The more fluent our own creativity is, and the more we foster that twinkle in our eye, the easier it will be to clearly interpret the information higher intuition is providing.

Ideally, relationships and pleasure go hand in hand. In an ideal world, all of our relationships would enhance our sense of love, protection, belonging, and safety. Unfortunately, this is not always the case. But the good news is that by bringing our attention to and balancing out our second energy center, we can enjoy more loving and fulfilling relationships and increase the pleasure in our life. We can learn to follow our own new thoughts rather than focusing on our own or others' remembrances of the past.

Intuition acts as our guide here. It shows us the role we ourselves play in clearing our own past life experiences and in creating space for the new. This can happen in simple ways. Maybe you follow through on an idea to create a painted image that pops into your head and clean out your old paint set to dig in. Or maybe you suddenly have a thought that you should eat more plant-based food to help balance your hormones in order to increase your chances of getting pregnant, and then you head right out to buy the foods that popped into your head. The possibilities are truly endless. When our relationship to our intentions is clear and we begin to get signs that show us our intuition was right on, we begin to more easily interpret and disseminate the intuition we receive as we are meant to. Following the above examples, these signs of correctly hearing intuition can come through in ways like the painting you decided to sit down and create sold right away or you became pregnant after switching up your diet.

We come into our second energy center, associated with the bright color orange, from the age of seven all the way up to around fourteen. We evolve rapidly during this important span of our growth. These years usher us from young childhood into adolescence, and a lot of growth and change occurs. Our families, while still important, are no longer the only focal relationships in our lives. As each year goes by, we become more and more dependent upon and invested in our relationships with our peers and our own bodies. We are now influenced not only by our parents but also by our teachers, coaches, and other adult authority figures.

As our scope of relationships expands, we develop other subsidiary relationships. For example, perhaps an eight-year-old develops a special bond with his art teacher. Not only does that relationship between those two individuals now exist, but it also likely affects the child's relationship with *art* as well.

So often in life, the literal and the figurative align—and the second energy center is a great example of that. Our second energy center is located around our sexual (or sensual) pleasure organs and includes our reproductive organs. This positioning is fitting because another influential element of those later, preteen years associated with the second energy center is that our hormones and stronger tinges of sexuality emerge. Our reproductive organs are where creation itself exists—and, as we've discussed, the second energy center is also the seat of our creativity in the more general sense. As we see more of the world and develop more relationships with the people and things around us, we begin to understand where our creativity and passion lie. We have an increasing amount of autonomy between the ages of seven and fourteen, so we can delve into these passions and creative urges in ways that are generally not possible at younger ages because we don't have as much access to or inspiration from the world at large and haven't yet developed our relationship with ourselves enough to fully understand what our passions are. This is exemplified in small ways that ultimately add up to us beginning to gain a better understanding of who we are—like starting to choose and make our own food, deciding who we want to play with at school, and picking what we want to wear. With all of this, we are starting to build out our own world based more and more on our own tastes and decisions, and through this, we begin to exercise our own creativity.

Already, we can see how each energy center builds upon the one before. If our first energy center is healthy and we have a solid foundation underneath us, it is easier and feels safer to branch out in a way that will allow us to know ourselves and have a healthy relationship with the environment around us because we have a safe home to come back to, both literally and figuratively. We are free to cultivate our creativity because, with the basis of safety and protection that the first energy center provides, we will feel more comfortable expressing our truest selves. Also, with a solid first energy center in place, we know what it is like to feel safe and protected in our relationships, so we are more naturally drawn to other relationships that will provide those same qualities.

As a culture, we are currently stuck in this sacral energy center. We have an extreme need to experience pleasure, we *expect* pleasure, and we wish for quick rewards, including the avoidance of both physical and emotional pain, which can numb deep pleasure. In general terms, we are imbalanced in that we pay ample attention to things that are outside of ourselves instead of within ourselves. This external focus includes too much emphasis on our status or rank within group activities, our outer appearance and the labels we wear, the size of our home, our children's accomplishments, and following trends no matter how much they adversely affect the environment. This also often leads to an unbalanced relationship with possessions. We want more. We put how we appear to others above how we feel about ourselves. We value quantity over quality when it comes to things like quelling loneliness or fatigue, and we are often on the hunt to obtain more possessions quickly. We crave more receiving rather than thoughtful giving, even if it's just information. This can be in our relationships with food, intense sensations, or pleasurable new images (such as those on Instagram, Facebook, and Twitter). *Easy, bigger,* and *more* are all big themes in how we live our lives today. The earthly world is paying the price for our collective second energy imbalance by not being able to replenish and realign what we use quickly enough. We are often not valuing connection as much as ourselves or self-desire. Natural resources are becoming more extended or polluted by our reliance on quantity; we see this in extreme in our consumption of things like soda and plastic toys. We keep needing *more*.

As we see in packaged food or branded label choices, this type of want does not often hit the intimate pleasure spot we think it will. This need for quantity can show up with food, in the home, and through social media, which "ranks" our relationships in terms of likes. This overindulgence can tax our relationship with our body, our intellect, our experience of intimacy, our hormones, and our resources. We may have a more difficult time getting pregnant, not have a healthy menstrual cycle, need sleeping pills to sleep, or experience yeast or dehydration within our body. We begin to go for quick adrenaline fixes with anyone or anything rather than real, intimate relationships. We choose what we can hold instead of touch. This begins to starve our deeper relationships with our intuition and our feeling worthwhile. We do not trust ourselves as deeply, and we turn to the outside for our sense of value. This breeds both loneliness and isolation. From that place, intuition cannot be heard in a healthy, creative way.

The fact that we as a culture are stuck in the sacral energy center also shows up in our overemphasis on sexuality. Sexuality and sensuality can be wonderful openers for intuition when engaging a mature mind and body. Sex and sensuality show up everywhere even for a young child—they are the basis of many advertising campaigns. We see them graphically portrayed on television, in movies, and on billboards. Even our children are sexualized at a younger age, wanting to emulate their creative idols in music, performance, and celebrity.

All of this results in an energy congestion in the second energy center and inhibits the flow of healthy chi, or energy, into both the heart and the part of the brain that houses intuition. We can help to combat this by being still. Stillness and quiet actually *increase* the flow of healthy hormones, bringing balance to our sexual organs. It creates a bridge back to intimacy.

On an individual level, we all must work on these imbalances and begin moving on up the energy centers from the very earthly sacral energy center to the third, heart, throat, and higher eye energy centers. When we become too attached to objects, our identity becomes tied up in them and we feel the need to collect and possess (and, in extreme cases, to hoard) rather than to give and receive with others in a balanced way. We are confusing love and attention with external commodities. This extends to the intangible as well—if we are imbalanced in the second energy center, we may not be able to value, or give and receive, those things that are free and infinite, like eye contact and attention.

So how do we correct this imbalance? We take a clear and honest look at our relationships. We look at how we can have healthier relationships with ourselves, our body, our family, our friends, and our community. We also look at our relationship with those things that provide a false sense of intimacy with each other, such as turning solely to social media and electronics for interaction. And finally, we nurture our creativity. With this chapter, we'll do exactly that.

The Second Energy Center and the Physical Being: Relationship with All Things

Intuition is a relationship with ourselves, our creator, our ego, and what our analytical mind is doing and *thinking*. This means that our fight-or-flight and warrior part of the mind needs to have a relationship with the *being* side of the mind, which values stillness. When we are physically healthy, we are more receptive . . . quieter . . . and we can more clearly hear our intuition when it comes to making everyday choices. This includes things like being more intuitive in our eating and more mindful about what we buy (*Is this good for me? For the planet?*), intuitively choosing when to act in pleasure and sexual expression (*Does my body feel relaxed and accepted here? Does my partner's? Am I here in this moment for healthy reasons?*), as well as what products to put on our face and body (*Does this add to my total health? Are these products wasteful?*). All of these situations rely upon the creativity and relational energy that resides in our second energy center. We want to use our intuition to maintain this physical balance.

It will come as no surprise that, particularly in the United States, many of us consume far too much—this extends to everything from clothes and other material items to digital media. This habit of consumption is perhaps most clearly manifested in our oversize food culture, wherein we consume in quantity rather than selecting the *right* things to provide our body with the sustenance it needs. We can see this through the broad overconsumption of foods that are lacking nutrients, our need for and addiction to sugar fillers, and our reliance on packaged foods—none of which fuel our intuition or our sensual organs with complete health and balance.

Many of us have developed a tendency toward using food for the wrong reasons, which can ultimately result in an addiction to food. This happens when we eat for reasons that don't have to do with physical hunger. You've probably heard the saying "eating your feelings." This is something that many of us do—we eat when we're sad, when we're scared, when we need comfort, or even when we're bored. Obviously, people do this for many reasons—because it's what we saw in our childhood homes growing up, because we are out of tune with our body, because we are masking pain, or simply because it's habit. In some cases, we do this because we feel empty, which becomes a second energy center issue when that feeling of emptiness stems from a lack of meaningful relationships or intimacy and pleasure with our selves or others.

Of course, some people also slant in the opposite direction by not eating enough or by going on extreme diets. This, too, is a second energy center manifestation. We feed into the images the outside world presents us with and ideals that have been projected onto us, and we may come to believe that we have to look a certain way so that we can be as good as others, fit in, or be seen and heard. A situation such as this represents a negative relationship with our body, intimacy, or self-image. Some buy into these images to a detrimental degree and are willing to malnourish themselves for the sake of appearance or attention. This mutes our intuition because when we do not nourish ourselves, it can confuse both our heart and our mind.

Whether it's eating too much or too little, these negative relationships with food that we've developed as a culture are not conducive to our health or achievement of pleasure, not only in terms of our physical body but also in our emotional, mental, and spiritual being aspects. When we are not providing ourselves with fuel for our life force, we are effectively stripping ourselves of the ability to experience joy and to open our mind. We must learn to tune in to what our body needs in any given moment and to provide it with exactly that. This requires presence. Getting into patterned eating, wherein we eat mindlessly or consume what we are served without consciously evaluating its worth, most often means that we are not listening to what we really need. For example, eating a turkey sandwich because it's lunchtime and that's what we always eat for lunch can be unhealthy, even though it's a pattern that involves eating "healthy" foods. In instances such as this, we're often not taking the time to tune in to what our body needs at any given moment.

Deciding what we need to eat in the moment can be a great practice in intuition. To do this, begin by asking yourself what your body is craving. This simple question unifies what we want and what we need. Our body will tell us what it needs when we take the time to ask. Begin by counting down slowly from twenty to calm the thinking part of your brain. Either close your eyes with eyes looking down under their lids or look down at your nose (with eyes closed) as you take between three and five deep, full breaths with equal inhale and exhale to still yourself; as you breathe, think of each color of the rainbow as a way of bringing balanced chi into the body. After maintaining these deep, full breaths for one to three minutes, bring your awareness to asking yourself what your body is deprived of, or simply call to mind seasonal vegetables, proteins, or whole foods that you have not eaten for a few days (or weeks). When one of these foods particularly catches your attention, you have your answer. Simple and mindful practices like this quiet one hone our relationship with our intuition and allow us to intuit what to ingest that is best for our body in the present moment.

With this kind of intuitive eating, you may notice you're hungrier than you realized (and, therefore, should not just stop at a quick mart or coffee shop) or that you're feeding something else that doesn't require food (like emotion or stress). Figuring out *how* to hear your intuition can take some time. Acknowledging the relationship with intuition is an important aspect of honing your intuition, especially when it comes to using it as a tool in making personal choices. We can become more aware of that other voice inside through breath work (see page 70 for a great breathing exercise). This calming of the mind around food can also help us be mindful of what is *really* in that package of our go-to food and how sugary foods can mess with our insulin and cortisol levels. It can help greatly to literally focus on your belly and ask what it needs (therefore creating a *relationship* with your stomach). Until we intuitively recognize that we are often making choices because of a craving, what those around us are eating, or what we were fed as kids, it can be difficult to make dietary changes. Do you need protein? Veggies? Some healthy fats? Or maybe you really do need that piece of chocolate in that moment. You will be coming from a more interactive, present place in choosing (and enjoying) your foods.

Until we practice a more intuitive relationship with ourselves, our eating patterns can be quite negatively affected when we eat in a rush. When we are in our doing, hurried state, our intuition just can't catch up. We are instead functioning from that fight-or-flight (or warrior) part of the brain that wants quick food, meaning food that is high in simple carbohydrates and is quick to eat and digest versus food that is slow cooked, high in nutrients, and slower to digest. Using our intuition to develop more nourishing eating habits plays a key role in beginning to trust ourselves and our intuition on a basic level. We are actually *hearing our body* more and providing it with the calming, healthy support it needs.

Allowing ourselves to stay present as we're eating so that we're fully satisfied and self-aware when we become full is also a good practice in being present. This helps improve our body's relationship with outside stimulus and is actually correlated with connecting to our intuition. Throughout history, we have never been so hurried around food except in specific situations when we sensed a threat. Today we see the ticking clock, weight gain, and fear of missing out as threats. In earlier days, people tended to have more awareness about food, and they cultivated a calmer, more interpersonal relationship with it through practices like spending more time in the kitchen for food prep, saying grace before a meal, and lingering over more traditional gatherings around a family or communal table without the distraction of television or electronic devices. In this day and age, simply turning off your electronic devices while you eat can be a good step toward more centered, intuitive eating. Give yourself the gift of fully chewing and savoring a bite, feeling that sense of nourishment spread through your body. Even noticing the texture and flavor of your food as you eat calms the brain and brings you into the present moment, where, again, intuition resides. Listening to your body in the moment is an intuitive act, and it's a step toward understanding that intuition requires your attention.

We can look at all of this as a form of connecting or *building* our relationship with food, but more importantly, we're building a comfortable relationship with time and pleasure. We will not always experience intuition instantly. We might ask the universe for more signs and need to wait patiently. Experiencing a presence in the current moment with something as easy (or not as easy) as eating food—rather than doing a dozen other things at the same time—balances your attention, your brain, your digestion, your adrenals, and your intuitive relationship with yourself.

Also pay attention to how you feel after eating quick or habitual foods. Notice whether or not you feel bloated after eating, if you have indigestion, if you feel uncomfortable, or even guilty. If you do experience any of these sensations, it might be that you are eating too much or too fast, or that you're eating foods that are not serving your body's need for enjoyment and pleasure. Speed, when it comes to pleasure, does not serve an open, balanced intuitive mind. Slow and steady actions often cause less reaction. This is important, in terms of connecting both with intuition and with your relationships with things in your life.

It is important to mention here how much acidity in the body can play a role in hearing and connecting to our intuition. Why? A balanced, clear mind and body can be a great asset to a healthy, strong relationship with our intuition. Acidity, however, can lead to confusion and imbalance in our blood, urine, and metabolism. An alkaline state greatly helps our relationship with a healthy body, our thoughts, and our intuition. (You can test the pH balance—alkaline versus acidic—through a blood or urine sample.) We want to get back to that natural alkaline state to maintain our body's minerals and vitamins, more easily eliminate toxins, and enhance mental clarity and emotional harmony. All of these qualities support our intuition as well as our longevity, radiant health, and general life experience. Cancer cannot grow in an alkaline body. Our relationship with our intuition can.

We live in a culture that, aside from dictating the value of the size and shape of our body, values youth to what feels like an unhealthy degree. Plastic surgeries, Botox, fillers, and other aesthetically "enhancing" procedures are a multibillion-dollar industry in America today. Every year, younger and younger patients are engaging in these procedures. Botox is no longer a way of smoothing wrinkles but now is also a means of preventing them from appearing at all. In doing this, we are fighting nature and time. But we are *meant* to be, to experience a rich, full, and expressive life that includes times of stress and times of laughter. Our physical body is a reflection of all of those unique moments and experiences that ultimately constitute our life. When we try to prevent or erase the passage of time in a physical sense, we are also disconnecting intimacy, expression, and shared experiences. We are eschewing our ability to fully emote with others in favor of a pristine physical appearance. Rather than embracing the aging process and the mark that living a full life leaves on our body, so many of us are trying to fight or override that natural process so that we can fit into the mold of what society and the media tell us we are supposed to be—eternally young and flawless. These physical tweaks represent not only a skewed relationship with our own body but also with our relationships with other people—how can we truly connect with others if we are not allowing our foreheads to wrinkle in concern or our laugh lines to become a bit more pronounced when we smile together over a shared memory?

As we know deep down, this can be an empty and losing battle. We are all meant to age, and this can be a beautiful and rich process. A natural order of things. We can all be whole in our own, individual ways rather than molding ourselves into a simplified form of beauty that may rob us of individuality and the wisdom that maturity naturally brings. We've learned that the way to be seen and heard is to look the part, act the part, or wear an item that will gain attention or validate us. I've sadly witnessed many fall into this trap only to find emptiness, immaturity, narcissism, depression, and anxiety as they try to cram themselves into physical or social molds that simply don't represent who they actually are. And with the proliferation of social media, our children are receiving these messages at younger and younger ages.

As we also know, today's media and pop culture put an increasingly heavy emphasis on sexuality. There is a lot more access to sexual imagery through commercials, the Internet, and headlines on magazines we read as we wait to check out at the grocery store. This can affect us in a couple of different ways. When we see graphic sexuality constantly on display through things like online porn, television shows, movies, and advertisements, we can all too easily lose touch with the idea of what intimacy is—a coveted, sensory act. Also, if our relationship with ourselves and our pleasure received through sexuality aren't strong, we can begin to mirror the images we see on-screen or the expectations of others. This does not completely fill our internal well of pleasure. Our intuition wants us to have more joy and pleasure in our own lives on a day-to-day basis through the way we dress, touch, and interact with one another. It's healthy! Sexuality is a beautiful thing and is *good* for our intuition. It calms and clears our body and our mind. It offers pleasure, both for ourselves and our partner. However, when we constantly need more and more stimuli in this regard, it ceases to create joy and deep pleasure, as is the case with any addiction or fixation, be it sexual gratification, food, money, drugs, or attention.

To bring your attention back to your individual senses in a way that will help you become more aware of them both in terms of sensuality and everyday situations, stop wherever you are—cease all activity, including speaking. Close your eyes briefly. Bring your mental focus to *just* the sound of your breathing for twelve rounds of breath, taking longer inhales and exhales than you are used to. Open your eyes once again and notice what's in front of you, but in a more detached, observant fashion than usual. Notice not only what you see but also what you hear and smell. Then visualize seeing, hearing, and smelling *only* what you think will enhance your health or your life experience. This is a way of transforming your experience so that you are not just a witness but also a *participant*. Practicing this way of being in an experience also lets us soak up intimacy in new ways. We begin to connect more deeply to the world and people around us when we focus on the simple yet powerful offerings our senses provide.

Simplicity works. If we truly stop and notice the *color* of a ripe strawberry and we *feel* what a ripe strawberry feels like, we will take better notice of the taste and smell as well because our senses are turned on. This is also true when it comes to the person in front of us, whether it's in a sexual situation or not. When we practice seeing others more clearly with our first five senses, the sixth and seventh senses tune in as well. We may notice a tiredness under their eyes, and we might offer them more compassion or attention.

Because the sacral energy center is tied to our reproductive system, hormonal imbalance (in women and men) and an unhealthy colon (in men and women) are often clear signs in readings that a client is experiencing a second energy center imbalance.

Intuition is a knowing, and if we begin to know what is going on with us physically, we connect our physicality to our intuition, thus allowing intuition to open all the more rapidly.

The Second Energy Center and the Emotional Being: Finding Balance in Relationships

Ideally, we all experience relationships with others and with ourselves that leave us feeling healthy and fulfilled. We experience a balance in which we give and receive equally, recognize and embrace others for who they really are at the deepest core of their being, and feel equally accepted in return. Achieving this balance often requires that we not only see others with compassion and love but also see ourselves through that same lens of acceptance. When we do this, we have achieved harmony in the second energy center.

I find that some of my clients stumble a bit with including their relationship with themselves in the same category as their relationships with others. Without honoring this important connection we have with ourselves, we are leaving our joy and pleasure in someone *else's* hands. This does not help *us* open our own intuition because we are inherently out of touch with ourselves. It also robs us of the pleasure we will feel when we know something intuitively. We need to have that inner trust and confidence that a good relationship with the self breeds in order to read outside situations.

As we develop relationships with others, we inherently begin to see ourselves in a different light because we are now seeing how we relate to and, for lack of a better word, "compare" (or contrast) to others. This is what those early, sometimes uncomfortable, grade school and junior high years are all about. Ideally, during this time, we will begin to see our own light and begin to understand what we will contribute to our community. We compare and contrast with others to hold space, contribution, and hopefully pleasure for the well-being of both ourselves and others. Unfortunately, many of us never get past the comparing-and-contrasting stage of relationships. This new understanding of responsibility for the self and for gathering our own pleasure is important for growth and finding space in a society, community, or group. It is not a step in our growth we can skip if we want a healthy, responsible relationship with our intuition.

One of the most important elements in any relationships we have, either with people or with things, is an understanding of how great a role our relationship to ourselves plays in them. Some of us allow the *other* to take precedence over the *self* in a relationship, which isn't always ideal. Women, in particular, still often think it is egocentric to put themselves in the top running for self-care or compensation or for wanting to control their own destiny or life experience. I feel this is in part our nurturing, communal nature, and it's also a leftover element of a more patriarchal society. Girls witness a lot of mythical imagery about being "saved" or "taken care of" through television shows, movies, commercials, and at times even in their own childhood homes. This theme that someone or something outside of us possibly holds the key to our happiness can take the place of intuition. There are often louder messages of feminine reliance on males (even a masculine God) and this can drown out the quieter, feminine voice of intuition. Both men and women learn consciously or unconsciously to rely on "other" for a relationship to joy and freedom. A shift to a more "centered" view is important.

One of the marks of a truly healthy and balanced second energy center is an understanding that we, as individuals, already possess everything we need to be the best and truest version of ourselves. While relationships enhance our life and are imperative to growth and balance, the relationship with our inner and outer self should be number one on the list. It's a powerful way to thrive and embrace aging with joy and worth. Others cannot bestow true power, worth, agency, or belonging upon us. This comes from within. Without this understanding, we run the danger of choosing relationships for unhealthy reasons, too often basing our decisions on needs that were not met during our younger years. We might look to others for security or self-worth, or to maintain a roof over our head rather than selecting relationships that provide the best means for organic growth and that allow us to be our most authentic selves.

When it comes to intuition, outside voices and opinions must take the passenger seat to our internal whisperings. This means we go to ourselves *first* and then let others weigh in with their opinions. This creates a type of bond with the self, which is internally what intuition is. This bond not only allows us to decipher what we feel and know to be true in a situation (versus someone else's projection) but also to own our feelings. We help everyone by doing this because then we, in turn, do less projecting upon others, and everyone can more easily tune in to their own voice. Intuition requires that we trust ourselves and that we are eventually able to freely express ourselves to others without fear of judgment.

On the other end of the relational spectrum of second energy center imbalance, we may choose relationships that feed into narcissism or, on the extreme end of the spectrum, abuse. This is often the result of skewed views of or experiences with power and self-worth, and it stems from insecurity or a feeling of lacking something. For example, we might choose relationships with people who we feel are inferior to us and thus allow ourselves to feel a sense of superiority or dominance—or, simply, to feel needed. Alternatively, if we do not feel good about ourselves, we may feel inferior or subservient to those around us and lose our sense of agency and worth in the process. In this case, many people end up choosing a mate they feel gives them a higher status, bragging rights, or more attention. None of these are healthy relationships, and they all create imbalances that can result in situations that are controlling, isolating, and quite empty.

By about second grade, right around the time we start developing deeper relationships with others outside of our family, we begin to have an awareness of our social status among our peers. This new awareness informs how we treat the world and how the world treats us throughout our life. As we move into adolescence, the opinions and perceptions of our peers only grow more important. By encouraging our children to have a stronger emphasis on emotional intelligence and by offering them the room and time for feelings to be expressed, we will have more highly emotionally intelligent thirteen-year-olds. Can you imagine? This very well could also allow our children to steadily gain more and more wisdom (and self-worth and compassion, as we will describe in the following chapters) because we are teaching them such a healthy relationship with the *whole* self at such a young age. Were we to do this, the entire *planet* would change for the better. I believe *that* would be the world that nature intended.

The early teen years are getting trickier and trickier as we ignore our "being side" and squeeze intuition out of our children's natural growth process. Think back to junior high and high school and the social patterns that you perhaps experienced or, at least, witnessed during that time. My guess is that many of us, either ourselves or perhaps through our children, have seen the queen or king bee versus wannabe scenario. Or how "popular" thoughts and trends do not leave room for a lot of empathy around those who do not fit into a certain mold or exude the current trend. Unfortunately, our society fosters this unhealthy way of thinking and interacting during these formative years. This scenario plays out a lot, especially among girls in their adolescent years, but we can often see the relational behavior pattern in our adult lives, too, whether we're seven or forty-seven. There is still a large fascination with who has what and what others look like, live like, or dress like; this is encouraged even further by trade magazines and award shows, which are built around comparisons and peeking into the lives of others to pass judgment.

I see this play out both in my parents' generation through eye-rolling and comments about one another's lives *and* in the park with four-year-olds who are telling their playmates they have more shoes than them while peeking out over designer sunglasses. Many are emulating this behavior from parental or media influences. Truthfully, this is tied to moving through those early teen years without learning emotional intelligence and evening. Without it, competition runs rampant.

Many of my clients have had this dynamic play out in their own lives, whether they were the king, the queen bee, or the wannabe—or both. One of the examples that stands out the most in my mind is Ashley, who was a self-professed quintessential queen bee in high school and greatly enjoyed the status that came with that role. Throughout high school, Ashley ruled the roost—she had a sweet gaggle of girlfriends who followed her every move. Many young men wanted to go out with her. Even as a thirty-eight-year-old adult, Ashley looked back at those days fondly and felt an ongoing sense of confidence based on the "it" girl status that had been conferred upon her in high school. Once high school came to an end, Ashley left town to go to college. A few years after graduation, she moved back home and was surprised to find out that those who had followed her so closely in high school didn't exactly welcome her back with open arms.

When Ashley came to see me, she was confused and depressed. She couldn't understand why none of her high school friends were returning her phone calls or inviting her to gatherings. She claimed it was because she was ahead of her time and more "evolved" than her former classmates. Despite the fact that it had now been two decades since graduation, Ashley was still dressing in the style that had been popular when she was in high school. She was stuck. The reading with Ashley quickly showed that she had never grown out of that queen bee dynamic that she felt had served her so well in high school. In any situation she was in, she wanted the attention to be focused on her. She was, in effect, stealing energy from those around her and had a tendency to unconsciously use fear tactics as a means of keeping others near and loyal to her.

You have probably experienced an energy stealer at some point in your life. This is when a person sucks up a lot of the air in the room or stirs the pot to draw attention back to them. It's taking someone else's personal power. It is also a violation of a person's boundaries or self-contained energy reserve. This can include things like continually calling a friend to come over for support, getting an adrenaline rush by encouraging someone to chime in to a rude comment about a third party, or something as subtle as catching someone's eyes to draw them into an eye roll. We can feel quite drained and emotionally deprived after being with this sort of person or group. Such scenarios often happen when a queen bee or dominant person is present.

While Ashley may have gotten away with energy stealing in high school, it did not work so well in the adult world. Those who used to follow her now had confidence of their own. Ashley did not recognize that her wish for status and attention had taken energy and, at times, resources away from her friends. She was blind to the effect she had on others because she had spent the past two decades more self-absorbed and caught in her own mind to see what was happening to anyone else around her. Understandably, Ashley's former friends no longer wanted to partake in this dynamic.

Ashley's twenty-year high school reunion rolled around, and she was excited to attend. Once she got there, though, she had several difficult conversations and awkward situations, through which she came to realize how many bridges she had burned in her relationships with other females. She also understood how many people she had hurt in high school. I commended Ashley for her quick understanding of this situation. She had stepped out of her ego to see more of the whole picture.

As Ashley and I continued to meet, she began to understand that she constantly felt the need to be the leader in most situations. Much of this, it turned out, had to do with her need for control, which stemmed from her own insecurities—a low self-esteem; a competitive nature, which led to unhealthy views of relationships with other females; and an unrealistic expectation for everyone else to consider her needs first (a form of narcissism). Ashley didn't feel confident about herself in her own right, so the easier way to achieve a feeling of self-assurance was through having importance conferred upon her by her peers. Put simply, Ashley didn't enjoy herself very much, so she tried to fill that void by controlling others so that they would act as if they enjoyed being with her.

Through our readings, Ashley realized that she was ready to let go and grow into the person she wanted to be today. She came to understand that although she had been getting what she needed, it often came at the price of those around her. One by one, she went back to her friends and made amends by admitting that she had required a lot of attention and, in achieving this, had taken attention and space away from them. Then, Ashley began to work on herself emotionally. She worked through *The Work of Byron Katie,* a book about self-inquiry written by Byron Katie. She also began to exercise, which provided her body with endorphins, allowing her to feel good from within. Furthermore, Ashley wrote down five traits she admired about each friend from high school. She then expanded the list to teachers and, finally, her parents. This helped Ashley to see the world outside of herself. She began to see that her entire life had been focused on creating an external image rather than fostering her own internal gifts and accepting herself for who she was rather than who she appeared to be to others. She bought a bright-blue journal to help in her healing. She wrote down notes about her feelings (mostly about insecurity, loss, and not feeling seen or heard) and the feelings of others. Her growth was astounding.

The process took months, but the rewards were significant. Once Ashley started to become comfortable with and more compassionate and accepting of herself, she attracted a very smart and caring mate, who eventually became her husband. Once Ashley gained confidence in herself, she was able to shed that fear of allowing others to see who she really was, and with that she found the most real and rewarding relationship of her life. Although she wasn't able to salvage all of her high school friendships, she eventually cultivated some new ones. In these friendships, she was very mindful about giving as much as she received and relinquishing control. She now understood that it was just as important for her friends to be themselves and to have the opportunity to do and achieve the things they desired as it was for her to do the same.

The transformation I've seen in Ashley is profound. She has a new peace about her that is the result of not only being a more authentic version of herself but also of being surrounded by people who truly care about her for who she is and vice versa. Ashley has learned to bring a sense of compassion and caring rather than competition to her relationships. Her entire world has changed be-cause of this, and her second energy center is now more balanced and healthy.

Ashley is not alone in this pattern. The world is equally full of people who are stuck in either the queen bee or the wannabe category, which often stems from an ungrown relationship with both the self and with others. Neither of these roles lends itself to healthy relationships. No one wants to feel stuck in a stunted growth pattern. If we are not choosing to be confident in ourselves, true to who we are or who we wish to be, we are often unable to cultivate authentic, balanced relationships. And without healthy relationships, our growth and energy become more stagnant. Just like Ashley, we can get stuck. Our children and intimate relationships often mirror this and can stagnate along with us. We often see our own stagnation reflected in how our families deal with deep emotions, how intimate friendships bloom and are sustained, and how emotional turmoil influences our DNA and mental health.

In our culture, we have a tendency to let our peers determine our value—this goes beyond school age and includes our peers through all areas of life, whether it be at work, in our social group, or in our neighborhood or community. The truth is that we're hardwired to be communal . . . and this is lovely! Our peers and community will always influence us. But it is important that we learn to trust ourselves enough to be secure in who we are on our own, stripped of labels and comparison. Value that stems from emotional intelligence does not come from the outside. It radiates from the inside out. Without a strong sense of self, we run the danger of letting our peers, celebrities, or the media dictate our worth and who we should be.

The Second Energy Center and the Intellectual Being: Showing Up in the World and in Our Relationships

If we move our thoughts and experiences only through the fight-or-flight or competitive part of the brain, our relationships will not be whole or satisfactory. In today's world, they need the creative side—the feminine, nurturing, inclusive side—and the emotional intelligence that comes from that part of us within. If experiences are only funneled through our "doing" side of the mind, they will have a more linear, ladderlike feel, while emotions are more circular and need a hug more than they need the application of logic. Much as we try, we cannot rank our emotions or determine that one person's emotions are more important than another's to solve them.

When we get into a highly emotional place, and we do not trust the environment, the brain triggers cortisol, insulin, and adrenaline. Often instead of going straight to the source of our emotion or discomfort, we seek comfort and peace of mind through outside sources like pretty visuals, sugar, stimulants, distraction, and other quick feel-good pick-me-ups. With this, the part of the brain that needs to rest and acts calmly and mindfully will remain dormant. This can lead to an unhealthy mental desire to control or forget emotions through reason and compartmentalization. In the extreme, this can lead to a complete disconnect from pleasure of the things our mind uses to numb disappointing relationships, circumstances, and emotions. This is, in a word, addiction.

When we are in this cycle of plowing through old pain or broken relationships in a mind-over-matter sort of way, intuition is often muted. Yes, there might be moments when intuition or signs become stronger, leading us to break addiction cycles and accept help. But, for the most part, when addictions are going, we are not in a place to listen to *anyone,* let alone intuition.

Addiction is found in the second energy center because it is a relationship with something external or "other." It often occurs when a lack of pleasure or joy is present in one's life. Addiction can also be thought of as an *illusory* means of achieving mental ease (pleasure) around (among other things) an unenjoyable relationship with a person, memory, self-loathing, or abusive or disappointing experiences. There is no way to have a life without interacting and having deep, intimate relationship to something outside of us. This starts at birth with our mother and father, whether they are present or not. Often, the catalyst for addiction is filling a hole someone or something created. The relationship to the stimulus represents a warped relationship with pleasure—or at least some temporary relief from pain. Obviously, addiction is not a sustainable form of healthy relationship with pleasure. The analytical mind will trick us into thinking this or that object will fix a situation. The intuitive part of the mind knows this is not true. When we are addicted to something—which, unfortunately, so many are in this day and age—it represents an unbalanced relationship with self and the current moment.

Sitting with the pain of the past or not being able to keep up in the modern world leads to escapism in various forms, which only further exacerbates the lack of intimacy and compassion in our life. We become imbalanced, we feel disempowered, and with this, we often do not know when to stop consuming. Or perhaps we use this consumption as a refuge or a way of blocking other unhealthy relationships, deficiencies, problems, or difficult emotions that we do not feel empowered to handle in a healthy way. The soul is sometimes referred to as our personal power, and if we feel disempowered in a relationship, especially at a young age, the imbalances of loss of intimacy and agency can be all-consuming and extremely difficult to bear.

Addiction is a self-perpetuating cycle that affects our relationships with other people. When our focus is on addiction, it becomes very difficult to cultivate other relationships outside of that. This generally results in displeasure or isolation, which exacerbates the situation further. We tend to recognize drug addiction the most, but there are so many other types: addiction to food, sugar, shopping, gambling, or another individual, just to name a few. Anything that we rely on as a crutch and unhealthily depend upon can become an addiction. Any of these things can be a way of escaping other relationships, the world, and our struggles. They provide a mental escape, when we can't physically escape a relationship, situation, or emotion. In our culture, we have been trained to avoid pain at all costs, in addition to avoiding many other feelings. It is a part of the patriarchal, Puritanical basis our country was founded upon. When we are addicted, it is particularly difficult—at times impossible—to show up intuitively. Not only this, but addiction is also often judged by others, which causes the spiral to intensify, often adding more shame and driving us toward even more addictive behaviors.

One of my favorite readings to date was with an old surfer named Chris. He had a heavenly house on the ocean and, from the outside, his life looked like idyllic California living. It didn't feel like that to him, though. He came for a reading because his relationships with his family and friends were falling apart due to his self-involved tendencies. Like most self-involved people, Chris couldn't see this quality in himself, but he'd heard it cited as the root of so many failed relationships in his life that he finally had to pay attention. Our reading showed that Chris was stuck because of his deep fear of abandonment and the fact that he was constantly seen by others for his external talents and achievements rather than his passionate heart. Because of the resulting isolation Chris felt, he spent many, many years cycling through a rash of addictions, most notably drugs and alcohol. As a result, his adrenals, pancreas, bladder, and male organs took a hit. He also did not have the ability to trust. This in turn caused his nervous system to remain on high alert, and thus, his cycle of addictive tendencies spiraled. He would take his pain out on others in an effort to release his own discomfort, and not surprisingly, all of his relationships ultimately suffered because of it.

Of the most interest to me in our reading was the information that Chris was stuck at about age nine or ten, not coincidentally the age he was when his parents got divorced. This happens often in readings, and when the client looks back, they intuitively know the breaking-point moment. It is ingrained. In other cases, seeing at what age memories are blocked (after the age of three) also helps. From here, many clients know how or where to get help or unlock old mental images and memories. Ah, intuition.

Also not coincidentally, this was the same period of life when Chris believed that he *had* to be number one in every single sport he played . . . but he also did not remember any of his experiences from this time period of his life. Technically, you could call this need to achieve his first addiction. Sprinkle some burgeoning hormones on top of it all, and Chris completely spun out, never to move beyond that point. Even if we do not spin out in as big of a fashion as Chris—a big personality—did, there may be smaller spinouts, like looking back at a certain age with a feeling of disdain or not wanting to touch food or a place from a specific period in your life.

Through his reading, we learned that the best way for Chris to clear his addictive patterning was for him to write letters to his nine-year-old self. This helped him begin to uncover, recognize, and heal those old wounds that were perpetually dragging him into addictive tendencies. In doing this, over time Chris was able to heal his own pain in order to treat himself, as well as those in his life, better. He was then to go surf the waters he loved with the intention of filling the new space created by releasing his pain with light, fresh, clear, new energy. He used the saying *I am loved* to help process the pain and release his past disappointments in love. By processing his feelings, he was able to work through a proper mourning cycle for those people he had lost. No matter how far beyond loss we move, until we mourn it, it is difficult to heal.

Chris took up a faithful meditation practice, and by the end of our sessions together, he'd mastered three different types (because that's what the competitor in him does). Without fail, every day around 3:00 P.M. he could be found meditating—he knew that was historically the time of day when he became most agitated, so he used meditation as a tool to combat turning toward his addictions. Slowly but surely, he developed a true, compassionate, and accepting relationship with himself, his body, his disappointments, and his past. With this, he mended some of his relationships with family and friends and was able to mourn and healthily let go of those that needed to be left in the past. From those relationships he lost, Chris gained a deep understanding of and compassion for others, which ultimately allowed him to develop new relationships in their place. As Chris and his relationships healed, his addictions alleviated. I'm happy to share that today Chris is healthy and addiction-free, and he has surrounded himself with healthy relationships.

Just like Chris, so many of us use addictions of all stripes as a crutch or an escape from old losses and our struggles with feelings of worth. Working through addiction is never an easy battle, but it *is* possible—even if you have tried before and failed. In the case of addictions, we often need outside help from rehabilitation or step programs to combat physical, mental, or emotional dependencies; they give us the clear, supported space we need. I still work on my addiction to sugar cyclically. When I do not, my insulin and cortisol raise too quickly in readings and life events.

What I have seen and experienced time and time again is that without getting to the root of our broken or disappointing relationships, relapse or cyclical behavior looms and clarity of mind is unattainable. The other integral part of letting go and facing mental blocks is surrounding ourselves with healthy, supportive thoughts or mantras, serene actions, and openhearted help so we can engage with ourselves, our past woes, and our thoughts, beliefs, and neuroses. It also helps to surround ourselves with the influence of intimate loved ones in a trusted, calm environment.

Intuition surrounds us not only with the love and the security that community provides but also with the love and security that the *universe* provides. The intimate relationships we cultivate with universal law, universal love, and universal support are important for the mind, even for those of us who have become trained in critical or analytical reason. Try opening up to the side of the mind that thinks new, creative thoughts (much more on this in the next section).

Sometimes I call the mind a husband-and-wife team because we want to make sure there is dialogue between those masculine and feminine parts of the brain. This will pave the way to a more intimate and much improved relationship with our thoughts, and it will allow us to have an honest conversation with ourselves in the case that we notice overconsumption of any one thing or theme. With that intimate support we find in our relationships, from the universe, and within ourselves, we can then find and implement a solution for wellness and rebalance. Intuitive being will then feel more balanced.

The Second Energy Center and the Spiritual Being: Experiencing Creation

We are all born as creative beings. What this means is different from one person to the next. Maybe you have a knack for gardening or for woodwork; perhaps you are a phenom in the kitchen; maybe you express yourself on ice skates or a skateboard; or maybe the muse moves you to paint, act, write, or sing. Creativity can be expressed in any number of ways, all of which are valid and true. It is a response (or alchemy) to what we see and know through our intuition *and* what we want to contribute back to the universe. It is an offering of new life, new creation—and often we do this with a response so natural to us and so ingrained in us that we don't even realize this response is happening. When I am in this mode, I can think of a meditation and want to teach it; I see a tree, and I visualize how I can plant three more; I have an emotion, and I translate it into a deep breath or a musical composition; I have a good thought about a friend, and I translate it on paper to send to her or him. Creativity is action and movement, both of which are key for the second energy center. It's also working with the spiritual side of life and the world outside of my self.

Creativity is a beautiful exchange with and within the spiritual body that happens when we are open. Often, joy and peaceful feelings radiate from our being, almost as if they are coming from our heart, and they create a glow that extends a foot or two around us. This life force is something that flows to us and through us, often fueled from a place that, I believe, is higher or lighter. It is almost like the air and sunlight combined. It comes through us, but it doesn't always come *from* us. It also represents the even combination of our masculine and feminine aspects when in harmony: creativity flows through the feminine emotional side of our being and is executed through the masculine doing side of us. We'll discuss this in much greater detail when we move our way up to the sixth energy center, which governs the third eye (see chapter 7). The second and sixth energy centers are intricately tied together through creativity, and the heart lies in between them, so the work we do in the earthly second energy center has a profound impact as we move up to and open our heart and our intuition.

Exercising creativity on a day-to-day basis is one of the best ways to bring the second energy center into balance. It clears and opens our mind. When this flow and our creativity are stifled, we learn to rely on relationships outside of us for creativity, and that doesn't always directly promote our own creativity or uniqueness. It's almost as if new ideas are too risky. This is something that I think was trained into many of us long ago. Maybe as a child we had a good idea that was squashed by an adult or that required materials or a quiet space to execute but these were not available to us. Maybe our parents mistook our creativity for laziness or a lack of structure, so we turned away from our creative, interactive flow with the earth and the sky. We may have become heavy in the masculine, logical, and doing side of our relationships and moved away from the feminine, intuitive, emotionally intelligent, creating part of relationships. As a result, we were inadvertently trained not to create from our free, creative spirit.

Sadly, creativity that doesn't fall within a certain set of parameters still isn't always deemed worthwhile in our society. Today, if it is not electronic or digital, ideas are often shelved before they hit ground. There are many types of genius in this world, and these different types are all necessary, in both small and large ways. We are, unfortunately, more prone to recognize those ideas within a certain subset, largely because of the way our patriarchal system is focused on material goods and productivity. We can learn to create more ways for our souls to contribute on a spiritual being level by doing things like growing food outside our doors or windowsills and giving that bounty to the neighborhood or by starting a company that helps new mothers get a five-minute break to rest or shower. We might be able to find new ways to conserve water or create a business that teaches twelve-year-olds how to cultivate boundaries.

When schools begin to narrow the focus to traditional academics at the age of seven or eight, we tone down that creative side of our children, which represents a huge element of the second energy center. However, our spiritual being needs to feel free to create *new* relationships, new ways of thinking. This would ultimately work for the betterment of all, which is something we have begun to forget in our more heavily capitalist society.

We've begun to tell our children what they need to do to achieve greatness. These parameters for achievement are more narrowly controlled, often heavily dominated by competition and fear-based thinking, thus further stifling creativity. And focusing on outer worth.

Creativity is also important because it helps us understand duality. Duality is learning "difference" and that division between black and white, to later bring different sides together for a more powerful, stronger "whole." Children ages seven to fourteen *need* to learn duality so they can begin to see that they are different from their peers (in a good way) and that they have something to offer their friends, their extended family, their community, and possibly the global community. As we reach the ages of thirteen or fourteen, we come to know our differences, then bring these gifts to our community. It is crucial for children to learn what makes them different, special, and eventually, what worth they will contribute to themselves and to the world as adults. As we will discuss in the next chapter, then we are using power, worth, and self-assertion for the good of all, not simply for the sake of an inflated ego. The inflated ego is stuck in duality, whereas a healthy ego sees that the power of one equals power for all. Once this realization sets in, duality becomes unity. In other words, as we mature, we want to grow into the idea of oneness and universality—but first it is important to understand who we are and what we have to offer individually.

This is one reason why, as parents, it's important to nurture and encourage whatever forms of creativity our children display without attaching judgment, logic, or any kind of ranking system to it. If those negative reactions are in place, children grow up to be adults who are stuck in that duality mind-set of better than or worse than. Or, when children's creativity is not encouraged at all, the result is a narrowing or complete loss of their connection with their naturally embedded talents and their connection with their direct higher self, spirit, universe, or God. This is the connection that keeps the ego in check, so a lack of the connection further feeds duality. On the other hand, children who grow up in homes where their creative spirit can thrive and stay open cultivate a stronger sense of self, more compassion, intimate friendships, and a more vibrant second energy center, which often results in less disease, less anxiety, and less critical judgment of themselves and others.

Perhaps creativity was not encouraged when you were a child. If that is the case, now is a great time to get back in touch with your uniqueness and your messy fun side. Many times when I encourage clients to do this, I'm met with a blank look or they are completely overwhelmed about figuring out where to start. "But I'm not creative!" they protest. Sure you are—we all are. Finding your creativity has a lot to do with uncovering what it is that brings you pleasure and silencing the critic inside of you. It's about being honest about what is inside of you. Think back to what you loved when you were old enough to make your choices but young enough that you weren't yet programmed or embarrassed about what you liked to do to express yourself—before you had those ideas of *should* and *should not*. For most of us, this time period falls between the ages of five and eight, but I bet you had clues long before then. Back before you listened to others' viewpoints about what you were doing and not to do, what you were wearing, or how dirty your hands were—when you were just following your own happiness.

Once you make this lighthearted connection (and if it is not lighthearted, that is the intellectual being coming in, so get talk therapy for that), *just begin*. Anywhere. Do whatever you have to do to nurture your creative nature. Maybe that means taking a class you've always wanted to take but have been avoiding signing up for or simply have not had enough time for. Maybe you liked to pretend as a child, so bust out the group party board game or join a local theater class. Maybe you like to sketch—get out some pencils, look at a picture in a book or online, and begin to draw. Or maybe it's just carving out twenty to thirty minutes to putter around in the kitchen and see what happens. All of these are ways to connect yourself with your inner creativity, your inner voice, and your freedom to hear your authentic self. All of this also prepares your body to tap into your intuition. You don't have to be a prodigy or even good at whatever creative endeavor you choose.

Intuition uses our being side to connect us to the outside world and to harmonize so our needs are met in it. Simple creative practices can bring life not only to our innate creative talents, but they can also bust open the part of the mind where intuition resides. You can think of it like muscle activation. You just have to have the sensation of pleasure from whatever this creativity is you're bringing to life.

Once we do this on a consistent and sustained basis, the effects can be profound. We become more lighthearted and joyful, more naturally energized, and more present in the current moment at work, at school, or with our children or family. Our attention might become more focused on our internal life and self rather than on external noise, opinions, and cues. We begin to tune in a little easier, both to ourselves and to those desires that run through us. We may begin to associate pleasure with fulfilling our true internal needs rather than on material, external ideas of what we need to be happy. We give ourselves the chance to be a more true and complete version of who we are. Best of all, we have some fun.

Sacral Energy Center Meditation

Begin by reflecting on which of these sayings most resonates with you (or, if you'd like, create one of your own, beginning with the phrase *I am*):

> *I am healthy.*
> *I am creative.*
> *I am abundant.*
> *I am calm.*

Once you've selected your saying or mantra, find a comfortable spot to sit, either on the floor or on the ground. Lengthen your spine and feel your seat connect to the ground. If you are outside, become aware of the ground beneath you, supporting you. This helps connect to the feeling of being supported and safe while meditating.

Your eyes may be closed or slightly open, whatever feels more comfortable or natural to you. If your eyes are open, it can help to look down at a direct area, keeping your gaze on a spot on the floor in front of you.

As you begin to settle in, connect to your breath. Notice your breath and take stock of how fast or slow you are breathing. How deeply are you breathing? Breathe slower and more deeply. Maybe this time, for a few minutes, let your exhale be longer than your inhale. Count to three, visualizing your breath going all the way into the bottom of your lungs. If this doesn't come naturally to you, try repeating the following in your head: *I am breathing in,* as you inhale and *I am breathing out,* as you exhale. The more slowly and evenly you repeat this, the better. Again, notice your inhale and exhale. Drop your shoulders down away from your ears.

Once your breath is slow and even, connect your *I Am* mantra with your breath. As you breathe in and out, visualize these three words and what they mean to you. Use this to calm your mind to the point where you think about very few things or nothing at all. Silently continue to repeat the saying to yourself until your brain begins to calm and your mind can become a blank slate; you can think of the saying or mantra as a tool for the brain to chomp on. This can take time, so be patient. The key is to perform this practice with a calm, opening heart, using breath as the vehicle to calm your mind and feel more present in your body, more able to focus on yourself, your breath, you sitting in this space, and nothing else.

After connecting your thoughts with your breath, it can help to simply notice your chest and stomach rising and falling. Feel your sits bones grounded to the earth, and visualize yourself flushing the energy out of your second energy center and back down to the earth. Visualize new energy drawing up the base of the spine to your pleasure organs. This also helps improve reproductive and penis function as well as alleviate menopausal symptoms by both increasing and decreasing energy in this region.

Continue breathing in new energy and life force, exhaling out old thoughts or energy from past relationships and past feelings of lack or disappointment. Remember to give yourself between three and ten minutes per day for this practice, perhaps increasing the time from three to five minutes, or five to seven minutes, per sitting. Repeat this practice for seven to nine days in a row.

The Sacral Guide

What it governs:	Reproductive system, sensual organs
Ages:	7–14
Color:	Bright orange

In balance:	Sense of other and self as even; healthy relationships; feelings or disposition of pleasure and joy; focus on internal as well as external to learn balance of both; harmony, lack of addictions; balanced, healthy hormones and reproductive system; creatively alive. Creating abundance.
Imbalanced:	Addictions, overemphasis on sexuality and self-pleasure, need to fit into a specific image, hormone imbalance and infertility issues, fighting the natural aging process, lack of self-acceptance, externally motivated, creatively stifled. Higher craving for external stimulus.
Supportive foods:	Eating what the body requires for optimal health and sustenance including earth and trace minerals; foods with a high water element in them; orange foods like cumin, turmeric, ginger, rooted foods with deep orange, and spices and teas that soothe elimination and balance hormones (calming). Carrots, peppers, squashes, oranges, tangerines. Foods with vitamins C, B, and A.
Beneficial practices:	Self-affirmation, listening to what your body tells you it needs. Yoga for balance. Walking, swimming, slow hikes. Journaling feelings of desires, destiny manifesting, and dreams. Intimate touch.
Sayings:	*I am healthy.* *I am creative.* *I am abundant.* *I am calm.*

4

THE THIRD ENERGY CENTER: THE GUT

The Clear Ego

Our gut is one of the primary physical locations in our body where we connect with intuition through sensation. Our gut acts in partnership with our intellect, our brainwaves as well as outside information. It offers an instinctual and physical feeling in our body when intuition strikes, which signals that our instincts are real, mean something, and that we pay attention. Intuition ignites like a flame burning brightly in our bellies, shedding light upon a situation. When our third energy center, which resides in our solar plexus in and around the gut, isn't in balance, we mute this flame and our intuition can be dulled.

The third energy center also governs our feelings of power and worth. When we do not feel an internal sense of power or worthwhile, two things can happen in terms of intuition: 1) we may be scared to share or act on our intuition because we do not feel powerful enough to trust in our ability to have or share this knowledge, or 2) we may use our intuitive knowledge as a way of obtaining power from or wielding power over others in an effort to seek a sense of worth externally rather than from deep within.

The third energy center informs how we create boundaries, governs our self-worth, and is the source of the power with which we energize ourselves and meet the world with vigor. It also helps us to burn off unwanted energy from the second energy center (as well as the fourth energy center—the heart—which we'll delve into in the next chapter). This is important because if this unwanted energy remains latent in our body, it can negatively impact our gut instincts. That unwanted energy can confuse our gut into thinking information left over from *another* source—which can include anything from food pumped with hormones to someone else's thoughts or fears—is important to listen to. That other information can feel so loud and overpowering that we miss out on or dilute what our intuition is trying to tell us. Of course, the gut is also where we *literally* assimilate the energy, through calories, that fuels our daily life. The solar plexus energy center is represented by the vibrant color yellow, which is appropriate because an easy way to think of this energy center is as our own personal source of sun rays. It is the warm fire that burns within us.

We've all heard the adage "Listen to your gut." This comment refers to the presence of strong instinct in the third energy center. The role the gut plays in intuition is *extremely* important. Without a properly cultivated third energy center and the sense of worthiness and deep self-trust it instills, it can become difficult to tune in to our gut instinct, let alone to trust it. Being intuitive, we all make a choice about whether or not to trust the information we receive—and this choice happens in our mind. The more in tune we are with our gut, the easier it is for us to recognize these intuitive signals. And the stronger the signals are seen physically, the easier it becomes to mentally accept this information as truth. Then we can act from an intuitive space.

Intuition (or higher knowledge) exists both within us and outside of us. Our brain and heart read this intuitive information that comes from the outside, thus synthesizing it inside of us. *Outside* in this context can be any external stimulus, person, occurrence, or situation and also includes our inner voice sharing what the universe is showing us. While all of our energy centers in some way feed into our intuitive powers, it is through the gut, heart (fourth energy center), and brain (sixth energy center) that the reading and *receiving* parts of intuition occur. For example, our first energy center grounds us so that we don't get carried away by intuition—therefore, it plays an important role in how we *process,* use, and release intuitive knowledge, but it's not a point where we actually *receive* knowledge. It is a "doing," or masculine, energy center. In the third energy center, we're actually *detecting and absorbing* information, which is a masculine, doing task. Remember how we discussed the sixth and seventh senses at the beginning of this book? Our gut and heart provide us with sixth-sense information. The sort of *hmmm* of intuition, almost a tug on our logic that tells us something is up. It is in the sixth energy center that we process exactly what that information is, getting into that seventh sense.

When our gut is healthy, it is lit up and cleared out by a powerful energy within and by what we "accept" in, both attracting and making way for intuitive information. We are more connected to those sensations that intuitive information incites in it. The stronger the flame—which inherently involves strong feelings of worth and a feeling of physical connection with our gut—the more aware or sensitive we become to intuition. We can more easily *recognize* and sometimes literally *feel* that ping of intuition in our gut, whether it be through butterflies or a feeling of excited, or strong, energy in our bellies. And, as our intuition grows, we can distinguish between the different sensations in our belly and what they mean—for example, while a more gentle fluttering is often the soft tug of intuition, more painful, aching feelings in the belly are generally a reaction to stress or overthinking. When that feeling is distinct and easier to identify, it becomes easier for us to then mentally accept that intuitive information as truth and to act on it from there. The feminine, feeling part of our brain instinctually knows very well that intuition is a real thing, yet we have been trained to draw from and trust the masculine, analytical side of the brain. We need that strong, healthy flame in our third energy center to clear all of that mental analysis and stimulus we've been programmed to apply to our life.

The instincts our "second brain" picks up on connect us to our higher intellect. From there, the strong boundaries we cultivate in this energy center give us the space from outside distraction and influence to think through what our gut is showing us. Without these internal boundaries in place, our instincts might not actually be alerting us to intuition but may merely be a by-product of fear. *Remember that intuition is fearless.* Instinct is movement based and primal. It had to be this way in earlier times for survival. Intuition, on the other hand, is of higher intelligence and is connected to the collective. When it is intuition our instincts are alerting us to, it will not be accompanied by a sensation of fear. This is one of the primary ways you can tell when it is intuition that is stirring in your belly—instinct alone will often be accompanied by a sense of fear, fight, or fleeing thoughts; intuition will keep thoughts more level.

The healthy boundaries we formulate in the third energy center not only contain our own energy and resources but also help us to share and execute our power wisely and appropriately. With boundaries in place, we have more internal reserves to both listen to our gut and to act accordingly in a fair way. These boundaries also help us to understand that our gut instinct and our health in general are our own responsibility; we balance this with the understanding that we should apply what we have and know to the betterment of others in a *healthy* way. After all, it is not truly empowering to have a higher knowing if you're not able to apply it in ways that will improve both your own life and your environment in general. This is yet-another function of the third energy center: it is important that we become clear about our own boundaries so we can treat others with worth, and share what we know for exponential good, while not sacrificing our own power.

Boundaries create the space to listen to or pay closer attention to our gut and what it is pinging. From this recognition and *connection* to our gut, we are then more empowered to understand and act accordingly. Boundaries are healthy. They help us care more and have more energy to see and assist those around us because we are not depleting ourselves or putting the interests of others above our own. This can be a foreign concept, especially to women or minorities who were taught to be a *servant* instead of to be *of service*.

We need to burn off old molds and types of self-confinement (like acting smaller and less powerful than we actually are or being followers instead of leads) for fresh boundaries that are empowering. The gut is about empowering personal choice and seeing one another with a view of worth and agency. With boundaries in place, we can better trust our own worth and, from there, feel powerful enough to bring our intuitive knowledge into our body, our community, and the collective. With this, prejudice and subservience will disappear. For this to happen, we must choose not to ignore our gut and not to default to the competitive, fearful side of our brain, which tells us to keep power and resources away from others. This is the antithesis of using our intuition wisely.

This solar plexus energy center is able to come into its full strength between the ages of fourteen and twenty-one. At this age, the body and mind have reached the point of maturity where they are ready to incorporate gut instincts as a tool in the self-help belt. It is right around these ages that self-power and self-awareness can start to become natural by-products of our growing independence. Not coincidentally, in many cultures this period of life is viewed as the beginning of adulthood. It is this age range that offers us the peak opportunity for self-discovery in terms of cultivating strong internal self-worth and discovering what we can offer to society as a whole. For most of us, this means that we are learning the lessons the third energy center has to teach us about our worth, our access to inner wisdom, and our ability to create healthy, unapologetic boundaries. We can experience these lessons of powerful self-worth by trusting the internal wisdom that comes from our gut and relying on our decision-making skills. This also happens through our relationships and by mirroring the behaviors of those power holders whom we look up to. This is the age where we can really begin to add worth and contribute information to the world around us.

The third energy center also influences the sense of worth we attribute to others. When we do not ascribe worth to other genders, sexual orientations, age groups, and ethnicities, division and grief result. A healthy gut does not enjoy this. It can cause weight gain, stress, and indigestion when we are empowering ourselves but leaving others in the room disempowered. Some say gut imbalances are due to the rule of worth: what I give to you, I give myself. This includes our gut instinct knowing if our brain chooses to deprive another person.

As we'll discuss throughout this chapter, gender dynamics and understanding the feminine side of worth are particularly important today. Many call this time in our history the time of truth, or the Aquarian age. Gender roles are changing rapidly, as males and females alike are taking on more nurturing roles in the home as well as more powerful roles in work and society. The feminine, more emotionally intelligent and nurturing side is rising to the surface in both men and women, which offers more freedom and opportunity for all. We all need our gut instinct to see our way through these changing times. It is through our instincts that we will discover the great power in seeing others as ourselves, and letting them see us in turn. When your intuition lets you know who is calling on the phone ahead of time or clues you in about how to help someone without being asked, your connection with others will skyrocket. This will bring more equality, intimacy, and joy to any task at hand, which will fuel greater feelings of worth in each one of us.

Despite the fact that outmoded beliefs still exist, the world is very much in flux today, and there is a new forward motion toward empathy. We are in an age that is focused on mass information and choice. If we began to allow our intuition to guide us toward choices that serve all people and not just ourselves or our loved ones, we will quickly notice a domino effect. When we offer someone a smile and they smile back, we may be more patient with others at a stoplight or might even feel better about putting a new idea into practice simply because we feel more connected. Listening to our gut is a choice. Empowering others is a choice. We have the choice to either join in or dam the flow. Your intuition matters both to you and to others: if you decide to ignore those in need around you, you might also increase the chances of damming your own flow. Intuition thrives when we use it for good. When we don't put it to use for that purpose, over time, it goes quieter.

This solar plexus energy center is especially pertinent in the modern world because how we experience and express power is often intricately tied to our professional lives and our output into society at large. Some of us have had negative experiences on our way up the corporate ladder, whether that has to do with power struggles, unequal pay, or falling into workaholic patterns. When our solar plexus energy center is stoked, all of our experiences with worth become simpler, clearer, and far less stressful. We can begin not only to adjust our own thoughts and habits for the better but also to more clearly understand some of the negative aspects that plague so many workplaces and relationships today.

The Third Energy Center and the Physical Being: Knowing Our Gut

The stomach includes a cluster of nerve endings that are commonly referred to as the second brain. It is these very nerve endings that are pinged when intuition comes through. This is to say that our ability to pick up on or feel intuition is *extremely* tied to our general physical gut health as well as to our general awareness of this second brain. The mechanics of this are important to acknowledge in order to satiate the masculine, logical side of our brain. By simply creating a cognitive link that explains and acknowledges how intuition works, intuition becomes that much more powerful and easy to pick up on. In terms of the logical brain, it ascribes more worth to those pings we feel in our gut and thus makes it easier to understand what those pings are trying to tell us.

In scientific terms, that second brain is known as the enteric nervous system (ENS). The ENS is its own nervous system, separate from the central nervous system (composed of the brain and spinal cord). The ENS is embedded in the lining of the gastrointestinal system, which begins in the esophagus and extends down to the anus. This second brain is scientifically recognized as affecting our moods, decisions, and behaviors. Those butterflies we feel in our stomach when we're excited, nervous, or scared? They're the neurons in our second brain firing away. To grasp the extreme importance of the second brain, we should also understand that, although less commonly referenced, this second nervous system is actually the *original* nervous system. According to *New Scientist* magazine, the system made its debut in the first vertebrates that dwelled on Earth more than 500 million years ago and is believed to have potentially even given rise to the brain itself.

Our gut health is important not only physically but also in terms of our emotional balance and intuition. If our physical gut health is muddled or mucky, so too will be our ability to hear or decipher intuition. Our emotions can also wreak havoc on our stomach, liver, and bowels when they become stagnant. Through sensation, emotion, and mood, our gut offers clear indicators that support our heart and brain in picking up on intuitive information. All of this is to say that clear gut health *is* clear intuition. The link between a healthy gut and healthy intuition is not any different than the link between whole foods and balanced blood sugar. One leads to the other. Since we house so many stress hormones in our gut, a physically healthy gut plays a big role in keeping us emotionally balanced. When we are emotionally balanced, our brain stays out of fight-or-flight mode or notices when we are tapping in to this region of the brain—since intuition doesn't operate in fear alone; when we're in fight-or-flight mode, it's *very* tricky to pick up on what it's trying to tell us when we're in this state. How can we center our mind when it is in that mode of fast muscular movement that fear instinctually requires?

Through intuitive work, I've noticed men and women from all over the world experiencing power struggles that are more internal than external. These manifest as issues about "deserving," worth, and self-awareness and cut across gender, cultural, and socioeconomic lines. Our sleep, digestion, and the body's acidity are all greatly affected because of this. Both stress and sleep loss are of-ten rooted in the feeling that there are no choices, options, or ways to avoid or decrease life circumstance. Much of this is a result of the way we live today—we are over-*doing* and under-*being* . . . constantly overstimulated and rarely quiet or alone. Our gut not only senses this distress, but it also senses the helplessness that results when we ignore our body's signals to slow down and relax.

When I have clients come to me with stress, sleep, or digestive issues, the readings often tune in to their third energy center. A balanced third energy center will physically present itself through a smoothly running digestive sys-tem, a well-balanced diet, a healthy metabolism, nutrient absorption, low stress, hormonal balance (especially cortisol and insulin), and rejuvenating sleep pat-terns. If we find ourselves having difficulty with digestion, habitually eating too much or too little, engaging in emotional eating, relying on fatty or sugary foods, feeling sluggish, or experiencing chronically interrupted sleep cycles, this may well be a key sign that our third energy center is out of balance.

Just as the brain in our head generates dopamine (a hormone for pleasure and reward) and serotonin (the feel-good hormone), so too does the brain in our gut. Together, these hormones prevent depression and anxiety, and they help regulate sleep, appetite, and body temperature. They also serve the purpose of repairing damaged cells in the liver and lungs, and play a role in regulating bone density and heart health. Suffice to say, we've got some pretty important activity going on in our belly.

Our body has two nervous systems: the sympathetic nervous system, which triggers fight or flight, and the parasympathetic system, which calms us after the fight or flight response is triggered. These two systems both inter-act with the ENS. Because fight-or-flight mode induces stress, we can *really* physically manifest life's stresses in our gut and in the digestive process. Our feelings of self-worth and being worthwhile are also tied up in this. Feeling unworthy in the world often induces feelings of stress on many levels. It also stops us from doing things that may very well provide us with happiness, such as taking an exciting new job or going on a first date, even when our entire being is saying to go for it.

When discussing our third energy center, it is good to address how many of us use our gut instinct as a trigger to emotionally eat. When we feel ner-vous or push down emotions, our insulin and cortisol levels go into overdrive.

This can easily lead us to make the choice, be it conscious or unconscious, to turn toward food. When our stomachs are not healthy, neither are our gut instincts. We are *ignoring* or *overriding* that second brain in our gut. Rather than tuning in to what we really need to do to more permanently alleviate our feelings of stress or negative emotions—such as having a difficult conversation or going for a walk, both of which will ultimately bring those levels back into balance—we are making matters worse by causing an insulin surge. When we feel stress or exhaustion, we can tend to gravitate toward sugary or packaged foods or, alternatively, to limit our food intake to a detrimental degree. We might also choose comfort food that reminds us of our childhood or a more comfortable stage in our life. Until we consciously change our eating patterns, we will likely continue this cycle of eating foods that don't activate our power.

The gut produces a hormone called ghrelin when the body is stressed, which reduces anxiety and depression—with the side effect of making us feel hungry. It is thought that we actually do this instinctually as a means of alleviating our sense of stress and increasing comfort in the moment. *The Journal of Clinical Investigation* recently reported that study volunteers who had a dosage of fatty acids inserted straight into their gut had a decreased response to music and pictures designed to make them feel sad. The downside of this is that it's easier to overeat. Overeating or eating unnecessary foods can create a vicious cycle of sluggishness, acidity imbalance, and exhaustion. Rather than eating for quick energy or to soothe ourselves, the food we choose to eat should make us feel nurtured, supported, and like we are taking care of ourselves.

Tuning in to our eating patterns can be extremely empowering and can greatly enhance the energy and power reserves in our stomach. Noticing how our thoughts, mood, and emotional triggers affect our cravings is quite enlightening. When we feel ourselves reaching for unhealthy fats or sugary substances, making a concerted effort to stop, shift, and adjust is a powerful form of establishing boundaries and worth. From this space, we can select more whole food options by asking our gut what we *really* need and making more intentional choices that better serve us. Often, it is not food we want at all, but a feeling of worth. One of my favorite ways of doing this is by creating a simple feel-good experience for myself—almost like a date. Choose a time or day of the week to go on a field trip to an open-air market or anywhere else where you know you can find good, fresh ingredients. Maybe doll yourself up a little before you go—like you're someone *worth* splurging on and taking care of. Shower and put on something you enjoy wearing. Take your time in the market, picking up new foods, fruits, or vegetables you have yet to try. This is also a great opportunity to tap into your intuition. Take your time really feeling and smelling the fruits, vegetables, and breads as you go—make it a sensory experience. Select the ones that pique your interest and create joy. If you feel particularly compelled to throw something into your basket, chances are it provides nutrients your body needs. When you get home, search online for delicious ways to put these ingredients to use. As a bonus: if you find you need more fresh ingredients, ask a neighbor, friend, or family member if they have extra to give you. This way, you're not only nurturing your gut health, but you're also stretching your worthwhile and assertion muscles!

Giving up "dirty dairy" (dairy that is not in raw form—in other words, dairy that is pasteurized, has hormones added, or is sold in plastic containers) or processed grains for a week can help kick-start better gut health. Or simply declare it a "no-wrapper week," during which all of your food is prepared fresh. Healthy and easily digestible food choices—mushrooms, squash, herbs, small quantities of fruits, probiotic yogurt or kefir, lime and lemon, a variety of green vegetables, seeds, broths, sprouted raw nuts, avocado, and ginger as well as free-range, high-quality meat and fish; delicious oils like olive, sesame, or coconut oil; and sea salts—can soothe and balance the gut, essentially resetting and supporting our system. Having "earth" in your belly will help you to be balanced, centered, rooted, and supported. At times when we find ourselves making snap judgments or becoming easily upset, we are either hungry or crashing from too much sugar, caffeine, or alcohol. It is a physical response due to our adrenals and nervous system going on a roller-coaster ride. The effects are no joke. When we're stressed or suffering from low blood sugar, our body responds by producing the hormone cortisol, which suppresses the immune system, inhibits metabolism, and decreases bone formation. Cortisol, in turn, affects the production of insulin, which controls our blood sugar levels. So it follows that supporting our gut can smooth out our mood and drastically shift both our physical and emotional life experiences.

Our sleeping patterns are also connected to and affected by our gut health. When we are not rested, our nerves become frayed. When we are tired, sluggish, or lethargic, *all* of our responses are slower (or snappier), it's that much more difficult to understand what our gut and intuition are trying to show us, and we tend to get into fight-or-flight or power-through mode. I know that when I'm stressed, my sleep eventually takes a hit. I fall into a cycle where I'm exhausted, yet either I do not choose restful actions or I do not have the time to get quite enough sleep. My adrenals go into overdrive, and I fall into a self-perpetuating cycle of not sleeping enough. Of course, stress in and of itself can cause this to occur; another culprit is eating too much or consuming the wrong things too close to bedtime.

If you find yourself lying wide awake in bed at night, one solution is to calm the activity in your brain and your gut. To do this, focus on your breath to clear the mind of words or energy. Try putting your hand on your stomach and breathe "into" your hand like blowing up a balloon in your stomach. Watch your hand for twelve deep breaths. This is easier to do when your hormones aren't running haywire—this particularly applies to insulin and cortisol, both of which can be revved up by eating fatty or sugary foods. Not coincidentally, many of the same foods that aid digestion also help with sleep. Regulating insulin and cortisol not only helps keep weight off of the stomach and hips but also helps achieve peace of mind and heart. A healthy gut breeds rest and rejuvenation, but to foster this we must keep our adrenaline from surging, whether from stress or unhealthful dietary choices. Burning off energy and calming the mind through activities such as brisk walking, stretching, twisting, meditating, swimming, and yoga can also help calm the nervous system and tire out the brain and body.

A big step to a properly functioning third energy center is finding physical balance within the gut. On a purely logistical level, the ways we eat, sleep, move, and handle stress play a huge role in creating a physically healthy environment for the gut. Incorporating the simple changes discussed in this chapter, such as multisensory whole food shopping adventures and wrapperless meals, for even a few days, can renew the gut. It's well worth the effort; you might be amazed to see what a difference small habit shifts make in your overall state of being, including your intuitive clarity. You will feel less stressed, have more energy, and most of all, have a healthier gut that you are more in touch with, making it easier to feel it when your intuition begins to softly or more loudly ping.

The Third Energy Center and the Emotional Being: Feeling Worthwhile in the World

Intuition helps us understand our emotions and leads us to see the signs when it is time to clear out our emotional well or take a time-out. Emotions cloud intuition because they are a buildup of past experiences; intuition lives in the here and now.

I believe that when the universe begins to notice an emotional imbalance, it sends signs cascading in to alert us to clear them on out so that we can connect to our intuition and life more easily. I notice that when I'm on emotional overload but either don't yet consciously realize it or choose not to do anything to combat it, the universe starts to point the way. When I'm on overdrive, I start to crave coffee, which only gets my adrenals going more and makes it more difficult to sleep. When I'm in this state, I find that I'll start constantly stumbling upon articles advising me to limit my coffee intake. Or when I need a break, friends begin to call me to suggest we go walking, do yoga, or go on breakfast dates. And they are not coffee drinkers. I'll hear the word *rest* in almost every good quote and television interview I come across. And each meeting or children's activity I go to offers me water instead of coffee. I have been using intuition so long, it has become a lot like what you see in the movie *The Matrix*, including when I am tired or feeling more emotional and need the right tools to press through a bit louder.

Emotions are represented in dreams and in the body aura by water, so I always find it healing to be *around* water when I need to clear them out. There are so many ways to do this—swimming, kayaking, taking a sauna or steam, to name just a few. Increasing water intake also helps with this and, as an added bonus, helps the gut digest and eliminate the leftover hormones that emotional thoughts and experiences leave in their wake. Releasing emotions helps us feel more secure in our worth, which lays the groundwork for tuning our gut instinct.

When we clear out these stuck emotions, it is much easier to get in touch with our sense of presence and worth. We don't talk as much about the issue of willpower and worth once we reach early adulthood. This is not necessarily about how present we feel in our house or neighborhood—although these logistical elements *do* play into our general sense of well-being—but about how we feel in the life we've created, in our worth, in our relationships, and within. While we will never be able to control others or have them give us the security and worth we desire, life and the world around us can become peacefully present, "in the now," when our inner worth is activated. This has nothing to do with outside elements but rather with an emotional and deep gut instinct or feeling within. When we have self-worth and our choices are not reactive, we can rest easier in knowing that, no matter what happens, we have the strength to make it through the various situations and life events we encounter. *This* is real worth. And we soon realize that no one and nothing can take that away.

When we feel more worthy, we can also achieve the understanding that we are worthy of the powerful gift that intuition is. We are worthy of this deep, universal knowledge. With that present thought, we can better trust our intuition, let it open more, and become more attuned to it by being at peace with whatever comes our way. We spend less time questioning the information it provides us with and are able to more easily act on it. This means applying the information to our own life or sharing it where we find useful.

When our self-worth is developed, our intuitive voice naturally becomes stronger and more easily discernable. We trust and *hear* our gut. This leads to greater emotional intelligence and a more constant attunement to an inner compass we may not have previously realized we possessed. We might wake up just *knowing* we need to dress a little more snappily for work (and, *lo and behold,* the big bosses just happen to unexpectedly drop in). We may begin to intuitively know what our body needs to stay in tip-top shape to keep healthy when everyone else in the office, home, or school is getting sick. Or we might listen to our gut when it tells us it is time to end a relationship that no longer supports us or our feelings of self-worth and empowerment. We no longer need to wait for those more logical cues to take action; we can simply trust the feeling in our belly when it indicates a course of action. Those "logical" cues will never fully understand emotion.

Trusting our gut is similar to having an angel on our shoulder. I use my gut instinct and intuitive part of my mind to navigate through traffic, know what to say to a friend at any time, or how to handle emotional disappointment that hits deep. Our gut has many incredible gifts that bring us peace. In addition to all of this, the brighter our solar fire burns, the greater the clearing power of its internal flame can be for the mind and body.

When our gut has the capacity to clear, it is either transmuting or altogether obliterating our fears, jitters, nerves, poor food choices, or emotional belly knots. This clearing can take many different forms, including a brave conversation, jumping higher in a track meet, focusing on a test, or maintaining a calm demeanor during a public performance. This internal flame can clear guilt, allowing us to act rather than wallow. It can clear the nerves in our belly when we have to do something scary, new, or intimidating. Some believe it can even fight cancer by helping expunge our emotions before they have an acidic effect on the body. This clearing gives us more freedom to take chances, to address pain and scary situations, and to express ourselves with centered, clear intention. Not only do we gain energy when we function from such a true place, but so does everyone around us. We can handle feeling both brave and vulnerable at the same time. We can proceed with our missions in life—even on the days when this simply means getting out of bed.

For those of us who don't feel safe and secure in our own power—and we can cycle in and out of feeling this way—finding this sort of comfort and stability within ourselves sounds like an extremely tall, if not impossible, order. I find it helpful to break worth down into two main components: boundaries and power.

Establishing Clear Boundaries

Human beings are communal creatures. Most of us want to surround ourselves with loved ones, family, significant others, friends, and like-minded people. When we function in close connection with others, reading both our own needs and those of others is necessary for intuition to be fruitful and expansive for everyone. Listening is key here. It is difficult to have a truly loving and supportive relationship if we are so tuned in to our own wants, needs, and ideas of the way things should be that we are unable to work in cooperation with those in our life and to recognize their wants, needs, and preferences. Intimacy is not linear; it's a circular flow. Also, when we get too attached to our idea of the way things should be, it makes it difficult to hear and follow through with intuitive knowledge that isn't in line with whatever our own personal vision is.

With this in mind, for the good of our own sense of worth and to protect the sense of worth of those around us, it is important that we are cognizant of our own emotional and logistical boundaries. This allows us to keep our energy clear and to offer more empathy and understanding to those situations we find ourselves in. To identify where those boundaries need to be drawn in your own life, notice those situations or people that trigger you to feel "messy" or unworthy. What elements in your life stir you to feel less than par or, in the case of the opposite extreme, unwilling to be flexible for the sake of your or others' happiness and well-being?

At times it can be easy to confuse worthiness or being needed with a violation of boundaries, especially with the dynamics of modern society. In the world today, we are often moving quickly about our lives. We are constantly multitasking, communicating in quickness via texts, emails, or exchanges. When we're moving at this rapid-fire speed and not tapped into our gut, we can read attention of any kind as empowering or as establishing our worth—even when it's doing the opposite. For example, an inappropriate sexual innuendo from a boss may make us feel powerful or worthy in the moment, but it's ultimately not doing much to instill a *true* sense of worth for the right reasons. We can also perceive doing too much as empowering in and of itself, when really all we're doing is depleting our own resources—most importantly, the resource of energy.

Learning to find that balance between caring for and empowering others and finding worth and empowering ourselves can be tricky for those of us who are people pleasers or who give too much. Women and men have been taught we are being unkind or even rude when we offer a dissenting gut feeling about a situation. We can end up giving too much away or feeling denied or unheard as a result of trying to fit into these social expectations.

Because of our society's patriarchal roots, self-worth is not often the main priority for females. The feminine side of us quiets, and this shows up often in the gender of women. Women tend to base their worth and power on whether or not they are making *others* happy rather than on whether or not they are making *themselves* happy. Often, this comes at the cost of taking care of ourselves.

We all find our power and self-worth when we listen to our own voice. This connection feels like having a mentor inside showing us signs and signals. Balancing this energy center gives us a clear line to what we are looking for in our intuition—ownership of our life experience, a guidance compass in our center, and more sensations of hunches and tugs. We will notice the benefits *in our own body*, not just in someone else's or a group's success. We learn to listen by correlating our thoughts to a rooted, powerful relationship with our body's signs and signals, and we can clearly hear what our own body is saying to us at any given moment, despite anyone else's influence. For example, when I meet a new person and feel a slightly nauseated sensation in my belly, I understand that I should remove myself from that situation. I do so kindly, and then I move on. Once we own our own worth, external voices and recognition will not matter as much. Moreover, when we weaken our boundaries to please others, we are acting from an inauthentic place, which does not serve us or the people we interact with. I've definitely done this as well, and it can be a weekly intuitive ritual to check in that I am not slipping into old patterning. This is where meditation helps me greatly.

Healthy boundaries involve three specific criteria: 1) knowing what a boundary feels like and understanding the importance of that feeling of containing our energy, 2) having the confidence to define and communicate to others what does and does not feel good emotionally, and 3) knowing (and believing!) that we are okay no matter how other people react to us and our actions. We want our gut to feel good about our *interactions* with others rather than basing how we feel upon other people's reactions. *This* is the essence of boundaries. Boundaries are the energetic equivalent of a lovely home surrounded by a lush lawn. Our physical body is the house, and the lawn of fresh space creates a kind but controlled property line. We invite people in and extend our space to a certain point. We take care of only what is our responsibility.

When we do not have our own boundaries, we end up operating in accordance with *other* people's boundaries. This gets us out of touch with ourselves—and it is through our own self that we connect with intuition. When our boundaries become fuzzy enough, it even becomes difficult to determine what feelings or emotions are our own versus those of someone else.

We began this chapter with a discussion about clearing past emotion because the less emotional turmoil there is in our life, the easier it is to establish boundaries. To establish or strengthen your boundaries, begin by noticing what comes to mind when you hear the word *boundaries*. Many of us have thoughts about boundaries (or a lack thereof) that were ingrained in us from a young age—some of us are told that our boundaries are inconsiderate or that we need to let them down for any number of reasons. Remind yourself that, when applied with love and empathy, boundaries are a *good* thing, both for you and for others.

Now draw your attention to your thoughts and feelings about who or what takes care of you. Really take your time with this—the more attention and time you put into listening to your gut, the more it is empowered to speak. When our boundaries are in place and our intuition is activated, we can interpret the information we are receiving and give ourselves the final word. Are *you* the number-one decision maker and the loudest voice in your own life?

Take ownership of your thoughts and feelings so you can come from a more energized or clear place when creating space for yourself. This can be as easy as taking a fifteen- or twenty-second pause before you respond to someone (yes, this might feel funny at first) to find and connect with your inner well of self-worth or assertion before answering from that place. Another tool is doing three full minutes of deep stomach breathing each morning when you wake up. You can do it right on your bed. Watch your stomach fill like a big balloon with each slow inhale; then visualize creating your healthy, clear boundaries as you exhale, using the air you just inhaled to make that boundary. I practice this breath work regularly in the several days leading up to public speaking engagements or seeing someone that I have found myself cowering to. I find that usually this latter scenario involves an intimate relationship with an untrustworthy history.

Because we generally develop the third energy center in our midteens to early twenties, there is a tendency to mirror and react to the behaviors of powerful figures in our life rather than truly *developing* our own actions and reactions around self-worth and boundaries. This can be another area where gender roles come into play—particularly for those of us who were raised in households that operated according to traditional gender roles. Growing up in my house, for example, I saw through the actions of my parents, grandparents, friends' families, and the media that the male assumed a more dominant providing role, and it was my job as a female to be more polite, pleasing, physically attractive, and subservient. Like many, I was implicitly given the message that women were meant to be seen more than heard and to serve without exercising power. Ironically, the women in my family were very opinionated (which, at times, came out through passive aggression) and they experienced deep, quiet anger as a result of squelched opinions and low self-worth. They were not seen or heard for true thoughts or feeling.

Up until my late teens—a time during which power is extremely important—if I was anything other than sugar and spice and everything nice, I was doing something wrong or "not behaving." I was so busy trying to cater to others—especially friends, peers, teachers, parents, coaches, and those of the opposite sex—that I did not have the energy or space to create a powerful sense of worth and assertion on my own. It was challenging, and I know that my experience is by no means uncommon. I developed a pattern of letting males take the lead and assume the worth in our relationships, only to be crushed when simple needs like respect and honesty were not ultimately met. I was left to clean up the resulting disappointments until I figured out that I was not giving myself what I was asking others to provide for me. Once this clicked, I learned to find my own power from within and to brighten that inner light.

Boundaries allow us the space and time we need to grow and flourish rather than consistently placing our focus and effort on others' growth and needs. Ideally, boundary setting will begin around thirteen or fourteen. Unfortunately, most of us in this culture are not so lucky to have parents that both have their own firmly established boundaries *and* are able to enjoy truly intimate relationships, so we don't necessarily have this example to emulate. Intimacy, vulnerability, and trust in the self are a vital part of boundary setting, but combining these three elements takes a lot of courage and self-awareness. I feel this is also one of the reasons so many people struggle to hear their intuition—intuition needs the trust in self and deep support that boundaries create.

When our parents, teachers, coaches, team leaders, and other authority figures understand the value of vulnerability, intimacy, and taking the time to see and hear teens clearly and with complete lack of judgment, then boundaries are set naturally and freely in those years that precede leaving the nest. When trust and self-worth are mirrored, teens are more equipped to make more confident, thoughtful decisions. This room for personal expression and reliance should be balanced with boundaries by parents, such as curfews, and family/school obligation since witnessing boundaries allows us to be better able to create them for ourselves.

For me, it wasn't until I was out in the world on my own in college that I learned to radiate boundaries and assert myself with kind, empowered empathy. This required a lot of forgiveness and self-empowerment to cultivate more balanced relationships with both males and females who did not help me feel empowered, seen, or heard. I did this in long-term relationships and in day-to-day interactions. It did not always work to use my voice during my upbringing, but once I was out on my own, intuition became an absolute constant confidant. I began using intuition to cocreate my destiny.

There were a few moments of trial and error. Yes, it probably would have been better *not* to hitch a ride on the handlebars of my best friend's bike at 1:00 A.M., but it was actually (an arguably ill-advised) practice in intuition because I found I knew how to swerve or act moments before a possible catastrophe hit. I knew I was safe even when exploring situations that appeared unwise. These are parts of intuitive growth that I feel are imperative to become a reliable, trusted adult.

And importantly: intuition offers a wellspring of reserved energy because we are not expelling as much energy worrying or taking the long, "safer" route when we pursue tasks or adventure. Intuition also lets us know what situations will have high consequences, and it can help us catch ourselves before diving into a situation that might bring a lot of repercussions with it. We are working *with* fate, not against it.

In practical terms, the boundaries I instated that allowed my intuition to rise to the forefront gave my gut more of a say, as if it were sitting in the passenger seat of my everyday life experience. I began to hear my inner voice all the time. Not only that, but I had confidence to *use* intuition. When a friend needed her or his self-worth supported, I would show up at just the right moment. I also heard and followed through when my intuition guided me to reach out and call a loved one and, alternatively, when it told me to wait. Basically, I learned to trust myself.

Empowering the self in a balanced way keeps the voice of the ego in check and gives the more quiet, graceful inner voice room to rise.

Self-empowerment gives us that confidence and drive to see what it is like to live independently. We begin to seek answers from our own inner voice more and from our peers less. Valuing friendship and our peers' perspectives is important, but when we intuitively connect to our self-worth, we add *more* value to our friendships because we're not overly dependent upon them. We develop a balanced, worthy exchange of ideas. The truth about solid, healthy boundaries is we let *more* love and intimacy in, not less.

Even after I learned to set boundaries in my life outside of my childhood home, it still took a lot of practice to break ingrained old patterns and set boundaries with my family and closest friends. In fact, it took me until close to my early thirties to feel powerful enough to set beautiful, strong boundaries and not be moved by the tide of someone else. Once I cracked this code, my feelings of complete worth and power were unlocked. This is when I knew intuitively it was time to have our first child. I had spent all this time recognizing the value of others but not taking the time to recognize the full value *within*. And because I knew intuition well, I knew I needed that kind of value within before I was ready to raise another person. (This is never too late to acquire, even if you've had children without this value. It just takes a bit more forgiveness and outward conversation. This will be discussed in the next chapter on the heart.)

Intuition has helped me see that the relationships I have had throughout my life that lack proper boundaries are simply mirroring my own lack of self-worth—and this is *my* responsibility to change. It is not selfish to consider yourself worthwhile. In fact, it is imperative. Everyone benefits.

This can be a difficult realization to come to, but once it sets in, it's amazing how things click into place. Social, romantic, and parent-child connections reconfigure, and a beautiful new cycle begins. You will begin to automatically draw people with whom there exists a mutual sense of respect, worth, and boundaries. Old friendships will blossom in new and powerful ways. Few things are as empowering as surrounding yourself with this sort of positive, supportive energy . . . and it begins with finding that careful balance between establishing clear, firm boundaries while still treating people—especially ourselves and those we love—with clarity, compassion, and respect.

There is a deep correlation between intuition and setting boundaries. We must hear ourselves, we must have an intimate relationship with our gut, our inner voice, and our body's cues of stress and distress. We can think of our boundaries as older siblings who hear and understand everything about us and all we have been through. It is very hard to trust our intuition if we have not carved our space to: 1) *hear* our gut and 2) *trust* our gut and turn what we hear into action. Boundaries give us the space to hear ourselves think. As the world gets more populated and moves at a more rapid pace, our boundaries will keep our antennae clear of static and unworthy influences. I usually keep my boundaries in place by, most importantly, always reminding myself that they are there. Then I fuel them with meditation, yoga, time with intimate friends and family, and quiet walks outside—all of those things that bring us back in touch with ourselves and remind us how much we are worth.

Power

There is no doubt that status and wealth confirm a certain sort of power in the youth culture. The issue with this kind of external power, though, is that it is: 1) often insatiable and 2) always unstable because it is based on outside flux and perception. Those who derive their power solely from their job, appearance, or financial resources often experience a certain sort of appetite wherein there is no such thing as enough. As a consequence of this, there is a tendency to function by taking power from others, whether that means constantly aiming for higher positioning, craving more symbols of prestige, or obtaining more money or things from others. This represents an unhealthy relationship (second energy center) with power and worth (third energy center). It is not the gut but the ego at work here. The ego is on overdrive.

I have found that one effective way to identify *true* power is by paying attention to whether or not action is utilized to *empower* ourselves and others as opposed to demeaning or taking away power—even in subtle ways. We may empower someone without even knowing it when we give a tip or a look in the eye and smile as we walk by. We can disempower others in our intimate circle—for example, family members and friends—by being disrespectful to those we think of as being beneath us or different from us. Often, we do this subtly and energetically, without even being aware of our actions. We can recognize if we are empowering or belittling others by taking an extra moment to watch the eyes and body language of each person we interact with. Cues such as warm eye contact, facing their body directly toward us, standing taller, or openly exposing their chest by drawing their shoulders down are all good, visible indicators that someone feels good and worthy in our presence. In some cultures this is called *kimochi*, this acknowledgment of the feeling we bring to others or a situation. Making the conscious effort to smile at each person you come across throughout the course of your day is a simple form of power with feeling. Watch their bright (or surprised) reactions. This is such a simple way of empowering both others and ourselves in a way that does not come at a cost to either party. And feels uplifting.

This awareness also can unfold by paying close attention to how we use or interpret the gut responses we feel in certain *situations* and by noticing what our intentions are when we take action. Are we helping others or just ourselves? True power—that internal solar warmth we've been talking about— grows and thrives within, and also empowers those around us. This doesn't mean that everyone who comes into contact with us will feel positive and perfect. What it *does* mean is that those we interact with will feel slightly elevated simply by our interaction and proximity. *Kimochi*.

It is important to mention that this empowerment has nothing to do with any sort of material item or source of external prestige. It's also important to note that internally powerful people often can and do enjoy wealth and have a radiant glow about them, generally because the fire in their belly is burning brightly and their gut is clear, fearless, and forging ahead for the sake of all rather than just for themselves. An authentic glow.

Another key difference between internal and external power is that when the power comes from outside sources, we often lose touch with who we really are because someone else holds the key to our "success." Our sense of self becomes enmeshed with the source from which we are deriving power. This is often accompanied by a sense of fear—if our identity is outside of us, what happens if that source vanishes or shifts? This is not true power. A momentous cycle is born when we are working from emotions such as fear, longing, or greediness because it becomes harder to connect to our intuition and our gut can become clouded. Our third energy center operates from a place of neutrality. Even if the information we receive lends itself to a resulting positive or negative emotion, we are equipped to handle and digest such information . . . without completely losing our glowing spirit . . . but not if our worth and power hinge on outside entities.

External power can lead us so quickly off of our true path. The more difficult it is to tune in to what our intuition is telling us, the more difficult it becomes to identify those signs, synchronicities, and cues that exist in the present moment. Picking up on these external signs requires no more than simply listening and witnessing the world around us. The combination of this awareness and the creation and activation of boundaries helps us lean into our intuition. Intuition thrives when we are both working with those external signs and attentive to the cues of our internal signals, without the interference of emotions or dominating outside influence.

As we have discussed, to feel empowered and possess a strong sense of self that involves both internal strength and trust, it is important to clear emotions out of our gut by stoking that inner fire with self-worth and boundaries. To stoke this fire, notice how you handle tough emotional situations or scenarios that feel daring or new. Do you simultaneously feel a sense of calmness and strength from within? Are you able to witness other people's physical cues without getting too involved—in other words, without going on a mental journey about their life just by standing next to them? The outside world is just that—outside. It's not meant to emotionally squeeze its way into *your* gut and be empowered by *your* flame. Yes, you can help empower other people through kindness and consideration, but that *doesn't* mean taking ownership of others' story, well-being, or journey. In my experience, no one really wants to be helped or led by *my* flame. Rarely does anyone else want to be stoked by *my* internal fire. They might think they do, but I think that deep down, they all intuitively know that it's far more important and productive to learn how to gain self-worth for themselves. This includes children and teens. The influence of others must remain minimal and our internal fire or drive must empower ourselves first. To the givers out there, don't worry—ultimately, you'll be able to give more by empowering your own center. This drive balanced with an open heart, as we will talk about in the next chapter, creates a great force of empathy in action.

It is extremely difficult to tune in to the gut when we have linked our power to external sources (whether that means we've given our power away or we've attained a sense of external power) because, in doing so, we have given outside influence free rein to put toxic thoughts and emotion right back into us. When we do this, both our gut health and our emotional intelligence suffer. The stomach area is extremely sensitive as it is extremely powerful. To be sure, no matter how secure life feels, currents of new energy will present us with new goals and obstacles . . . knowing that we have the will, fortitude, and stomach to get through whatever we are handed makes all of the difference.

The Third Energy Center and the Intellectual Being:
Power from the Inside Out

We now understand that authentic power, empowerment, and self-worth emanate from the inside out. Much as we may know this, it's all too easy to fall into the societal trap of gauging our power by outside factors, such as money, position, and social standing.

All of this is compounded by the fact that we live in a world that is currently in a great state of flux. In many ways, conventional and traditional gender roles are breaking down. Women now have the choice to remain at home or enter the corporate world. Men are no longer necessarily the bread-winners. We are taught that, regardless of gender, we can design a life of our choosing. And, in many ways, this is true.

However, in other ways, we are still living in the remnants of a patriarchal society. Some of this is the result of a world that's in transition, still moving along the spectrum from point A to point B. We see this in the workforce, where men and woman are not necessarily paid equally for doing comparable jobs. Men who stay at home as primary caregivers, even by choice, may feel as though they are somehow out of step with society.

I cherish when a male is brave enough to come in and see me, even if only at his partner's or family's urging. Stan was such a case. He initially came in for a reading with me because his daughter and wife urged him to do so in the hopes that our time together would help him find a solution for dealing with his domineering and egocentric coworkers. They also hoped it would help him determine if (and how) his long professional career was affecting his health and if he should retire. I came to learn that Stan felt stuck: yes, he was in a power struggle at work, but he also felt that if he retired, he would find himself in yet another power struggle at home. During our reading, a lot came through about worth, shallow breathing, and letting go of duality (for example, feeling there is a winner or loser or that certain scenarios are either good or bad).

Stan began to understand that his thoughts and fears, which resulted in adrenaline and cortisol surges, were creating not only brain fog and stomach fat but also an aversion to change. His fears were bringing on more confusion and fear, an easy self-perpetuating cycle to fall into, especially as we age and our gut flora and cellular immunity decrease. Mental clarity can be affected by decline. His power source and once-honed gut instincts were dimmed and buried by these effects. We discussed what factors and old thoughts and judgments were currently holding Stan back as a way to change habits rather than point blame on age. He began to realize that he had been hanging on to the false feeling of power that came from being "the man" or "top dog," even though it was ultimately causing him great distress as well as getting harder to physically maintain as he was getting older. Stan felt that if he were to lose this top billing, it would devastate both his work and home lives. In fact, Stan had not created boundaries and true inner strength because of these fearful thoughts and hangups with labels. Blaming others for being "devastated" was a label as well.

Our reading offered Stan strong reprogramming tools in terms of his self-worth and asked him to take a good look in the mirror in terms of his value system and where he was choosing to put his energy. Stan soon realized the great power in giving and receiving *equally* rather than just taking. He also reexamined past choices that had been based on ego-centered insecurities.

I checked in with Stan almost a year later. He was retired, and his health had never been better. He was enjoying his relationship with his wife with an ease they hadn't felt since before they were parents. His blood pressure and cholesterol had gone down. Most importantly, he felt powerful, youthful, and brimming with creativity in new, innovative business ideas. His power was now real, and he had established boundaries so that when old fear crept in, he had the tools to balance himself out and find true power in staying present. These boundaries also allowed Stan to maintain reserves of energy. His sparkling eyes and smile said it all. Even his granddaughters noticed Stan's new "fire." He no longer felt inferior to other males in business or relied on titles for powerful connection and self-value. *Now* Stan truly was the man.

The state of our transitioning society is compounded by the fact that human beings tend to learn from mirroring the behavior of authority figures of the current moment or past influences absorbed during times we were searching for role models. On a large scale, Generation X, for example, was raised by baby boomers who fell under a more rigid patriarchal structure than the one we live in today. As a result, we still hold that "normal" way of doing things. Many of us grew up in households where our mothers and fathers exhibited more traditional roles and where feminine power wasn't encouraged in either men or women (both genders can—and, ideally, *should*—exhibit feminine power through emotional intelligence and trusting their true nature). And in these roles of a more patriarchal form of raising children, both genders, both the mother and father, fought for power and agency and often followed a more straight-lined, expectant form of hard-line routines, rules, and discipline. There was, at times, a struggle for power and agency in place of leaving room for emotions (and listening skills) having stake at all. Or in households where we were taught to treat others how we had been treated rather than how we would *like* to be treated. We do not need to replicate these roles in our own lives today if they do not serve us. We may have to work a little bit more consciously to break these patterns though, as the world begins to shift toward a more feminine way of being.

It's important to briefly look at how we view power, assertion, and self-worth from a historical viewpoint. The feminine side of our collective power as a society has been mostly ignored in U.S. history (and in most first-world histories, for that matter) because feminine qualities and the mother or women's empowerment have not been found worthy of equal billing to the blood-sweat-and-tears version of history we salute. In history books we do not talk about the American dream in terms of its feminine intelligence, and this keeps our intuition unconsciously tucked away. Religion, too, has often distinctly lacked an equal emphasis on the feminine.

In the modern version of change, I've witnessed empowered businesspeople, stockbrokers, athletes, and celebrities use this internal connection to their intuition to create alchemy for themselves and their families. To get in the zone of accessing internal power, both the acceptance of the self (self-importance) and healthy boundaries are key. But still, so many *don't* use intuition when going after a job, trade, career, or performance. Instead, we fall back on the whims of our second thoughts. Too often, we settle because our dreams have not materialized, and our creative nature is put on the back burner for a job that is more mainstream or "acceptable." If you have done this, it is important to recognize you're making a *choice*. Once you realize that, you can begin moving in the direction your heart desires, trusting that the current moment will bring you to your highest potential in *whatever* sector your heart sings out for you to be in as long as you trust in your intuition. External views about what is and is not worthy might be part of why we do not ascribe worth to our gut feelings. Our third energy center and our intuition encourage us to dream bigger for ourselves and for the greater collective, and they give us access to the ability to create these dreams in real-life terms. Using intuition creates dreams that catch wind and fire. Dreams that will become real-life experience.

The good news is that we are here now. What an exciting time to ignite our gut, dreams, and intuition! The third energy center holds those gut instincts and the clear intentions that allow for the expression of our true worth and happiness. It also carries the road map that leads to igniting these dreams into reality. It is time to merge our daydreams with our intuition.

When tapping into our third energy center to create this new reality from a place of self-worth and empowerment, stillness is crucial. Presence is key. It allows us not only to hear our inner voice and feel our gut feelings but also to organize the wisdom that comes in with what feels right in the now *regardless* of old models or outside influences. In the present moment, the thinking mind cannot think several things at once. If our body is moving, our mind is thinking about movement. Stillness offers our brain, our body, and our soul a sense of peace and centering so that the intuitive space in the mind can open up wide. From here, what we hear can take a front seat in our decision-making process. From here, we learn to listen.

I take a lot of quiet time, less now that I have children, but still *some* time daily. It keeps my intuitive mind open, receptive, and aware of a lot of the more subtle energy around me. It helps me not become convinced by all the fast, loud outside messages I encounter. I encourage you to spend some time in quiet, any way you can. To think less—and simply focus on breath, feeling inhales reach far, deep down through the lungs, and into your belly. Connecting with this space brings us in tune so that we recognize the sensation when something fires or our instincts kick in from an internal place. Notice how you feel in the moment. Peaceful? Wandering? Centered? Butterflies are often a sign that good change or movement is occurring. Or maybe your stomach is churning in disagreement. Perhaps you feel that stirring that we call fire in the belly. If so, notice what visions of your life cause that stirring. Maybe you can even feel your nervous system picking up or calming a little bit with joy or excitement. Nerves are okay. Breathe. Remember that your true power and worth do not lie in social constructs. It is in the light and fire of this energy center, the inner power of regeneration that creates room for worth in the new and in the now. Bring your ideas, your invention, and your worth into the world, and watch your chances for success increase. Situations around you begin to transform. This is bravery.

The Third Energy Center and the Spiritual Being: Trusting Our Gut

When the body is humming along in a state of equilibrium and we are powering ourselves and our choices from within; when we are secure in our value and place in the world and existing within the confines of healthy, thoughtful relationships; and when we have a clear sense of self-worth and clearly established boundaries, we become stable within ourselves. It becomes difficult for the world, those around us, or even our own mind to rock the proverbial boat. We are stable and steadfast, even in the midst of the storms that erupt throughout the course of our life. When we are clear and strong, it becomes easy to tap into our truest self. We can hear what our gut is telling us because its signals are not convoluted by misrepresented external messages, thoughts, or situations. We are not trying to decipher what our gut is telling us through the cloudy vantage point of emotion or fear.

A wife, mother of two, and pillar in an affluent community, Kristy came to me to see if there was positive probability she and her family would move to an adjacent town with better schools and, if so, if her husband would be able to find work closer to home. Kristy also worried about her son's cognitive learning.

Although Kristy likes to credit the gift of my intuition for the experiences that followed her reading, they definitely transpired through her own intuition and ability to begin to trust herself and tune in to her gut. To get to this point, Kristy began regularly practicing breath work, taking walks, and actually conversing out loud with her intuition. As she did this, she began to notice how much better she felt physically, emotionally, mentally, and spiritually. As Kristy became more in tune with her gut instincts, she manifested great, almost overwhelming changes. First and foremost, within weeks, Kristy and her husband were able to sell their home and move to the town they had dreamed of living in, closer to their family and friends. They were able to get into the public school they felt was right for their family. Shortly after settling into their new home, Kristy's husband was able to secure a lucrative job minutes away from the house. They were making business connections that kept their social life rich *and* their financial security abundant.

Seeing these positive results, Kristy began to rely on her gut more and more frequently. She swore she began to hear her gut in words and sentences, even when she was driving or in the shower. She began to hear actual advice and anecdotes that she had not personally experienced. She noticed calm new sensations and a lack of tightness in her stomach region. She began to let her stomach release instead of holding it in and squeezing its power source. She now uses it regularly to intuit and manifest her dreams for her family, including everything from good health and parenting ease to lovely vacations and fulfilling community outreach. She started a business she had dreamed of since she was a teenager. Also very importantly, she now feels in control, happier, and more confident in her decisions than she has in the past decade. She looks more vibrant, and her quality of life has reached a new pinnacle. Kristy can breathe easier and feels as though a heavy weight of worry has been removed from her shoulders, simply from knowing everything will be all right and as it should be. She handles each day with more confidence in her role of manifestation.

A clear and healthy third energy center allows us all to listen to our gut and take graceful and efficient action as necessary. I know it can seem daunting to come into our deep power. The good news is that our body wants us to live in this way—and our gut holds the clues that will steer us in the right direction throughout the rest of our life. We can use our belly awareness to tap into and notice the cues it provides us through sensation—it might be a sinking feeling, a sense of elation through a clapping vibration, somersaults, butterflies, or a dropping, as if you were in an elevator. These feelings can help us gauge whether we are in our power or not, adjusting as necessary until our boundaries, worth, and sense of self come into full bloom. We can write these sensations down when they occur so we can log them and get to know their qualities.

We might then also understand how to clear emotion and connect to a higher source of strength and support because we see and feel when an intuitive feeling is coming. In chapter 7, we'll explain how to use these signs more intelligently. Once we achieve this connection, we'll start receiving information in a variety of ways: a certain piece of advice that comes from somewhere "above" will filter down to us with ease; the choice we should make appears to us clearly and visually, almost like a movie; or we hear something specific giving us an answer to something we had been wondering about.

I have seen in my own life and in the lives of my clients that self-worth, self-belief, and clear boundaries create a beautiful self-perpetuating cycle. When we are able to hear our gut and respond as necessary, we begin to build even more trust—trust in ourselves, trust in the universe or space around us, and trust in our place in that space. When we act on our gut instinct, the actions we take are connected to choices that are good for all and empower ourselves, our children, and our community. Making decisions from the gut represents a win-win for all, even when it involves change.

Gut Energy Center Meditation

In this chapter, we'll veer away from traditional meditation in order to incorporate some Lion's Breath to ignite the internal fire of the belly. We will use this to activate, clear, and balance the stomach region as well as to strengthen our breath and direct our attention to our gut.

Begin by reflecting on which of these sayings or mantras most resonates with you in this moment. Or, if you'd like, create one of your own that feels 100 percent empowering and helpful in letting go, beginning with the phrase *I am* or simply using *I am* without a third word. This is your time to be in your third energy center, to empower your meditation with ownership and self-assertion. Trust your gut.

I am worthy.

I am strong.

I am powerful. (Or, *I am power.*)

I am confident.

Find a comfortable seated position, and lengthen your spine. As you inhale, recite your *I Am* mantra silently and begin your Lion's Breath by taking a deep breath in through your nose and imagining the air traveling all the way down to your belly and filling it up. Hold the breath there for a couple of seconds, imagining whatever saying you have chosen filling up your belly. Open your mouth wide and stick out your tongue. Exhale strongly and audibly with a *haaaaaaa* sound, pressing all of the breath out of you as you imagine yourself expunging whatever the opposite of your saying or mantra is (powerlessness, weakness, worthlessness, and so on) from your belly.

Continue your Lion's Breath, inhaling what you need and expunging what you do not. Give yourself between one and three minutes per day for this practice, perhaps increasing the time by thirty seconds per day to do two times a day totaling three minutes each sitting. Repeat this practice for five to seven days in a row.

The Gut Guide

What it governs:	Power, self-worth, boundaries, confidence
Ages:	14–21
Color:	Yellow
In balance:	Feeling worthy of all things that offer progress, warmth, and comfort; good at setting and keeping boundaries; feeling of self-worth; balanced power that comes from within; healthy digestive tract; trusted sleeping patterns; balanced cortisol and insulin levels; ability to tune in to gut feelings. Trust in yourself. Intimacy.

Imbalanced:	Lack of self-worth; feeling powerless; others taking advantage of your time, personal space, and divine gifts; unhealthy digestive and sleep patterns; feeling stress in the nervous system, adrenal fatigue; falling into outmoded gender patterns that do not work for you; cannot easily distribute power; poor listening habits. Acidic body. Lack of giving eye contact.
Supportive foods:	Digestive-friendly foods, such as kefir, yogurt, oat bran, cinnamon. Lemon, yellow vegetables, and healthy fats and oils. Light-green vegetables with a high water base (celery and cucumber). Melons. Banana, apple sauce. Aloe juice. Avocado. Fennel and mint. Soothing chamomile and herbal teas.
Beneficial practices:	Meditation, slowing down and doing gentle exercises without outside distractions, belly breath work such as Lion's Breath, and yogic twists. Releasing stomach muscles.
Sayings:	*I am worthy.* *I am strong.* *I am powerful.* *I am confident.*

5

THE FOURTH ENERGY CENTER: THE HEART

Love

Love, the heart, and our intuition each know that we are all one. Intuition relies greatly upon an open heart because it holds the intelligence we need to act on our intuition for the good and forward movement of all people. Our heart reads what's happening in the present moment to help clear old patterning, feelings, or actions to pave the way for the new. The heart can pick up on the vibrations of others, thus connecting us and picking up information that feeds into our intuition. When working together, the heart and our third eye (the sixth energy center) are the equivalent of Mother Teresa and Nelson Mandela in terms of their ability to facilitate *healing*. They create new situations and ways of being with power, grace, efficiency, and forgiveness. The fourth energy center is all about love and breath, and it includes the heart, the chest region (including the lungs), blood circulation, skin tone, and hand, wrist, elbow, and shoulder health.

The heart energy center is the bridge between the more earthly, lower energy centers (which include the first, second, and third energy centers) and the more expansive heavenly, upper energy centers (which include the fifth, sixth, and seventh energy centers), where intuition and intuitive support reside. This bridge must be open and strong for intuition to activate and flourish. But if the lower three energy centers are not open, balanced, and recognized, our heart can get stuck in the hardships or strife of our own story, other people's stories, or the collective story of humanity. A closed heart might feel blissful in some ways because it is sheltered from pain, but it also lacks the capacity to find and sustain great love and intimacy. And what is life without that?

The faith and support that the heart gives to both intuition and our overall quality of life are priceless. With an open fourth energy center, we feel loved and we give love at all times—or at least we are able to recognize and recalibrate to support the heart in those moments when our heart is not making either of these exchanges. The fourth energy center loves, loves, *loves* love, and it finds great peace and grace in bringing love in. This understanding helps the broken heart mend and also attracts intimate relationships to us that offer new love, understanding, and support.

Jesus spoke a lot about the heart, as did the great Buddha, the Dalai and Panchen Lamas, Nelson Mandela, and Mother Teresa. Today, we've somehow put the heart on the back burner, even with all of this historical knowledge from leaders about the compassionate strong heart. It is easy to choose to mute the heart, particularly in this day and age when we are overloaded with painful information, imagery, and fear-based propaganda. Muting the heart's connectivity dulls not just intuition but *all* aspects of life. If we never move beyond worrying about only our own needs, the heart energy center (and possibly the upper energy centers as well) won't have a chance for activation at all. An openhearted person understands that there is more than just "me" involved in all situations. This awareness can be exemplified through something as simple as becoming aware (with love, not guilt) that a family member needs a meal, a local school lacks art supplies, or that leaving our windows open might negatively affect our neighbors' early bedtime. (Note that the catch is this awareness must come from *love* rather than from liability.) Recognizing our heart's open vibration can be as easy as feeling a nudge to pay for the person behind us in a line at the coffee shop (and *doing* just that) or just *feeling* that our child needs an extra hug and ten minutes (or more) of tune-out time from an otherwise organized schedule.

Our hearts serve as a means of connection, in terms of both intuition and those around us. All of the energy centers we've discussed so far have had to do with more earthly, individually centered elements, such as getting our basic needs met, enjoying relationships, and cultivating self-worth. The fourth energy center, through love and the heart, begins to lift us up out of our self and connect us with the world at large in a more equal, loving way. Our heart operates at a higher or lighter vibration than the previous three energy centers; in fact, it's often represented by air. This vibration makes it easy for a healthy heart to pick up on a lot of intuitive information quite easily. The heart is our greatest ally in hearing, seeing, listening to, and assimilating energetic information. To do this, we must: 1) let the heart stay open and brave, and 2) be aware of what our heart is picking up. This awareness can be thought of as the air we see or feel between two trees. The heart picks up on what's in the air. In this equation, the person or people we are picking up vibrations from are the trees emanating that information into the air.

Since a healthy intuition works for the greater good of all and the heart is connected with all that is in the air, the purpose of the two entities is naturally aligned. It's almost as if intuition and the heart are kindred spirits. The more fresh air we get, the more we open and support our intuitive nature.

The intuitive part of our brain can understand and interpret the information that our heart collects. A strong and brave heart allows us to connect with not only those in our life but also with all living things; from this heart-centered place, we can share the information that intuition provides us in a compassionate way that works for the good of all. This is love. And love inherently makes everything better, calmer, and stronger. It organizes priority.

While one energy center isn't more important than the others, the fourth—the heart—is particularly integral to connecting to and deeply understanding our intuition. It bravely considers everything that we've learned in the first three lower energy centers and brings it all together in union, serving as the bridge between those and our upper three energy centers, where intuition and our sense of "something greater" exists. The heart is the intersection where we can learn to slow down and be aware of everything and everyone around us. Intuition will open and help more with a passionate, clear heart to function and connect the upper divine with more earthly matters.

If you would like a quick litmus test to determine how healthy and sturdy your fourth energy center is, ask yourself this one simple question: *How much joie de vivre do I feel today?* Do you feel joyful, happy, and peaceful about life, or do you feel weighed down? Are you able to give with conviction and without expecting anything in return? A balanced heart energy center results in precisely these feelings, so if that sounds like you, chances are you have a happy fourth energy center. If you feel like you could use a little bit more joie de vivre in your life—and, let's be honest, who doesn't want more of that good stuff?—the wonderful news is that bringing a little more balance to your fourth energy center will do precisely that *and* will help you decipher whether or not your intuition is clouded by old emotion or judgments. When your heart energy center is vibrantly loving, you feel lighter, calmer, and free, regardless of what may be happening around you at any time.

Our heart energy center can come into full balance, wisdom, and maturity between the ages of twenty-one and twenty-eight. When you think about your life experiences (or the experiences of those around you), this timing actually makes sense. It is during these years that a lot of us begin to invest in deeper romantic relationships, often becoming more committed and possibly starting new families of our own. Some of us begin to build our own lives with those who we *choose* as family because of love rather than heritage. We also may begin relationships that involve leading or taking care of others, through situations such as moving up the ladder at work, taking on more responsibility with elders, or raising children. The fourth energy center is about love in both deep and simple senses—love of ourselves, our family, our community, or the caregivers and teachers who invest in our children. This simple sense of love and openness can also be found in the workplace through the care and empathy we feel for our caregivers. The key is saying, "I see you, I love you, I thank you" not necessarily in words (although this is great), but also through action, eye contact, and open body language.

This vibrant energy center is represented by the color green, and, at times, it might be bright pink for some. This is fitting because the color pink is often used to represent love, health, or empathetic support. Because of the alchemy heart-based action can facilitate, some also feel that the heart energy center is represented by pure gold.

For our purposes, though, we're going to concentrate on the traditional color of the heart energy center, which is green. Green is very important for the heart energy center because it's all about air and a feeling of spaciousness. Green is the color we associate with thriving plant life: trees, leaves, fresh herbs, and chlorophyll. These all offer the heart fresh oxygen, mineral vitamin support, cleansing and flushing assistance, heartbeat balance, and increased energy. Foods of all shades of green also help the nervous system, skin, and blood alkalinity. All of these physical elements promote an enriched and supported intuition.

In Western society, the heart and love are viewed as inseparable, but although they are indeed closely interrelated, they are not always one and the same. This is similar to the way we associate the brain with intelligence and knowledge. But, in fact, the brain is *not* knowledge in and of itself. It is a network of nerves, synapses, and pathways through which intelligence flows and information is sent and received. The brain and intelligence also are not the same thing—they're associated with one another because the brain acts as a channel and storing house for information. Now, take that same concept and apply it to the heart. The heart is a channel through which love and emotion flow, and at times it is also a store house for lodged old pain and stagnation. In both the heart and the mind, too much energy, intake, or stored pain can lead to a rapid increase in movement (including in our thoughts and heartbeat) or a complete short circuit. In this chapter we will see why it's important to feel the inclusion and unifying energy of love in order to understand and support the heart's intuitive power. And we'll also discuss why this energy center is so important for cleansing and dumping those things we no longer need.

The Fourth Energy Center and the Physical Being: The Heart in Motion

I admire the balance and synergy of life—the way that the literal and symbolic mirror one another. The heart is a perfect example of this. Think about what the heart does energetically—which is to balance and connect energy between the lower and upper energy centers. Now think about what it does mechanically—it filters and channels blood, oxygen, and nutrients through our body. It's gorgeous, really, how the physical manifestation of the heart tells us everything we need to know about its more figurative work.

Let's start by looking at how the heart functions in a literal sense, in our physical body. First of all, there is the sobering fact that, as a society, our hearts are stressed. According to the Centers for Disease Control and Prevention, heart disease is the leading cause of death for both men and women in America. Every single year, about 610,000 Americans die of heart disease.

Disease usually goes to the weakest part of the body. I feel that this pertains not only to the weakest *physical* part of the body (although this is certainly true) but also to the weakest emotional, mental, and spiritual parts of the body. Enough people suffer from heart problems that most of us have probably been touched by the disease in some way, shape, or form.

As I was in the process of writing this book, I found out that my dad needed heart surgery for the second time in his life. Specifically, the outer layer, or glove, of his heart needed more room for the heart to expand, and he also required a bypass surgery to clear an obstruction. There was a hardening in his pericardium, which is the double-walled sac that surrounds the heart and the roots of its vessels.

My dad, one of the kindest men on the planet, showed me how the muscle can physically bounce back. Born and raised in the Midwest next to the beautiful Black Hills, carrying that kind, neighborly sensibility that Midwesterners are so known for with him throughout his life, long after he left his hometown, he also carried with him some other less helpful generational and learned values, like keeping emotions in and not letting the heart say its piece (or peace). This dammed energy literally started to squeeze his tender heart. As has been very common in our culture for many generations, at a young age, he learned to tuck his feelings away inside and keep them hidden. Not only that, but he also learned to compete—to always try to excel at whatever it was he was doing at any given time—for the purpose of self-worth and value. His first (security), second (relationships), and third (power) energy centers were not quite fully matured and balanced. Since these lower energy centers are foundational to heart health as we age, his heart was not balanced either. It was unable to flush out emotion and disappointments, or to express deeper feelings as they arose.

My dad has always liked being in relationships, which ultimately drew him to two lovely long-term relationships, both of which, unfortunately, ultimately ended in divorce. Both of my dad's heart surgeries corresponded with his impending endings of each. Both of these surgeries were highly invasive, massive procedures that were necessary to physically clear and rebalance his heart. In the physical sense, he was given support for clearing and mending his restricted heart as well as a few mental tools to help with his recovery. He was not, however, provided with emotional and spiritual tools to assist with recovery. He is learning those now, and it is beautiful to see it's never too late.

Like a lot of us, I initially learned about the heart from watching my parents' relationship. My mom, strong in her convictions of the heart, grew up in San Francisco, close to her extended family. Her family had emigrated from Italy, where there was less discussion of emotion. They tended to react to the world around them by building stronger walls around the heart. Even as a child, I saw that my dad had a soft heart with a harder shell around it, and I understood that this was not quite a healthy scenario for intimacy and deep, honest connection. I felt my dad close off his naturally soft and open heart because as a child he was taught and disciplined to be "strong" and to refrain from showing emotion. This affected his heart and his love and trust for himself and others profoundly. In other words, he was not always true to himself and his feelings, and this may have stymied his relationships. He was raised to believe that was how a male should act. Emotions equaled weakness. This blockage of emotions not only failed to serve my dad in his relationships, but it also manifested physically—as the years went by, his heart exterior literally became hardened and blocked. It has been difficult to watch this manifest in my aging father, not only in terms of his physical state (which right now is actually strong), but also in terms of the internal pain he went through before, during, and after his divorces. Pain that was a result of blocking off emotional truth, vulnerability, and love in order to be "right," "masculine," and a "provider."

My dad has physically recovered well from his latest surgery. Physically, he's healthier than ever. He's cleared out plaque, regulated his blood pressure, and lost almost thirty pounds. One might say that it's helped him go deeper into his heart and love. But that's only the beginning. With the aftershocks of the surgery and the conclusion of his second marriage, my dad has had to clear out and unblock his heart emotionally for his health as well. He's shed physical weight, but he's also shed emotional weight by letting go of old sorrow and knocking down some of those emotional walls that have blocked him for so long. He sees his family more and makes more time to connect with nature again. He's less fatigued, less prideful and competitive (sorry, Dad, but this is a big one!), more attuned to the needs of others, and more present with his family—most notably with his grandchildren.

All of this has resulted in a beautiful cycle. Because my dad is more emotionally open and has fewer walls up, not only is he able to give more love, but he's also able to *receive* more love in the present moment. The more love and kindness he receives, the more he is able to give. In his seventies, my dad is incredibly vibrant and alive, more relaxed and present, with his healthy, open, unblocked heart. We've always been very close, but I now feel more seen, heard, and valued for being myself in his presence. And I see his relationship with my children deepening as well. It's invaluable.

I wish my dad's scenario was more common, and that more of us had a chance to open our hearts for healing and to cultivate strength (figuratively, of course) and room for newness. When I'm doing readings, there are a few key signs and signals that alert me to the fact that my clients' fourth energy center needs more opening, and a safer space for love and loving. You'll notice that all of the symptoms that are red flags in terms of the emotional, mental, and spiritual blockage of the heart energy center are also hallmark danger signs for physical heart health. Some common physical indicators of imbalances in the heart energy center include: an irregular heartbeat (this is not necessarily a sign of an arrhythmia—although it certainly can be—but can simply be a result of stress and the way in which it initiates our fight-or-flight impulse which, again, does not jive with intuition); coronary heart disease, which results from stored energy that becomes plaque (stored old emotion is often at the heart of this—no pun intended); high blood pressure; high levels of cortisol or insulin; or craving sugar or uppers. Notice that none of these issues help us locate or trust the intuitive part of our mind or heart. The heart and intuition both respond well to a safe environment for opening up.

Another flag for fourth energy center imbalances is when I pick up signs of lung issues in clients, often accompanied by shortness or shallowness of breath. Our heart and lungs work in tandem to filter oxygen throughout the body. This is the fourth energy center. So many of us never "get things off of our chests," and those emotions and pains ultimately lodge squarely on top of or within our heart, unbalancing the energy. Stuck grief can often feel like congestion or heaviness in our lung or heart space. If any of these symptoms sound familiar to you, you are not alone. We do still live in a culture that feeds into stress, racing, winning, isolation, and overstimulation, all of which lie at the root of many of these physical manifestations of heart-related issues. The heart likes to calm back into its balanced rhythm, to be able to connect to its intuitive radar. Grief and imbalanced emotion can be like rocks lodged in a stream. Plaque and irregular heart function can show up from this congestion, and a healthy intuitive connection can be compromised. As well, intuition can support the heart's healing.

By the time we reach our late twenties and early thirties, we have access to all the resources we need to take care of our heart. A heart that is well cared for supports a healthy, open, and even mind-blowing intuition because an open heart can read and interpret the wisdom of the current moment—a moment that it has taken the world eons of experience to provide. In my intuitive work, I've found that there are a few relatively simple physical practices we can incorporate into our life to better our heart health in the physical sense.

Remember that the heart is about giving and receiving love and life. Following that same general idea that what we put into our body is what we get out of it, the food that we ingest is critical to our health. Because the heart energy center is next to the solar plexus (gut) energy center—where we burn off and assimilate energy—a healthy gut calms and centers the heart. It gives the heart support to clear off old emotion, feeling, and pain. Clearing is key for "listening."

We want to keep that process as smooth and supported as possible, not only for the well-being of our gut and digestive system but also because this third energy center plays a key role in supporting the heart, heart health, and heart function. The heat in our belly ignites the vibration of love into action (the heart cannot do this). This is a very important connection for using our intuition clearly and for a loving result. This exchange helps the heart feel free, light, and vibrant without too much density or obsession about sustaining those feelings, and it gets our body ready for making a choice about what we will do with intuitive information, including the love it brings.

This density of or obsession with a loving feeling is an attachment, and we want to let go of attachment. This idea of nonattachment is especially pertinent when it comes to both intuition and the heart. The heart does not like attachment because it weighs the heart down. *Attachment*, meaning holding on to a moment, a memory, or intuitive information that becomes too judged or emotional. Sometimes intuitive information is filtered through the analytical part of our brain and deemed important, but if the heart is not included in this process and intuitive information gets "stuck in our head" it might not be used or heard appropriately. This often happens because of an unhealthy, overpowering third energy center, a louder unbalanced voice center, or an overdeveloped ego. Love, like intuition, is meant to be enjoyed *in this moment,* without trying to grab it, hoard it, or fear that the feeling will never return.

I see this sense of attachment happen often when I teach clients about their intuition. As we sit quietly at the beginning of a session, focusing on the sound of our breath, the heart-mind connection can begin to sync and information can be witnessed or read quite easily. We make room to hear that inner voice, almost like it is coming from within the heart or from the very center of the mind. The stillness we have spoken of is key. The awareness is key. This gives our mind and heart trust that we are here in this present moment, feeling safe, and out of our pure thinking (going-doing) mind. The heart can energetically expand its vibration in these moments so information can find room to come into our conscious mind.

This should begin to feel like a warm bath or a supported hug for the heart. Just like people, the heart likes to be heard and to have its experience cleared. This part of connecting to our intuition can be broken down into three steps.

1. The stillness of being present helps the heart connect to our quiet voice within.

2. Information can float up toward our conscious mind with the heart vibration almost being like a pull or guide. This is the quiet voice of intuition.

3. Using discernment—or the union of the heart and the mind— we can ask our "self" (as the heart is neutral or detached from the earthly energy centers) what we are seeing or knowing intuitively in the present moment. Then we wait a few moments and see if we hear that inner voice arise. This is a deeper connection of "self" and "soul."

We can have a *conversation* with this information that is heart centered and calm. This state of being connects to the signs and guideposts that are of this higher knowing as a form of both attraction and seeing what is. The soul and self are awakening or intersecting.

I often say intuition is a conversation, like that between two in a marriage or agreement. It is a soulful, heart-centered understanding of what a kind but powerful voice is saying.

Information seems to get louder or is heard more clearly when we begin to understand the union of our ego with our heart. Intuitive moments grow with this understanding. There is more of a conversation and grounded trust. If our heart does not feel grounded and safe, intuitive information can feel false or fleeting. There can also be a fear that when an intuitive moment goes away, there will not be another one. And then we do not *trust* we can hear our intuition. But when we have trust in our powerful heart, moments go, as the heart knows, and another one will arise.

Clients can latch on to that moment of first synchronicity or hearing the inner voice and want it to happen again right away. I help them see that information and synchronistic experiences will come again. Like a flower, intuition will open when feeling safe to do so. It might feel like a start-stop at first. Yet intuition, like the heartbeat, is always there, supporting the mind and body, never stopping or hiding. Like a flower, it can choose to open or stay closed, but it cannot hide its existence.

If we begin to think about this too rationally, we can miss reading or feeling the heart's radar, which is inferring information constantly, and instead activate a more closed state where we do not feel the gut tugs or hear the heart's collection of information subtly caught through its radar or delicate petals. Visually, how intuition comes or is received can help us understand that the heart is reading and holding things until we release the tugs or the knowing. This release or letting go can be through action, such as when you use the information to help yourself or another, or simply in breath work as you exhale energy out of the heart and lung space. The relationship of in-out, or know-assist, is an important one.

The heart likes to keep the neutral rhythm of flushing the body, blood, and mind to not hold too much of anything foreign in the body (not as mushy as one thinks). Too much outside information (or too many thoughts) can load the heart, and too many emotional walls can keep the heart from creating its alchemy. When we receive information from the heart's radar and try too heavily to rationalize *that* information, running it through an analytical filter to try to make sense of it, we risk missing its true meaning or why the information came to us at all. If, for example, our heart knows that a friend or family member is in distress, when we tap into our intuition, or quieter part of the mind, we might see why and then be in a position to gently, or more boldly, help. It is important here to make a choice to act from the heart—will we choose to act and help our friend physically, or will we take a quieter route (hopefully using our intuition to decipher this step as well) by sending good thoughts or flowers . . . or do we exhale the information out and intuit that the friend just needs good thoughts sent her way? Discernment and a brave heart are important here. It is also key not to get stuck in or with the information, feeling polarized. The heart does not like this, as the heart likes flow. We must be present and brave, the heart calm and open to achieve this.

Through readings, I've learned that the heart is very supported and energetically flushes well when we eat as many whole, clear foods as possible. Clear as in water content, color, good fat, and protein. Clean, organic protein sources are wonderful with greens and a simple whole carbohydrate, like rice or oats. This helps the energy center of the heart vibrate and refresh its clarity. The green color of great vegetables, including light-green vegetables and fruits with darker skin like limes and apples, also cleanses and calms the nervous system. Darker leafy greens and cruciferous vegetables greatly help the heart function at its best and minimize the damage caused by too much insulin, stimulants, or ingested cholesterol. In particular, this energy center thrives on the nutrient-rich green vegetables (leafy greens, broccoli, and sprouts), foods with chlorophyll and soluble, saturated fats (such as avocado and olive oil) mixed with green herbs (such as parsley, cilantro, oregano, basil, and thyme) that detoxify and balance the blood and, thus, the heart. The lighter green foods are important for adding water nutrients and alkalizing minerals to blood and organs, easing the nervous system, and supporting the skin. Celery, cucumber, green beans, cabbage, zucchini, and even watermelon are fantastic here, especially when paired with a good protein or fat. These foods richly help the nervous system for bravery. Easing up on processed dairy is also helpful. Eating too many fruits is not advised when opening our intuition because they can contain high amounts of sugar, and this can make your nervous system react more quickly to intuitive information (notice *react* versus *act*). If you opt to juice, try to keep it as green (and alkaline) as possible. You might also consider easing up on certain acidic foods like tomatoes and flour.

Remember that food is one of the main energies that influence your body. It is the fuel. In other words, if you're eating meat derived from animals that were killed cruelly or who lived fearfully or in poor conditions, your body is ingesting some of that animal's fear and adrenaline and incorporating it as your own. That fear and adrenaline, and possibly the animal's life experience, are going through the heart, both energetically and even in terms of cholesterol and blood, which is something we want to do our best to avoid. You can think of your heart as a sponge. When it picks up unwanted or foreign matter, it makes it difficult to keep other parts of the body clean. This applies both literally and energetically.

Whole foods help to keep the heart de-stressed and supported. They can also support the life force around the heart. The heart does not enjoy the heavier elements that course through our body through our foods, our thoughts, or our emotions, even if we are not cognitively aware of the connection. Many believe this also applies to our breast health, breast cancer, lung disease, and many nervous and brain disorders. Our heart and brain can kick into fight-or-flight mode as a reaction to the foods we eat (and how they are raised or grown), the thoughts we choose, or the emotions we stuff back down. These are all forms of ingestion that are often not accompanied with complete elimination.

We want the heart to be calm and regulated, and good food choices play a significant role in accomplishing this. Not only do these clean, alive foods pump more vitamins and minerals into our body, but they also help *keep* them in our body rather than quickly eliminating them. This helps our intuition stay calm, alert, open, and supported. Also, the simple act of putting time, care, and attention into nourishing ourselves is an act of self-love. Food plays an important role in this. This connection to self-love and self-care is important for intuition to be received, openly listened to, deciphered, and used. Just like we fuel up for a test or a performance, we also need to fuel up for intuition and to keep our heart calm, centered, and wise.

Another huge key to heart health and a clear intuition is breath. Our lungs hold a lot of oxygen (both new and old), emotion, and calming mechanisms, and they also hold on to emotions that are more difficult to move through, like grief or loss. So how we choose to use our lungs and breath is as important as how we choose to open our intuition. If we choose to let the mind and heart focus on loss or grief, this can keep us feeling held back or stuck in life, and it leaves our heart stuck in the past. Intuition cannot thrive in that scenario, as it likes to be in the current moment. What's more, if we do not move through feelings of the past that are still hanging around as grief, these feelings can become lodged in our heart. This is not helpful to either our everyday perspective or to opening our intuition. Our breath can help us channel and expunge this and other emotions. It's the best vehicle there is to link to your intuition. And, of course, breathing is how we oxygenate ourselves, which is key to physical (and emotional) heart function. Despite the fact that breath is essential to life, many of us breathe quickly and shallowly. This means we breath into the top half or third of our lungs instead of breathing *all* the way into our lungs. When we do this, not only are we failing to provide our body with the oxygenation it requires, but these quick, short breaths also amp up our nervous system. It is through full breath that we receive the *calming* aspect of breath, which in turn calms the heart and helps open intuition (are you tired of me connecting the two yet?). Practice deep, diaphragmatic breath by slowly counting to five as you inhale through your nose and channel your breath all the way down to your diaphragm. Hold the air in your diaphragm for another five count, and then exhale slowly through your mouth, again counting slowly to five.

Breathing like this may feel a bit unnatural at first, but when you see the profound difference this relatively simple tweak makes in terms of how calm, centered, and open you feel, there's no going back. To build this deep breathing habit, I recommend practicing diaphragmatic breath for three to five minutes a day and building from there. Making a point of bringing your attention to your breath when you feel stressed, harried, or scared is very helpful but can literally feel like a cramp or stone in your heart. Keep breathing. I bet you'll notice that, in those moments, your breath wants to be particularly quick and shallow. Instead, breathe deeper and notice the calm settle over you.

You can also burn off nervous, edgy energy and stimulate your lymphatic system (part of the circulatory system) and immunity by jumping on a rebounder (a small trampoline) or a larger jumper. This moves the heart, enhances the circulation of blood returning to the heart, and tapers down adrenaline and cortisol levels.

Finally, it's imperative to think about literally opening up your heart space. Remember how connected all of our systems are: physically, emotionally, intellectually, and spiritually. Time and time again, I've watched my clients open their hearts emotionally (which we'll talk about a lot more later in this chapter) by beginning with a physical heart-opening practice. To open your heart, concentrate on opening up and broadening while relaxing your shoulders.

One specific practice is to helicopter your arms. Stand up with your feet planted about hip-width apart, and open your arms out into a T shape with your shoulder blades gently drawn down away from your ears. Keeping your arms open in that T shape, begin to slowly rotate your torso in one direction, back through center, then over to the opposite direction. You can also use this as an opportunity to bring your attention to your breath. Exhale each time you open to the side; then inhale as you return to center. These conscious breaths will also help to modulate your movement so you're not moving too quickly from one side to the other. We all like to speed around quickly these days, so any practice that helps you slow your movements down a bit and move intentionally is a wonderful reset physically, emotionally, mentally, and spiritually.

If you're in the mood for something a little bit more relaxing and restorative, simply lie down on the floor or earth—or even in bed—with your arms spread out into a T and your shoulder blades gently drawn down to lengthen your neck. See how far you can draw the backs of your shoulders to the floor while keeping the motion soft rather than rigid. Just as with the standing posture, bring your attention to your breath, keeping it nice and easy and full. Let the air travel all the way down to your diaphragm as you inhale, and release it completely as you gently exhale, bringing awareness to that feeling of your heart opening up to the world. This opening helps your heart connect to and work alongside your intuition in new ways you might not have thought possible.

The Fourth Energy Center and the Emotional Being: An Open Heart

An open heart is priceless—and sometimes hard to maintain. Emotions do not often have the room nor are they given the time or listened to enough to be fully processed and then released. An emotionally clear heart vibration is not to be overlooked or skipped when trying to open and connect to your intuition. A heart that is more (often unintentionally) closed off to love and emotional movement will have a more difficult time reading and absorbing intuitive information. This is often because there is already too much energy in the heart from past emotional situations or from too much strain leftover from overeating, overexercising, or either overexpressing or repressing anger or rage. There can be a fear of the heart shutting down as a result of things like panic attacks, heartbeat irregularities, and heart attacks. All of these things—as well as the fear of knowing—block our connection to intuition. We can tend to shut off to others and, subsequently, to their heart vibration when we are emotionally overloaded, too stoic, stunned, closed, or irrational. Intuition does not like shut. How can we see when we are shut?

Almost everyone I read or teach intuition to wants to see situations clearly, and some want to learn how to differentiate emotion or opinion from fact. To do this, it is important to get the heart involved in a *nonemotional* way. I still sometimes have a difficult time giving intuitive rather than emotional information, especially when it comes to loved ones. I have to truly separate my feelings for a minute. When this happens, I usually catch myself by seeing that I am tapping into my emotion (remember, intuitive information is never emotional, but our response to the information can be) and redirecting my attention back to pure intuition or asking the universe for more time and information. It is important to tap into our intuition when we are *not* feeling emotional. This difference can take time to recognize, but if you tune in to your body and thought process, the answers are right in front of you. Are your body and heartbeat calm? Do you feel passive about any intuitive information you are receiving? If so, these are good indicators you are acting from a centered, nonemotional place. Is your heartbeat amped up? Does your breath feel shallow? Do you notice egocentric thoughts, agitation, pride, or happiness about any intuitive information you are receiving? All of these cues indicate that you're acting from an emotional place.

I often see clients who want to protect their hearts from pain—sometimes it's the result of a failed romantic relationship; other times it's the result of negative experiences in platonic relationships or programming or hurt during their childhood. The pain or reasons why they feel wary of love and allowing their heart to feel to its full capacity become a block in the road to understanding themselves and unlocking their higher wisdom. This is a high price to pay.

An open heart is a brave heart, but that requires vulnerability. Protecting our heart will keep it closed and lock in those stagnant negative emotions that make us want to close off in the first place. Being brave enough to air out our emotional baggage is key to opening our intuition *and* opening our upper energy centers, as we will discuss in the next chapter.

When we close off or block our heart, we effectively cut ourselves off from loved ones and from the beauty and comfort of feeling their true love for us. Consider this beautiful fact: the vibrations of our hearts actually connect us with one another. Whether you are consciously aware of it or not, your heart is literally speaking vibrationally to the hearts and minds of others. While this might sound scary to some, an open heart that is able to connect to the vibrations of others is conscious intuition at work. Your heart is connecting to your intuition, and that connection is supported by love and honesty. Feeling other people's true love for you and being open enough to see the love flowing around you helps your intuition come out of its shell. It allows you to bravely step into the ring, and see where trusting your gut will lead you. You'll have a well of love as backup when using intuition becomes more challenging, such as in those moments when you pick up on things that are not always so easy to hold peacefully. You can trick the mind through logic, but you can never, ever trick the heart. And this is precisely why the heart is so important to the intuitive process: *When the heart is open, intuition can flow through clearly for all people. The third energy center is still rooted in the earthly ways of self and the ego. Our fourth energy center represents that first step up toward unity through its intention to connect us all in love and to put intuition—and all of our actions, for that matter—to use for that purpose.* A conduit of connection.

I don't mean *heart vibrations* in a New Agey way; I mean it in a *scientific* way. According to research conducted by the HeartMath Institute, an exchange of heart energy can literally be detected between individuals up to five feet apart from one another. Heart energy is like a love vibe, the warmth and glow that you feel when someone is giving or sending you love. It is buoyant and filled with grace. This is *kimochi*. It provides you with that feeling of being more worthy than the sum of your parts. Some equate this vibration of love to a prayer or good intention sent your way. Receiving this vibration is feeling the compassion and greatest love for yourself and learning how to give and receive this vibration for its universally expansive qualities. This heart energy exchange shows up in readings often; the deeper the connection is between the client and another individual in his or her life, the greater the heart exchange will often be. I feel there is limitless intuition when there is true intimacy, like when a mother knows her unborn child, or that inexplicably deep and accepting connection we feel with family members, lovers, or true, dear friends. When love is open and supportive, you often know each other so well that, yes, you may begin to talk to each other intuitively. A daughter might burn her hand in Paris, and a mother may feel it in Colorado. A gentleman might think of a woman and hear her name called minutes later. I often have entire conversations with a loved one in my intuitive mind, only to receive a call a moment later, during which the same story is repeated by that loved one. This also pertains to dreams and déjà vu.

That said, strangers absolutely feel one another too. When we are tapped into our heart, we become more intuitive about our community and fellow man. Not only this, but one person's brain waves can connect with another person's heart and even synchronize. Many times, even as I'm still prepping for a reading, I can already feel in my heart what my client is going through despite the fact that we have not met yet. This often happens to me in everyday life as well, whether that connection is with another intuitive sitting across the stage from me, someone next to me on an airplane, or the clerk who's checking me out at the grocery store.

I mention this here because it is important to understand that the heart acts as an intuitive antenna or Doppler radar. The currents and conversations it can pick up are truly miraculous. Once again, this might take time and practice, but it is real and it works. I watch kids use these all the time. In its simplest sense, this is exemplified when kids know how to behave in certain situations that should theoretically be beyond their experience or emotional capability. For example, when a three-year-old is around an adult who is grieving and automatically understands it is appropriate to remain quiet and offer that grieving person a hug or a pat on the back. Our hearts can catch a lot of vibrations, especially when they are open and receptive. Try tapping into this by grabbing a friend and sitting together in a cozy environment—

maybe at home, in a coffee shop, or in an empty yoga or meditation studio. Face one another and clasp hands. Close your eyes and focus on your breath for at least three full minutes. When you feel centered and calm, continue breathing deeply and evenly as you open your eyes and focus your thoughts by looking into your friend's eyes. Tell one another what information you intuitively received during that period of close, intentful silence. Keep practicing. Eventually you may know the exact sentence or thought he or she was thinking. Remember, this practice is meant to be light and fun. If this does not work or you feel yourself becoming frustrated, keep practicing the *I Am* meditations focusing on any area within yourself where you feel blocked. Then, try again.

Not only does a closed heart cut us off from those around us, but it also cuts us off from our own self. Without being able to accurately hear and translate the emotional intelligence that stems from connection and the heart, we end up acting from emotion or from lower vibrations that are not wise and leave us feeling like we don't have the skills to work through a situation. This can easily lead us astray. Emotions are feelings that are more primal and instinctive (although not always without rationality), whereas emotional intelligence involves bringing in the wisdom of the feminine side and applying the lessons we've learned throughout our life and in our interactions with other people to that emotional energy. It's witnessing an emotion without attaching to it. Remember that energy in motion we spoke of in chapter 1? We want emotion to keep moving like the energy it is. Emotional intelligence directs our emotions into a calm new space, whether that means sending the energy back out into the universe through breath, or using the energy for the forward movement that comes from learning lessons about ourselves or others, and letting love flow. We can do this in simple ways, like writing a letter to someone that expresses our feelings.

We can think that we don't see things, do not know how to be emotionally intelligent, or we're not intuitive, but the heart always knows . . . even if it's on an unconscious level. It's about *connecting* to this knowing. If we're clear and feel lovingly supported by both ourselves and others, this information is able to make its way up to our mind and become a conscious thought. When we are unable to hear what our heart is telling us, the signs around us get bigger and we start attracting the same situation over and over again in our life until we hopefully reach a point where we can address and acknowledge it. This point marks a maturation in our evolution toward a clear heart. It is yet another big step in our journey toward cultivating a rich intuitive life.

So what exactly is a clear heart? A clear heart is a heart in a state of peace, presence, and forgiveness . . . which just happens to be one of my personal favorite definitions of love. Love is not a heart that's on fire or a heart that is on overdrive trying to find and hold on to love. A clear and open heart gives us the ability to feel unity and understanding within ourselves, with others, with our emotions, and with the current moment. It is a heart that can pick up the signals that the hearts of others are emitting.

When we have walls up around our heart, the task of taking them down can feel quite heavy. With a little bit of dedication and awareness, though, the process is actually as simple as practicing the golden rule: kindness. Not only should we treat others as we would like to be treated, but we should also treat *ourselves* as we would like to be treated. A big part of this involves not forgetting to take care of our heart emotionally. Be gentle, honest, and present with yourself, hopefully beginning to see more moments as they are. What would your heart like to spend its time doing? Sleeping? Spending time in front of a large body of water? Hanging out with family? Taking the time to be kind to our heart, treat it well, and give it what it needs from an emotional standpoint ultimately helps us to see the highest form of a situation and to act appropriately within that situation. This can facilitate great forms of forgiveness, and it allows us to have those conversations that have been ignored until this current moment in time.

These walls that so many of us have up around our hearts are just like physical walls—they close us off and lock us in. Some see their walls as a sign of valor: "I have been hurt before and learned my lesson. I am strong, and no one can hurt me again." The problem with this attitude is that while it may protect us from hurt, it does not allow for the possibility of truly loving or feeling truly loved, either.

In this life we are *meant* to connect with others and the space around us, even when we are scared or disappointed. It's one of the most beautiful and fearless parts of being human. If you are even and clear in the lower energy centers, you are ready. Instead of creating walls and boundaries, I encourage you to instead think about *clearing* your walls and boundaries.

To be sure, taking a leap into the heart can be shocking and painful. It takes a lot of bravery to live from the heart, to know when to love and when to walk away, to be vulnerable. But when your heart is open and can pick up and translate the intentions of others, you'll ultimately have all the information you need to ensure your own protection. Just like a healthy physical heart has good circulation, so too does a healthy emotional heart. We are able to give and receive energy without being weighed down. The healthy emotional heart is less stressed by the action of loving. And also, since love is a vibration and a vibration is energy, like any other sort of energy, love energy wants to balance itself, to form a neutral charge—to take care of itself in one connective motion, to feel whole in uniformity and not lopsided. Clearing the heart of intense or old emotion helps intuition attract clear information. We can then feel and pick up on the vibrations of others in an intuitive, nonemotional manner.

With this vibrational attraction in mind, instead of blocking love, think about bringing the intention of love to every situation. Practice love and forgiveness of yourself, love and forgiveness of others, and love of life and the planet. Think detachment: detachment from thoughts about the future, detachment from the past. Live in the present, in this current moment. Think about practicing love when you're driving to work, getting ready in the morning, and making dinner. Make love an integral part of your life at all times. When you give love—in whatever way—you get love back because you're open.

Living and loving with an open heart doesn't mean accepting everyone into your life and loving them to your own detriment. Love is seeing and knowing, and forgiving anyway. Proximity to someone or something we think we want is not always the way to stay safe and calm in the heart. We are not meant to stay in a space—literally or figuratively—that does not calm the heart. Humans are the only living beings who force mind over matter in this way. But the heart knows (even when the head ignores). And the body responds to "threats," even if the threat is to our ego. We need to notice our heart's reactions in the moment and then clear our mind to listen to this reaction. Meditation and forgiveness are great methods for helping with this practice. The more we forgive, the more we can stay calm in any space, no matter who or what else is in it.

Sometimes we have to say good-bye, but we can say good-bye with love . . . and an open heart will let us know exactly when this is necessary because the heart sees the whole picture of every situation. For instance, we may intuitively know that it's time to break up with someone. The intuition coming from our open heart and open mind shows us how to follow through with compassion and the other person's perspective and best interests in mind, as well as our own. At times it comes in as, "You can love someone, and you don't have to invite them to your dinner table." Sometimes that love needs to stay out of your personal space for your own self-love to grow. Or it is just time to conclude. We can use our boundaries to facilitate this. I often include people who fall into this category in my meditations or prayers. It's a way to direct positive energy and still keep the heart vibration calm and supported.

So many of our misconceptions about the heart come from our misconceptions about love and about being open. In our society, we've glorified love—and particularly romantic love—and believe that it always is a magical thing. And, to be sure, love *can* be very magical. But love can also be painful. It can also elicit a lot of fear. When your heart is open, you feel a lot. This is okay once the first four energy centers are balanced, because you'll find it easier to come back to center, let go, or see energy coming and redirect (and not absorb) negative energy to be present. And this is where intuition is. In presence.

Feeling the entire range of emotions is an important part of the human experience. Many have been convinced that feelings do not matter or they are not important for our heart health. This is not true. Feeling the freedom and safety that being seen and heard provides and not getting stuck in and holding on to emotions are the clearest path to true love. Remember that emotions are not facts, even though sometimes the brain and ego trick us into believing that they are, which often ends up taking our hearts on a roller-coaster ride. Intuition has a tough time with this. An open, healthy heart is calm and even-keeled in most every situation, no matter what is happening at any given time. Yes, there might be moments of great loss or of painful memories rising up. Stay with your breath and support system, including counselors and energy workers. An open heart knows when help is needed to *support* its healing and when it is feeling complete, total love. This doesn't mean that the less openhearted are completely doomed to a life alone; it just means that the intuitive heart understands that the earth, God, or the universe (depending upon what your specific belief set is) will provide. For healthy love to come, a healthy heart must exist.

In the past, I've been accused of not feeling deeply or not being present because I haven't cried hysterically during every disappointment or breakup. In actuality, the ability to remain calm even in the midst of endings is because I've learned to listen to my heart and come from a clear, compassionate, intuitive space that knows when and if it is in everyone's best interest to end a relationship. My heart knows, especially in adulthood, that all will be okay when I act from this place. Honestly, sometimes it takes my thinking mind or my pleasure principle time to agree, but when the heart and inner voice knows it's over, there's never any use arguing. Staving off the inevitable just results in an uphill battle I will ultimately lose. When I'm coming from a knowing, quiet heart and intuition, I will rarely take the "wrong" action, even if it feels unfavorable in the moment.

So how do you know if what you're feeling is real, true, openhearted love, fear, or something else entirely? Here are some sure signs of love that is *not* coming from full wholeheartedness:

- Love that involves an agenda or expectation: This comes from our own needs and is rooted in the lower energy centers. True love is for all equally.

- Love that involves the quest for security, power, or ego or to fill up some sense of lack.

- An empty or low well of self-love: Loving the self is essential. Since love is vibrational—and therefore a form of energy—and like attracts like vibration, you cannot receive what you are unable to give.

- Emotions that are too dense or overwhelming.

- Defensive or possessive feelings in loving relationships.

- Feelings of ownership about loved ones or their accomplishments: This is very common in our culture in parent-child and relational/partnership dynamics, yet it is not a healthy, balanced, open heart because it is not with selfless intention.

Perhaps the greatest key when it comes to love and intuition is knowing we will not always experience things we can see with the naked eye or analyze with reason. Because love is vibrational, we can't always explain *why* we're in love when we are. It's not a rational thing; it's energetic and vibrational. The heart feels the clarity and warmth of love, and it rejoices in it. When you are in your intuitive mind, you will feel the same peace. But it might not seem rational until you start to understand that intuition is a lot like a loving partnership. You might not understand why the feelings come in, but it nonetheless makes sense. A bond of trust is formed at a soulful level.

The Fourth Energy Center and the Intellectual Being: Forgiveness Paves the Path to a Clear Heart

I had done a few readings with my client, Betsy, over the course of a couple of years before she was ready to open her heart and clear out stuck emotion. Betsy was a quintessential thirty-something New York businesswoman—smart, quick, and working very hard to make headway in her career. When she came in for her first reading, it was ostensibly for career advice. What we ended up talking about, though, was the fact that she "desperately," as she put it, wanted to find a loving relationship and get married.

Up to the point when I met Betsy, her entire life had been unconsciously orchestrated around finding the perfect catch and having a dream wedding. Her focus on her dream wedding and its accoutrements is common in this culture that focuses on *external* symbols of love achievement or happiness. But this emphasis on a dream wedding and an idealized marriage did not gel with Betsy's authentic heart. It did not give her heart those calm, supportive feelings that she knew love and union required. Her hands felt shaky, and feelings of worry replaced elation when she thought about love. She was worried about the choices she had made in her life like choosing to travel extensively and waiting to settle down. Her body often felt nervous, like it was unsupported; her cortisol surges and elevated heart rate proved this to be true. Betsy's blood pressure was rising, and her old feelings of fear and disappointment were rising as well. Betsy often found herself feeling nauseated when she thought about how different her life and choices looked from those of her family and friends. As we sat there quietly, the facts begin to pour in.

Betsy was suffering from a divided heart that was rooted in her childhood. She was trying to fill her well with an idealized dream of a fabulous wedding and an easy, seamless marriage (I am not sure any marriage can be described as seamless, but I don't have to be intuitive to tell you that!). Everything Betsy had been taught to believe about love went back to an idyllic Disney fairy tale in which a strong, charming prince came to her rescue and her wedding was the destination, not the beginning of a union.

There was another part of Betsy that was very happy being career driven—she didn't *need* (or really want) marriage to dictate her worth. But her ambition and drive to succeed in her career didn't fit with her more patriarchal image of love and relationships. Betsy was inherently (or so she thought) work driven, but she believed she would have to give that up in order to find her ideal mate. Because Betsy's heart was divided between the two things she wanted but believed were mutually exclusive, like all divisions, it ultimately led to a weakened spot, and Betsy's heart broke over and over again when she dated. Her heart was not ready for intimacy, but her exterior goals were set on the "whole" package. This was not helping her health or her life experience, and her mind was constantly flopping back and forth between the past and the future.

As I spoke with Betsy, I could clearly see her deep wish for complete and total love. Betsy had been a witness to her parents' long, happy marriage, and she was adamant that she wanted the same for herself. Yet, when we peeled back the layers of her heart, it was clear that Betsy was deeply conflicted about how to find a mate who loved her whole heart and would let her excel in her career without being intimidated or emasculated. This is a struggle very common to women today. Although Betsy's parents were, indeed, very much in love, they also had a more traditional relationship in which her mom was a homemaker and her dad brought home the bread. Betsy had no template for the sort of relationship she desired. To Betsy, it felt like following a career track and desiring achievement and accomplishment in this realm were selfish. At the end of the day, she was confused about what love entailed and oblivious to the fact that it was possible to simultaneously enjoy a loving, romantic relationship and a fulfilling, successful career. She also felt guilt about what it was that she wanted out of life.

As soon as Betsy's reading took direction and the two of us realized that what the always-business-minded Betsy really needed to talk about was love, we had a good laugh. Immediately, Business Betsy melted away, and I found myself speaking to a much softer, more compassionate woman. As Betsy's reading continued to unfold, it became clear how stringent her life had become—she was focused entirely on working herself to the bone, looking the part (at the expense of her own comfort), and following a very strict food regimen. Betsy's life was all about control, with no room left for actual *feeling*. The intellectual part of her life was superseding everything else. What Betsy was actually accomplishing through all of this—aside from never being in the moment—was bringing more competition, grief, and dashed expectations into her life. Not only that but because she didn't believe deep down that she could enjoy good love and a good career at the same time, she was attracting extremely unkind males into her life.

Betsy's reading revealed that it would be extremely helpful on physical, emotional, and physiological levels to take better care of herself in general and, specifically, to release the weight that her expectations, food choices and restrictions, and nervous energy were placing on her heart. Her reading showed she was counting calories to the point of restriction and was not consuming foods that supported heart, nerve, and brain health. Her reading also mirrored she could dress more comfortably while still being tailored, and she shouldn't stress about her appearance in her efforts to find a mate. It also showed she needed to let go of her judgment of other people and her analytical view of the world, which were always reflexively firing away. These tendencies were affecting her heart. Betsy was pushing kind people away and magnetizing those who were more self-centered. The heart does not resonate with numbers and restriction—it's the masculine side of our brain that does this.

As soon as Betsy began to let go of her need to control, she understood that her heart and brain could operate as best friends. She began to feel free and supported in ways she could not have imagined. She let go of her black-and-white thinking and came into more unity-driven thought, which is founded upon the idea that parts make a whole and the whole is greater than the sum of the parts (we often call this subtle energy). Serendipity started to happen. Betsy let go of the vise grip she'd been holding over the different facets of her life. She forgave herself for what she realized she had mistakenly labeled as incorrect desires and the notion that new desires were bad.

Betsy and I spoke again a year and a half later and, in that time, much had changed. Betsy had now struck a balance between her professional and dating lives and was seeing a grounded, kind gentleman. Her career was flourishing. The new softness she had discovered changed the way she perceived work, and she found that her coworkers now treated her as an ally rather than a competitor. Betsy's weight stopped fluctuating so drastically. In general, she lived with more heart and evenness, both personally and professionally. Synchronicity snuck in.

Betsy's life now felt manageable and *fun* rather than like something that needed to be managed. She was noticeably happier and more peaceful, more carefree and open to the present moment, which is where we find intuition. She was more in the *now*. She had a glow about her, and the dark circles under her eyes were nowhere to be found. She gave herself what she needed when she needed it. And although Betsy was very content with her male friend, she was no longer so attached to the idea of and need for marriage. This was yet another offshoot of living in the here and now because she knew today's world supported a more modern view of relationships and she had nothing really to fear. Her mate was compassionate, kind, and really saw Betsy. That was fulfilling in and of itself. The future would unfold as it was meant to. *Ah*, how the heart loves living in this space.

Obviously, in life, there is a time to use logic and intelligence. What we *don't* want to do is to live entirely from the head. Our heart is wise in a way that our brain simply can't be, and if we are not able to rely on it, we end up living an unbalanced life that lacks much of the richness our heart can provide. Our heart allows us to be in the moment and to connect. Ironically, as we can see with Betsy, it is when we let go that we are able to more easily achieve what we really desire and are destined to have . . . and, moreover, we are able to *enjoy* the fruits of the current branch in life.

The question now becomes, how do we get to this place of openness, presence, and going with the flow of the heart, the flow of whatever given moment we are in? As we discussed in the emotional body, our heart thrives when it is open and clear. One of the most effective ways to get to this place is through a concept that sounds simple enough but that can sometimes be difficult in practice: forgiveness.

It is forgiveness that allows us to be vulnerable, that helps us remove the walls we put up around our heart. It is forgiveness that ultimately provides us with the clarity and openness we need to be available to others and to act purely and openly to those people and situations that greet us at any given time. When we hold on to past hurts, we become guarded and our heart is clouded. That place of purity that allows us to trust what the heart is telling us is harder to hear and see. And, if we cannot interpret this information, what we are essentially doing is muffling our intuition. We are not sure we, or intuition, matter.

Forgiveness requires us to be able to step into our and other people's shoes from a heart-centered space and to see life through our eyes and their eyes, and then we can act from this space of enlightenment. As our heart is emptied of old pain and blockage, we begin to see the situations in our life through clear intuitive eyes; we see each situation as it *is*, not as we project or perceive it to be. We shed old pain, which when left unchecked, can skew our intuitive clarity. Unaddressed pain causes us to filter the world through the fight-or-flight or warrior part of the brain versus through the intuitive, open, *being* part of the brain. With forgiveness, we can let go of both the baggage of our own story as well as those stories we project upon others. Forgiveness alleviates those ideas about who or what is right or wrong; forgiveness clears out that fight-or-flight reaction that we must fight off pain or enemy when it feels as if we've been hurt. Forgiveness helps clear not only *our* pain but also the pain of others involved. When we remember that everyone has a story and when he or she does something in the moment that hurts or irritates us—even if it's a loved one doing it—the action stems from a past pain of his or her own and we can help with that pain (without taking it on as our own) in the current moment. Once we realize this, it becomes easier to recognize the fact that we must forgive to move forward. Presence helps us realize. Seeing a pain arising helps as well. We do not re-act, which helps everyone.

This relates back to another lesson the heart teaches us, which is that we are all one. What we feel is often triggered by our past experiences, but these are not helpful to intuition and understanding what our heart is processing. So much of the work we have to do is in clearing our own heart, our own memories, and our old pain. Most of us have either witnessed or engaged in prejudice or the repression of another person or group, even if it's been in a secondhand way, like on TV, and these need to be cleared too. Living in a world without mental divisions will lead us to a freer and happier heart once we move past victimizations. Someone who understands how to use a loving voice to create more forgiveness of self, of others, and of our old, worn-out views, is walking a direct path to intuitive prowess. We must forgive and have compassion for others to clear our heart . . . and we must also do the same for ourselves to mature into this idea of connection to a higher experience.

I learned one of my favorite forgiveness exercises from the renowned healer Dharam Dev Kaur Khalsa. She encouraged me to use a traditional Hawaiian mantra of forgiveness and reconciliation: *ho'oponopono*. This simple but powerful phrase means: "I am sorry. Please forgive me. Thank you. I love you." I've found that reciting this phrase while sending love to someone about whom I feel sadness or pain (including myself, when appropriate) is an easy and effective tool for release and forgiveness. This is one of the most powerful forgiveness tools or sayings I have ever learned, aside from *I am love* or *I am loved*.

I was taught another great visualization technique to help with letting go, feeling safe in forgiving, and moving on by the great yogi Julie Rader. She described a beautiful angelic leader named Archangel Michael, who watches over us all. He guides us on a protective journey. This is how it unfolds: Visualize yourself, the person or people you wish to forgive, and Archangel Michael all in a small boat. Row out to a lovely, pristine island. Once you're there, say good-bye to the person you need to forgive and let both the person and Archangel Michael off of the boat. The person you are forgiving is safe, and you know Archangel Michael is there to watch over him or her. From there, another Archangel Michael appears (archangels can be everywhere at once) and returns back to shore with you. You and Archangel Michael get off the boat. You are safe, you have let go, and you have support.

Finally, an old tool that I learned many, many years ago has helped me continue to function well when a relationship gets tough. I visualize healing bright-blue light—it can be any shade from turquoise to the color of a clear, radiant sky—and put this blue light around both myself and the other person in the troubled relationship. Sometimes wrapping this light looks like we're covered in a bubble, and other times I imagine it washing over us like a bath. I allow the blue to wrap around us both, clearing, cleansing, and energizing both of us. It is inclusive and doesn't play favorites. I then send healing thoughts, love, and harmony to both myself and the other person. I have found that this form of directing energy works wonders in forgiveness and moving forward.

Think again about where the heart is: in the chest. So it helps us tremendously to get things off of our chest, as the fourth energy center encompasses this entire space. This clearing is imperative for a light heart. We'll discuss this process of moving energy more thoroughly in the next chapter when we get into the throat energy center and learn how to give voice to those things that are locked up inside of us. But, for now, concentrating on the process of dislodging those things that we are holding on to—past hurts and transgressions—and letting them go is priceless. This can move heaviness, congestion (including literal phlegm), and weight off our heart and chest, shoulders, and upper arm region. It helps tremendously with hand and joint health, not to mention the health of the upper back, shoulder blades, and trapezius.

Give yourself, your upper body, and your intuition a clean slate to work with so you can interact with those around you in a truly authentic way, rather than reacting to your past or to emotions that you're holding on to based on a current trigger or stimulus. Intuition will flow more freely and clearly without triggers and blocks in your path. Along with forgiveness comes letting go of fear, projections, worry, guilt, and blame. Making this choice begins the clearing process. Next, actions of removal will emerge.

The biggest gift you can give yourself and your intuition is forgiveness. Holding on to grudges doesn't teach a lesson to you or those who you perceive as having hurt you. Also, when your intuition is not open and flowing, others can energetically pick up on this and will not trust you with their intimate heart space. This traps everyone in the past. Be free. Let go. And most of all, be brave. This might come in stages, which is wonderful. Like increasing your intuition, all of this is a process. After choice will come small and large action steps you and your intuition co-direct. It is easy to act from the ego, and our culture sometimes even rewards this. It might be part of the reason so many people in our culture can easily get trapped in the second energy center, a junior high way of relating to one another. Forgiving others and ourselves, and acting from a place of openness and joie de vivre—in which we empathize with the fact that, at the end of the day, we are all dealing with the same human experiences regardless of external differences—is the biggest act of bravery possible. Using your intuition *should* feel brave . . . because it is.

Are you ready for some mind-heart openers to hear your intuition more freely? Let's do it. Shoulder releases are a great way to begin to activate your intuition. Let's add a mental aspect of mind-heart dumping. Sitting or standing up tall, draw your shoulders up to your ears as you inhale. Hold there for a count of three. As you are counting to three, pull up a thought about a person, situation, or feeling you need to let go of. On three, with focus (and somewhat swiftly), exhale as you drop your shoulders down and back so that your shoulder blades almost touch each other like wings. As you release your shoulders to a neutral position on an exhale, guide yourself that the out breath represents letting go. Do this three times, releasing the same thing each time.

One more tool to clear your heart out for your higher intuition to have room to open is going to a yoga or meditation class that focuses on heart openers and heart-based letting go at least once a week. Make sure you find an instructor who is guiding you visually and offers a supportive environment for heart opening. Pilates, dance, and tai chi can help as well. Rolling down like a rag doll stretches the "back" of your heart and gives a start or ending to heart clearing practice. Roll back up slowly for an even stretch.

Allow yourself to live more freely in the moment and to honestly hear—and follow—what your heart is telling you. This simple mind-heart shift can entirely change your life. Through forgiveness, we leave space for light and magic to trickle in through our heart. This magic will often have a loving, intuitive flair. It's well worth all of the work it takes to feel this alive.

The Fourth Energy Center and the Spiritual Being: We Are All One

One of the most compelling elements about learning to live from a heart-centered place is that it leads us to realize that we are all one. Divisions such as gender, ethnicity, and socioeconomic status fall away. Think of how the world will transform when we reach a point where our hearts are vibrating and aligned with those around us. Collectively, we will live calmly, compassionately, without fear, without lack, and with each of us acting in the best interest of all. The impact of a heart led by Spirit is incalculable.

Spirit is the essence of that "something more" that is guiding us. Our heart is tapped into this. While the lower three energy centers master earthly matters, the heart begins to let spirit—or an understanding of that "more"—into the conversation. While the heart does not know why it feels what it feels (after all, it does not house a complete brain, but some brain cells possibly), it *does* know it feels many things and that all of those emotions and feelings *must* be interacting with something. Our conscious being is beginning to understand that we are connecting to *something* more than ourselves. It is understanding we are both *interactive* and *interacting*. Inherently, we cannot do this by being individually one. Instead, we are tapping into the collective *one*.

When we let universal spirit lead our heart, we are cocreating our thoughts and experiences with something greater than ourselves. Our heart is almost like a bucket collecting information for cocreation. Depending upon your religious viewpoints, this idea of Spirit might include God, or it may simply mean the fresh air, the stars, the universe, or guardian angels. Whatever this unity is to you, it greatly assists the heart and intuition with seeing information and situations more clearly.

Since the world is made up of billions of individuals, we can see all of the heart-related elements we've discussed in this chapter reflected in society. When we are close-hearted or more centered in ego or power, tragedy occurs and pain lingers in perpetuity. One of the greatest examples I can think of when it comes to this is the attack on the World Trade Center towers on September 11, 2001.

You probably remember the sorrow and deep, gut-wrenching sadness we felt on that date—a sadness that resonated not just through America but throughout the world as well. To this day, we continue to relive the moment through the media, through political speeches, and through the ensuing violent actions that have resulted in response to 9/11. Since the heart does not understand time, whenever we rehash 9/11, the heart may reexperience some of the fear, anger, and sadness we felt when the attack initially occurred. Our media and society have yet to understand that a true brave heart moves on from pain and generates more understanding to clear past pain. Instead, merely hearing that date is now enough to give us a tinge of post-traumatic stress in our head and in our heart.

By failing to truly emotionally work through 9/11 and forgive the perpetrators, we are, as a global society and particularly as an American society, stuck in this cycle of reactive negative emotion. This is holding back the *spirit* aspect of the heart (and its higher knowledge that we are all one). Holding on to this negativity or blame makes it impossible for us to collectively act from a heart-centered place in terms of moving energy onward and out of our collective psyche. The mind and ego like to retaliate, so violence begets violence, and hate begets hate. September 11 was a horrible and tragic event—and there has been more horror, tragedy, and death in its wake because, as a society, we have been unable to practice forgiveness. For the well-being of everyone, it's time to change the fearful (and sometimes vengeful) pattern we've been living in to one of listening and compassion. It's time to collectively clear our hearts and let go of our perceived separation from one another.

This also shows up in our current era of gun violence. Seeing a gun or weapon is enough for most of us to make our heart race. Now we "see" weapons quite often for all the shootings occurring. It's heartbreaking. Pointing fingers or guns has replaced hearing one another, replaced love, and put the focus on love's opposite—fear. We can see this in how we witness gun tragedy now or how we used large guns in response to September 11. Spiritually, we have let love take a backseat to fear: fear creates abuses in power, prejudice, pain, and judgment. Abuse of power and abuse of status dissolve the vibration of love. Ownership and control have become new spiritual rites. A gun in hand contradicts what the heart energy center wishes and knows to be healing. Light. Love. Balance. Acceptance. Oneness. Jesus and Buddha held hands to their hearts to signify compassion and grace, and as a means for diminishing the idea of separateness. These days, fear, rather than love, is often embedded in us, and it's even used as the basis to encourage us to act "correctly." But if fear is the basis (this even includes the fear of not getting into a heaven that some religions instill), then fear is the outcome.

Of course, getting rid of collective cultural pain is not easy to do. In order to move forward and release negative emotion from the heart, we must, on an individual basis, mourn what we have experienced and what we have lost, move through grief, forgive, and from this space, come to a clear heart that can again be peaceful and can be intuitive. Knowing we can *be* intuitive creates a more intuitive nature. As with all loss, it is by mourning on an individual basis that society as a whole heals and transforms. Such is also the case with any other tragedy or hurt, whether it is global or individual. At the end of the day, there is no difference or division. Infuse intuition into this fact.

We hurt others when we are hurting ourselves. We can see this play out through our reaction to all violence. We can see that retaliation and actions taken from a place of fear, anger, or not fitting in do not work. No one wins. No one heals. The part of us that feels the need to defend or stand guard must be balanced with our heart instinct, which works toward the good of the collective. When we choose fear or pain as retaliation without consideration for all parties involved, we chip away at the intuitive part of our mind by silencing it. Many of us do this in small ways that add up. But we can catch ourselves when we hurt ourselves or someone else. We can apologize more quickly. We can follow through with action after our apology. We can breathe. Many individuals in our society are in severe pain and are feeling loss or a lack of love. Helping even a few people in small ways helps alleviate this. You might feel exempt from this, but no one is exempt from this collective responsibility; your heart knows this, even if your brain is convinced otherwise. Because we are always connected, these days pain can be viscerally experienced from our own living room or phone, and it can feel extreme and constant. Many think they're tuning it out cognitively, but that is getting harder and harder to do when we're surrounded by quick-moving information.

This pain is also intricately connected to the extreme rise in mass shootings. It seems we are beginning to see a template in these shooter profiles—they are committed by people who often feel isolated and angry, and often by young men. Their hearts are shut off, and they feel unaccepted by society, by peers, and by parents. According to their own manifestos, some of them are angry because they feel that sexual love has been withheld or they are confused about intimacy or connection. As a result, they feel disconnected and rejected by the world around them. At some point, they were unable to see or did not understand that they were seen and loved, and their hearts broke.

The responsibility for this does not just fall on their parents. We *all* need to learn to see every child as part of the collective we are responsible for. Either these souls did not allow themselves to connect with the hearts of those around them, or love was not made available to them. The violent acts committed as a result of this disconnection ultimately build up more resentment and fear in society. All of our hearts begin to close, and the fear-based cycle spins out further, repeating itself over and over again.

Forgiving those who have hurt us or threatened our sense of safety is a difficult thing to do. Allowing ourselves to grieve what is happening in the world at this moment can be painful, but there are ways to do it. This may mean your main priority in your day includes acts of letting go on a spirit level of unity. You can designate a certain time of day to this act. Maybe each time you practice yoga, you can dedicate your practice and set an intention to help heal yourself and others, thereby transmuting your energy for good. Or you can volunteer to give a hand to a local shelter every Sunday for a month as an act of grieving poverty.

I have learned through intuition that there are many different ways to grieve a collective tragedy, and most of the time it depends upon how deeply the event hits a nerve or old pain within us. Our actions are key in letting the energy leave our heart or mind in a physical (or physiological) way. The more we can relate to the incident at hand, the more difficult it is to get past the collective grief. If it is especially raw and close to home, take extra time and care before engaging in an act of letting go of grief. Maybe a day or more of rest is best. The more we can replace the hopeless and dense feelings of grief with action (this includes resting) in a personal sense of service, the more grief can become forgiveness . . . and then love.

A good way to move beyond this is through being of service and helping to make your community or neighborhood stronger. Maybe you can help ten local families. Another way to grieve on a collective level is by taking three minutes per day to send love to all of the families involved in a given tragedy. Allow yourself to feel any feelings that come up in the process, and let them out by crying or even screaming into a pillow. Breathing deeply helps the grief exit, just as it would in a simpler, more personal situation. You can also send healing thoughts toward the mass energy of your community, country, or whatever place you feel needs attention. This can be done in as little as ten to fifteen seconds or can last as long as ten minutes in the form of a healing meditation. Any quiet or calming meditation can help mediate heartache.

If the grief feels like a heavier emotion in the heart, this might mean you're projecting your own grief on mass grief, and this adds to it. It might be a good idea to spend a little time on that emotion every day, acting as an older sibling to your younger self and asking why the grief feels so polarizing, so personal. Journal if you can.

Finding a soul-filled way to clear or fill the space in you that is filled with fear, worry, or something else by bringing in new energy can be very helpful. You can do this through little gestures, like by planting small trees or a patch of flowers, sending a monetary offering to a group in need, or writing a letter to a congressperson. It may seem small, but any act of kindness is a positively charged vibration that literally alters the collective energy. And people feel this. Change follows where our energy leads.

Yes, it might take time to actively clear grief, but grief takes up a *lot* of our time when it's left unattended. Our actions, large or small, create a healing vibration and balance energy. The larger the grief, the greater the action should be. It causes forward flow. Just one final note: these actions need to involve your hands and heart; for example, a quick message on Facebook, although kind, is not vibrationally strong enough to constitute an action—it's more of a thought. If you can take even just a few minutes a day or on a weekend to write your thoughts out in longhand, send a simple letter, or journal, these simple actions can awaken much emotion to clear or communicate from a more connective, whole-hearted space. Getting your hands dirty is even better.

Through doing this on an individual and communal level, we can begin to clear, transcend, and open our hearts—and touch other hearts, paving the way for more trust in the future—thus creating more of a society where we operate on love and openheartedness rather than on fear and barriers. It should only take a moment to figure out how to help. Do not let confusion derail you. Go on a quiet walk and ask yourself what the heart needs to help with grief. Intuition responds to present, heart-based action.

It is hard to do—trust me; I know this as a mother, a wife, an intuitive, and an openhearted being. But I feel it is only when we realize we are all one that the open heart, connected in spirit, can begin to prevail over violence and hate. Is it a tall order? Yes. But we literally have everything to gain. It's all about compassion and small actions. Unlocking this form of compassion unlocks deep intuition. This is the truth. I feel the universe loves it when it sees us give with an open heart. It gives us more back. And for many, this presents itself as a gift of higher understanding and more attuned intuition.

Heart Energy Center Meditation

Since we've already covered diaphragmatic breathing in this chapter (see page 134), this heart meditation will focus on the saying or mantra of your choice, spoken aloud. Select the *I Am* saying that most resonates with you or create your own:

I am love.

I am joy.

I am compassionate.

I am open.

The heart *loves* rhythmic sounds that resonate with its beat. Close your eyes for a moment, and slow and even out your breath. Once you have found the rhythm of your heartbeat, begin to speak your *I Am* saying aloud, maintaining your breath as you speak. *I* on the inhale, *am* plus the third word on the exhale.

Bring your focus to the words as you speak them, particularly emphasizing and drawing out the *m* sound in *I am*. This rhythm is so happy and joyful—I truly believe this is why the first cognitively recognized audible sound or word most babies speak is *mama*. I feel this is not necessarily the word *for* "mother" as much as it is the word *to* the mother, spoken with pure joy and exceptional gratitude for the nurturing the little one feels from his or her mother.

In many cultures, *maaaa* is considered to be the sound for the vibration of the heart. The vibration is incredibly healing, especially when we take our head out of the process and simply let the heart be guided in this graceful vibration of gratitude.

I say one of these mantras every day, multiple times throughout the day—at home, in the car, at work, and whenever my heart needs to express emotion, be it joy, grace, pain, sorrow, or grief. You may try this method of quietly reciting your mantra throughout your day, or make it a focused practice at a certain time once a day. If you choose one specific time, give yourself between three and ten minutes for this practice, perhaps increasing the time by thirty seconds to a minute per day. Try to repeat this practice for five to seven days in a row. Notice if anything has changed in your heart or if you feel more expansive or forgiving.

The Heart Guide

What it governs:	Heart, love, equality, unity
Ages:	21–28
Color:	Green, bright pink, or gold
In balance:	Loving love. Not afraid of love. Open. Calm. Able to communicate with others intuitively through the heart. Ability to forgive, understanding that we are all one. Letting go to be present or here now.
Imbalanced:	Closed heart, feelings of isolation, physical heart or circulation issues. Fear-induced body responses. Panic. Tension in chest. Shortness of breath.
Supportive foods:	Vibrant green nutrient-rich vegetables, cruciferous vegetables, green water-based alkalizing fruits and vegetables (like limes, green apples, zucchinis, and celery), clear water, and healthy fats. Raw nuts. Decreased dairy. More avocados. Green beans, lima beans, mung beans. Leafy vegetables. Water.
Beneficial practices:	Deep breath to clear the lungs, shoulders drawn back and down to open the heart, yogic heart and chest openers and stretches, exercises (such as rebounding) that stimulate the limbic system. Long, slow walks. Hikes. Swimming. Shoulder and neck massage. Warm baths.
Sayings:	*I am love.* *I am joy.* *I am compassionate.* *I am open.*

6

THE FIFTH ENERGY CENTER: THE THROAT

Speaking Our Truth

Whereas the first through third energy centers are connected to earthly matters and the fourth energy center acts as the bridge between the earthly and the divine, it is here in the fifth energy center that we first connect to the divine. The divine is inherently about the union of two or more. In terms of the fifth energy center, this idea of union includes the collaboration of our physical voice that we use to speak to the world and our inner voice or intuition. We bring these two voices together to *speak the truth*.

So far, we've talked a lot about the importance of using breath as a tool to let go of emotion, which is important both in terms of existing in the present moment and for understanding intuitive information without attaching emotional filters. Since the fifth energy center resides in our throat (where we mechanically breathe), this area is imperative for balance and for keeping our mind and body light enough to act rather than *react* to intuition. It is about receiving information as it is meant, without tainting or misreading it because of influences from either the outside world or our own intellectual and emotional inner world.

As with our physical voice, this throat energy center can be mighty. When used correctly and with full awareness, it can be an instrument for change; for whole, present expression; and for rebalancing and letting go of not only our own experiences but also experiences of others.

Have you heard people sing the praises of being in their thirties and the new wisdom that comes with it? Or have you heard a thirty-something talk about how she suddenly feels freer to speak up? Some people cite the thirties as the period in life when they learn to use their voice and not care so much about what others say—it's the time when they finally come into their own and are comfortable with their own vibe. What they might really be saying (in not so many words) is that their fifth energy center has come into balance—for most of us, this happens between the ages of twenty-eight and thirty-five. When the fifth energy center is balanced, we are able to speak our truth from an intuitive place. This serves as a powerful instrument that ultimately brings us peace of mind.

The fifth energy center governs the throat and thyroid. Here we learn how to use our voice to purify our thoughts and feelings, either by letting them go through mindful breath, meditation, or guided support or by neutralizing them before or as they come in. We also learn to unify our thoughts and feelings with the best interest of our own health and the health of others. At first, the throat may seem to lack the romance and intrigue of the energy centers beneath and above it—the heart, the higher eye, and the crown (where connection to higher guidance resides). But the throat energy center is where we experience liberation through its ability to clear the past and put rebalanced creativity and expression into action. New energy flow is put into action when we share what we feel, thus creating a new experience. If you've enjoyed the sense of liberation that comes from expressing yourself freely, then you know exactly how thrilling, euphoric, and freeing it is. And if you haven't yet had this experience, you're in for an incredible treat!

When we talk about intuition, we usually talk about *knowing*. But there's another extremely important element that comes into play with intuition, which is *speaking*. After all, if we cannot speak the truth intuition offers, what good are an open heart and open insight? By the time we get to the throat energy center, not only can we *access* what we're feeling and what we're compassionately connecting to in the heart, but we're also able to gracefully speak it in a way that is simultaneously bold, truthful, and compassionate.

I love that this fifth energy center is associated with a vibrant shade of blue because it is my favorite color—one that represents (and replenishes) health, infinite fresh air, and spiritual, nourishing support—like that of open sky and clear water. Many cite this color as healing and representative of peace and forgiveness—some of the same gifts that the fifth energy center offers. Imagine the color of a crystalline sea or a clear sky. At optimal balance, this is the color the throat energy center emits. It fills me with awe that the fifth energy center is precisely the color of those elements of nature that we associate with freedom, peace, calm, and open space. In other words, the colors of liberation, expansive support, and new opportunity. Not coincidentally, it is liberation that we can achieve by letting go, using our voice, saying our peace, and expressing our beautiful truth—all functions of the fifth energy center. The throat is a passageway. Here we can find a true release of emotion, motion, and rebalance. Talking things out with kind purpose instantly clears both the heart and the mind.

As it pertains to intuition, that feeling of liberation frees us up to express what our inner voice is saying. This further strengthens our intuition, gives us more confidence in our intuition, makes us braver, allows us to trust ourselves more, and brings more freedom into our life. Freedom to *be*.

This energy center is deeply and simply about: truth; purification of the air in our lungs and of our heart, body, mind, and spirit; and giving voice to what the heart and mind intuitively feel. Purification is how we can clear our mind of thoughts and our body of emotion, both old and current. Old thoughts and emotions take up space, the same way old emails, texts, and images suck up gigabytes on our computer or phone. We must purge and purify the old to make room for the new. Purification, or letting go, is imperative for our intuitive experience because it allows us to exist in the *now*. Purification is integral to the process of clearing, expressing, and enacting the heart and the mind. Remember how we talked about getting things off of our chest in the last chapter? We execute a lot of this through our voice and through breath—by forgiving people, including ourselves, by being brave, and by speaking our truth. The throat energy center connects our heart to our wise, intuitive space, or what some call the third eye or center of the mind. It connects our inner voice to our deep center space, to ourselves, and to outer shifts.

Here in the upper energy centers that begin with the throat, we often receive clues about issues that we must still deal with in the lower energy centers. If you recognize some of the throat imbalances we'll discuss in this chapter in your own life, it may mean that it's time to go back and revisit some of the key issues discussed in the earthier energy centers.

In his book *The Four Agreements,* author Don Miguel Ruiz explains very clearly both what the fifth energy center represents and how speaking our truth enhances our life experience. Ruiz provides four main pacts that we make with ourselves to achieve liberation, clear expression, and peace. Based on his beautiful work, I was able to strengthen my fifth energy center, my weakest energy space in my late twenties and early thirties. Before I learned these agreements, whenever I tried to use my voice in emotional situations, I would falter and fall back into emotional pain and quietness. Ruiz saved me and many others from communication styles that are all too easy to fall into—things like projecting and taking in the energy, pain, blame, or shame of others—which are confusing and damaging. He also offered great support in learning about what truth means in terms of the mind and heart. Even now, when I need to rebalance my voice or choices, or if I'm trying to find the truth or lesson in a situation, I go back to *The Four Agreements.* These agreements represent a true union between a peaceful mind and heart. They lead us to honor the truth of the matter by showing us how to find our voice, use our voice, and support our voice and heart with intuition. In summary, the four agreements are:

1. Agreement: "Be impeccable with your word."

   We learn to be impeccable with our words and wording. This requires bravery. As you will see in this chapter, the throat energy center is *all* about how we express ourselves to the world. Think about the fact that our words hold so much importance, they can literally begin and end wars.

2. Agreement: "Don't take anything personally."

   We make a choice not to take things to heart or into the heart. If we are balanced in the five energy centers up to and including this point, we learn not to take things personally. This one took me decades.

3. Agreement: "Don't make assumptions."

Not making assumptions can be difficult. Not only are assumptions a form of prejudice, but they also involve analytical judgments that result in hierarchy. This is not a good use of our voice. When we are balanced up to the fifth energy center, it becomes easier to not infuse or project our own past experiences and emotions onto the actions of others. Instead, we can act from a balanced and true place. When acting from a healthy fifth energy center, we are connected to our truth and not as concerned about what others are doing (a second energy center issue) unless it is something that inflicts severe pain (or abuse) on others. We use our intuition to decipher our inner truth. Our inner truth becomes more powerful than hearsay or the affairs of others. We are feeling the strength and passion of heart supporting our choice to be free to be who we *are*.

4. Agreement: "Always do your best."

We are capable of always doing our best. Sometimes this means holding our tongue; other times it means being honest and transparent as well as speaking up for those who do not have a healthy or safe way to use their own voice.

Now we'll learn how to put all of this into practice.

The Fifth Energy Center and the Physical Being: Using Our Voice

The primary physical function of the throat is to clear energy within the self and to put our soul's clean energy back into the world—it gives us a voice to speak with and is a channel for moving breath through the body. Both of these acts play a vital role in creating wellness in all aspects of being. Notice how you actually speak throughout the day in various situations—the tone, volume, and quality of your voice. All of these vocal cues provide signs about your inner truth, how open your heart is, and how much you trust yourself and your choices. Noticing your voice allows you to witness yourself and will show you how connected you are to intuition. Is your voice supported in a calm, yet confident tone? Can you breathe through an entire conversation and not rush the speaker on getting to the heart of the matter? How high pitched or fast are you speaking (this can be different for different people, but the *vibe* will feel non-soothing to the speaker or listener)? The vibe is a part of *kimochi*. Notice when you are speaking loudly in an effort to be heard or, alternatively, when your voice becomes quieter and meeker. Are you letting your adrenaline or nerves dictate your speech? Are you letting your "doing" side dominate?

Be aware of your tone and begin to practice finding that middle ground where your inner and outer voices unite. This can be done with a listening ear or a more open heart. It can be done by staying centered in the mind and not letting your voice be led by ego-based intentions (which would take you out of connection to others or the current moment). Identify those situations where you can speak more clearly, with more brevity, or when silence will be more effective than words. Practice this not only during big, emotional conversations but also during casual interactions at the grocery store, when you're speaking with children, or as you greet a stranger. This practice will help lead you to the center of your mind and heart, where calmness is accessible, or assisted. Notice when you are saying either more or less than what actually needs to be said to express yourself. Also notice how you *feel* when you are speaking. Sometimes when we lack confidence in ourselves or what we are saying, we use more words than necessary and feel our nerves kick in. At times we might know that the person we are speaking with isn't actually hearing us. Often, people hear us better when we exercise brevity and make our words as clear and concise as possible. Other times, we just need to calmly walk away.

Be patient: it might take some time to master speaking in this centered manner. But it's worth it—even this small tweak in awareness and witnessing how we interact and communicate with others can have a profoundly positive impact on how authentically we are able to express ourselves and, in turn, how the world acts and reacts to our words. Changes will take time, but they will come, small and big. We will build up more courage to have direct and honest conversations (which also ends up saving a lot of time), and our loving relationships will feel more mature and authentic. We will experience more bonding, trusting experiences with others. We may find that we have fewer conversations but that they're of a higher quality. This helps us feel more safe, supported, and empowered to be our unique self. How we communicate and what we choose to say will shift, as will how quickly we respond.

We can think of this particular period as a time of truth. Through social media and the Internet, more people than ever are now able to celebrate their own voice and expression. It is a time to be honest and speak our truths. So be more bold. Be brave and kind in your speech. I see this as a refreshing movement that can increase our world's general sense of goodwill as we begin to hear more and more voices (with listening ears)—even if we don't always agree on what is being said.

In addition to housing our voice, the throat also supports the heart by bringing oxygen into the body. Moreover, breath plays a crucial role in keeping all of our energy centers balanced, cleared, and radiant, which makes the throat crucial to our overall wellness not only physically but also emotionally, mentally, and spiritually. We want to continue coming back to that idea of deep, diaphragmatic breath we discussed in the previous chapter to richly connect with the action of the air flowing freely and fully down our throat and into our lungs.

The fifth energy center also does the important work of regulating the thyroid and glandular health, and it helps create hormone balance, all of which positively impact our overall health and longevity. Our quality of life, our brain health, our calcium regulation and even our weight are affected by our thyroid and glandular health. If you have issues in any of these areas, whether based on lifestyle or heredity, we can all strengthen and support this area by increasing chi energy flow. This can be accomplished by hand weight repetitions mixed with walking briskly up stairs or hills. This supports more oxygen flow, deeper inhalations and exhalations, and gives our body more detoxifying and empowering energy. Loud bursts of singing help strengthen this area too, as do sound baths, both of which move stale energy out of the neck and jaw. Hanging upside down works wonders.

From what I have seen through readings and group healings, it seems that issues of imbalance and weakness in the fifth energy center are often a reflection of holding words, emotions, and experiences back or shoving them down. Clearing these areas can be as quick and easy as spending three to five minutes per day concentrating on taking deeper breaths. In doing this or any of the exercises mentioned in the previous paragraph, you are showing your body and your brain that you are taking care of them. You will move subtle energy and help lighten the heart-brain experience. The combination of intentionally focusing on removing the energy and opening the throat and lungs will show you how good it feels when you *express* yourself with intentful movement.

You can think of the throat as your body's gatekeeper—it is where we ingest what is on the outside and incorporate it on the inside. This happens in a very literal sense through breath and with food. This is great news because it means we have control over what we take into our body and thus the balance that is created within. We want to ingest foods with life force— foods that do not contain an abundance of artificial colors and stimulants or preservatives. We can begin to create balance by being mindful about eating neither too much nor too little. This does not have to do with caloric intake or any sort of numbers. It has to do with being in tune with our body and understanding what we need to nourish, nurture, and support clarity; what we need to support ourselves, our thoughts, and our emotions in the best way possible. What our body requires to function optimally, especially as we age, may well vary from day to day. When we are paying attention and listening to our body and inner voice, we are more likely to be able to determine what we need. And when we feel balanced and healthy, we are more likely to react kindly and positively to those in our sphere—our family, friends, coworkers, and those we encounter in daily life. This helps create and fuel a positive cycle of energy in which those we meet and are kind to are more likely to pass that along to the people in their lives. Expansion.

By this point, we've likely already put these principles of deep, mindful breath and nutrition into practice in the lower energy centers. Now it's simply a matter of remaining aware of them in the throat area and being alert to those thyroid, glandular, and hormonal issues that may signal that the other three aspects of being need some attention. These symptoms can include a dry throat, frequent laryngitis, or swollen glands. Notice if you tend to be susceptible to getting sick following episodes when others use a harsh or loud tone of voice toward you. Maybe you hold your breath for too long in tense situations or in other scenarios where you don't feel like you have a voice.

Such experiences can cause insulin or cortisol levels to dip or peak, resulting in cravings for stimulants or simple carbohydrate foods (which are not helpful for hormone balance or for purifying our thoughts, fears, or emotions). Being aware of the *choice* and the *freedom* we have to nourish ourselves in the best way possible—both through food and wellness practices *and* through speaking up and knowing when to walk away—is the best gift we can give ourselves for fifth energy center physical health. This can help alleviate many physical ailments from headaches and migraines to panic attacks and shaking (tremors).

The Fifth Energy Center and the Emotional Being: Speaking Our Truth

We live in a culture that doesn't always like the truth—one that, I would propose, *rarely* likes the truth. America was founded as a patriarchal, puritanical culture, and although we are living in an increasingly liberal society, it has been ingrained in us to keep those things that are deemed socially inappropriate or emotionally weak or messy to ourselves. This is compounded by the fact that in this age of political correctness, there is a danger of choosing our words *too* carefully, of not saying what we really feel or what actually needs to be said for fear of offense. This does not serve our intuition nor does it support bringing new, helpful ideas to the table. Instead, we remain stuck in old thinking. It does not matter what political or religious group we may choose.

For some, not telling the truth is a hard habit to break. But dishonesty leads to disharmony, if not in us then in those around us. And not only does dishonesty affect those we love right now, but it also affects future generations by teaching those who learn from us to continue the cycle. "Groups" of people do not equate to exponential doses of "truth," as group mentality can hinder personal responsibility. Whether through our actions or our responses to people and situations in our life, our own truth is necessary for growth—even in cases where the truth might be difficult to express. When we consistently suppress the truth, those around us can feel the walls we have put up in place of sharing our honest experience. This does not help intuition see or connect with the outside world, and our body responds in kind.

When we are dishonest (including to our "self"), our breath becomes shorter, and it's more difficult to deeply inhale. Our thyroid takes a serious hit. Old energy gets stuck, and there is not enough fresh new air to help the glands release the old collected energy and rebalance hormonal flow. The thyroid becomes sluggish or, alternatively, tries too hard to clear and balance, like a motor without clean gas that works harder than it should. Holding on to old emotion interferes with our connection to the fresh new flow of intuition. The truth of the now cannot be lodged in past emotion. These physical issues and past emotions muddle our intuitive voice detection and connection. However, with the truth of the matter and without emotions stuck in our lungs or chest, we can breathe easily, offloading stress and stale thought, and we can support our hormonal function by releasing old matter. This helps us connect to new forms of creating space for our intuitive voice to rise.

In addition to not telling the truth of our heart or situation, some of us are emotionally dishonest. This involves the failure to connect to our honest, truthful emotions. Not only does this take a toll on a healthy, open, and vibrant intuition, but we also age faster and lose interest in pleasure. We don't rest as soundly. We do not explore the world with the same vigor and stamina we did as children or young adults. Intuition *loves* the curious, creative action of fearless exploration. Creative energy creates "new," which creates space. Intuition lives in this new space (which is yet another way of saying that intuition lives in the present moment). Intuition loves fearless action that does not involve fear-based thinking and interactions. Creative energy can remove emotional barriers and instills in us a clear sense of direction and fortitude that positively impacts how we follow through on our intentions, how we treat our loved ones, and how we are loved.

Everyone benefits when we speak the truth, when it is done with compassion, love, self-clarity, and self-awareness. This means clear communication is worth its weight in gold. It's a way to *connect* versus a way to rate or separate. This energy center does not want to be disconnected from the wisdom of the heart (and the wisdom of turning a new decade).

Obviously, there are as many styles of communication as there are people in the world, but a few simple guidelines can help. First, take at least three minutes in the morning to connect to your breath and give thanks for the gift of this breath, this life within you. Next, set an intention to be more truthful, brave, and honest in at least one interaction you have throughout the day. Write that intention down and keep it somewhere you will frequently see it—for example, on a mirror, on your refrigerator, in your wallet, or on a bedside table. If you'd like, you can also use this as a guidepost to repeat in your mind throughout the day. Whenever you recite your intention or look at that piece of paper, remember to connect that phrase to your breath, thereby creating an internal support system for staying calm. As you go about your day, keep breathing quietly and remaining mindful throughout your communication. When practiced consistently, this will begin to activate your calm heart—and it will possibly help you unbury old patterns so you can breathe them out rather than bringing them into your interactions with others throughout the day.

We may not always be able to verbally speak the truth we see in our or others' lives. When this is the case, we might need to channel the unhealthy energy or situation we see through intuition to prayer, to good thoughts, or to a yoga mat. We can also visualize emotions "flushing" down through our throat and downward out our feet. Maybe we need to take a walk or communicate with the angels or guides we feel surround those we love. If that doesn't fall under your belief system, maybe you talk to a counselor or trusted adviser. But know that if we shy away from direct assistance (which is what speaking the truth in whatever form ultimately is), our emotional intelligence and intuitive wisdom may stall.

Particularly with those we love, it can be difficult to speak with truth rather than fearful, stale emotions, even when we want to. It's ironic, really. We often have the hardest time speaking the truth with clarity and vulnerability to those we love most, and who most need our intuitive support.

On both a broad scale and in our personal lives, very few of us truly enjoy being whistle-blowers or voicing the truth of a matter, even when it's for healing. That said, speaking the truth is powerful beyond measure for our health and our body's emotional harmony. It puts energy in motion, as energy is matter. Moving energy—and thus our life and emotions—forward is cleansing, liberating, and gratifying. Not only that but it also makes more room for our intuition. This cycle creates a wonderful upward spiral that begins to feel exponential. It moves heavier energy, and lighter energy takes its place. Speaking the truth can be a catalyst for bettering the health and well-being of all parties involved, in pretty much any situation, small or global.

I've often found myself in a position where I know I need to speak the truth to someone, but I have to muster up a lot of courage to do it. I've found that it's incredibly helpful to begin by making sure I'm clear about my intentions for sharing information. If a situation arises in which you feel it is time to speak your truth, connect with a feeling of centeredness and balance in your lower three energy centers. Now bring in breath for your heart to stay open. Bring yourself into the moment by connecting to your breath and feeling your feet and the ground beneath them supporting you. From here, make a point of ensuring that you have quiet time to walk, contemplate, or meditate to connect with what your heart is trying to communicate before having the difficult conversation. Check in with your intuition, which will offer guidance. For example, maybe you plan on delivering information to a friend over dinner but your gut tells you that it would be better to share during a walk after you've eaten.

I feel it's deeply important not to mix the truth with high emotion, and these practices help to clear out and quiet emotions so that you can speak from a place of truth. When we act from this place, everyone will benefit in the end, even if it does not seem this way in the moment or immediately following a discussion. Keep breathing and releasing stress or emotional challenges.

Most of the time this process works incredibly well, but when it comes to speaking your truth with someone you are intimately close with or with whom you share a deep history or unresolved pain, it can be more difficult to reach a point of resolution where all parties feel peaceful. You might need more time for the information to settle or a few check-ins after the initial discussion. Layers of old emotion and pain can take a lot of time to clear and heal. But I have yet to meet anyone in readings who regretted sharing how they felt, providing it was done in a calm, prepared manner.

To prepare for conversations like this, visualize a blue healing light around your heart as you speak your truth. You may want to take this even further by wrapping that light all the way around both you and the person you are speaking with. It can be very difficult in these moments to stay grounded and to prevent emotions from taking us off of our loving track. I have found that, in these times, what works best is holding on to the knowledge that neither love nor speech are always going to be heard as intended, but showing up honestly, bravely, and kindly is half of the experience of using our voice. Knowing that we are acting from a place of honesty and doing our best will help us to recover more quickly from hard conversations where walls were put up or our emotions were jarred. Having faith in the blessings of imperfection and bringing forgiveness in the room with us will not only get us through such situations, but it will also preserve our relationship with intuition. We intuitively know whether or not we are being honest with ourselves or with others. So at the end of each day, if we are honest, we will notice that we have the support necessary to connect back with ourselves even after hard, direct conversations. This offers clarity and freedom on the other side of the experience, even if it's not immediate.

When we come to truly honor and embrace the throat energy center, we realize its function is to help create a more positive, clear situation or discussion. Sometimes this happens through speaking, and other times it's through listening to what others are saying. This energy center knows how to rebalance situations by adding pure, fresh thought or action as well as a purity in mind and spirit. When we choose to back down from bravery instead of engaging in truthful interactions that are born from a radiant heart and clear mind—when we do not speak our truth or offer our assistance when we know we should—the situation at hand will not play out to its full potential.

Even knowing all of this and having had years of practice, I still find it difficult to have direct conversations at times, particularly when it comes to loved ones. I often go back to the same tools—trying my best to be rested and clear before beginning any difficult conversation, knowing my intentions, sticking to openhearted bravery, and acting from an intuitively centered place.

The more tired or emotionally drained we are, the more difficult the conversations become and the easier it is for us to get defensive or to shy away from the truth. We must feel rested and ready to speak and live in our pure truth. An intentional life does not come easily, especially as we are growing or recalibrating. There is a saying at a great yoga studio in Manhattan Beach, called The Green Yogi, that speaks of fear being fatigue or/and loneliness. Let's connect and enliven "truthful" energy.

Emotionally sticky conversations can happen in any number of contexts, but one example I frequently see in my work is within romantic relationships. Most of us have learned to hold our tongues so as not to hurt our partner's feelings. This can create a divide wherein we speak and act in a way that isn't completely truthful.

This is especially true when it comes to ending a relationship. Women often don't want to listen to their gut in interpersonal situations and, as a result, can stay in a stale or broken relationship for longer than they should. Men, at times, hold back their true feelings for the sake of not rocking the boat, hurting their family dynamic, or because they don't trust that their partner will understand or be emotionally rational. As we discussed in earlier chapters, many choose an exterior image over an interior truth. Many people know in their heart that it's time to end a relationship or move on from a perfect-looking scenario, but they remain nonetheless. Those in such situations are often incredibly unhappy, which does not give their intuitive voice much room to thrive.

In romantic relationships, females usually communicate more of their feelings than males do, but as times are shifting, this is changing. However, these cultural imprints can and often do remain in gendered dynamics, especially in our parents' and grandparents' generations. As a result of this, I speak to many women—and men, as well—who stay in relationships at the expense of their own joy or authentic release of expression, in order to protect the feelings of their significant other. When we do this, we may believe that we are safe from change. We are not.

I have found in readings that if the truth is that it's time for one party to end a relationship, it's in the best interest of *both* parties, even if that's not immediately apparent. *Speaking and taking action from the throat energy center while using our heart and intuition as guideposts ensures that the steps we take based on the information we receive are good for everyone involved, even if they require us to say some difficult things.* Whenever you find yourself feeling scared or hesitant to have a conversation you need to have, remember that presence and breath can calm our fears and, in turn, lead to clear action that is not sabotaged by overthinking and nerves. You are ultimately acting in everyone's best interest through the simple act of speaking the truth . . . especially when it is done with open love. You are also giving voice to your intuition.

Having said all of this, I must add that it is also important that we know *not* to speak when there's danger of emotional or physical abuse, or when we know that we have discussed our truth repeatedly and our words are simply falling on deaf ears. When we are sharing with souls who are not capable of hearing our truth, boundaries need to be reassessed. This will become clearer when you witness or take stock of what occurs after you speak, both in your own body and in the other person's body and language. As you become more grounded and intuitive, you will be able to more easily determine when it is time to stop interacting with someone who has a wall up to your words and heartfelt expression. Sometimes it can be difficult to determine when this is the case in intimate relationships. I have learned to allow my intuition to guide me about when I should try to have a conversation and, just as importantly, when I should take pause. The truth can be heard when it has an open, receptive, and loving recipient. We do not want the pain caused by those who simply cannot hear us to derail our bravery in speaking our feelings.

We've all had experiences where we've dreaded a conversation only to find that, when it's over, a huge weight has been lifted off our chest. *That* is the feeling of liberation. The more you experience this, the more instinctual the action of speaking up becomes, and the more emotionally healthy, wealthy, and wise you feel.

The Fifth Energy Center and the Intellectual Being: Speaking with a Centered Ego

Speaking freely and truthfully has been complex throughout history for various reasons, but it is especially so in the world today, where it's easy to default to quick and impersonal modes of communication such as text, email, and social media. But these modes do not use our actual *voice,* so communicating like this can inherently cause our fifth energy center to lose a lot of its richness. When we're communicating electronically, others cannot hear our inflection, and we are not *using our throat, thyroid and glands, or voice.* This is problematic because our voice is like a tuning fork. Our aura absorbs the sweet sound of a loved one's voice (and vice versa) as our heart picks up on another's vibration while we communicate. Our intuition is more supported and powerful because of this. Such intuitive connections simply don't happen electronically. Intuition loves intimacy and life force. This life force moves through the heart and voice box vis-à-vis our breath, which ignites and supports our third eye of sight and wisdom (much more on this in the next chapter). Electronics simply don't offer the same sensory wholeness, which is a key tool for a stronger intuitive connection.

While life is certainly easier and more efficient because of this technology, it causes our interactions to lack important heart-to-heart communication, leaving us without information and direct connection. Some of us have fallen into a pattern where we overuse words and underuse eye contact and face-to-face communication.

Setting technology aside to have meaningful conversations face-to-face is vital for our intuition. Not only is it emotionally, mentally, and intuitively important for us to have these sorts of interactions and connections, but it's also important for the fifth energy center because our glands and organs (which our thyroid affects) thrive on deep oxygen, which comes when we do things like sing, relay deep feelings, and the sort of heart-clearing and understanding that happens during communication in the present moment. Electronics can offer immediacy, which is valuable for keeping a connection, but it will never replace whole sensory communication.

Along with dictating those things we need to say, the fifth energy center also helps us determine those things that we *don't* need to put voice to. When our fifth energy center is in balance, we are able to understand where to best direct our energy and where to help energy move, shift, or grow. This process begins in the second energy center as relationships begin to form and we start making choices and learning about ourselves, our personality, and our effect on others. By the time we've matured into the fifth energy center, we are able to bring shades of gray to the second energy center's black-and-white way of viewing the world. Our outlook is more nuanced, and this in turn brings increased maturity, which aids us in making educated choices that are wise for *everyone*. In other words, taking mature action during moments of anger might involve taking deep breaths instead of saying something hurtful we might regret later. We catch "energy" before it hits our sore spots. We breathe deeper instead of more shallow. An intuitive choice in emotional "clearing."

As we move up through the energy centers, our intentions and actions become more *all* focused rather than *me* focused. This is probably why it isn't until our thirties that the fifth energy center comes into focus. Before we can reach full maturity when it comes to speaking our truth, we must first have a solid grasp of what it means to be comfortable, confident, and safe in our own skin. Then we can act on behalf of a full, joyous heart rather than from a more ego-driven power trip. The next time you have an important conversation, take a moment to notice who it's serving. You? The other party? The greater good? Anyone? To effectively engage and reap the health benefits of the fifth energy center, your words should work to the benefit of everyone, to the benefit of the greater clear consciousness. Of course, your conversation may only be with a single other person—but when your conversation is in service to the good of that person, it will lead to an outward spiral that has the potential to ultimately have a profound and wide-reaching positive impact. *Kimochi.*

Before we can truly speak with love and without high emotion or ego, we need the clarity that comes from a balanced and strong root, stomach, and heart. All of these elements are inextricably linked to support an open, clear throat that allows us to more easily speak our truth. Because conversations always involve others—even if it's just between us and whatever our version of the divine is—they can only be truly productive and proactive when we use our voice from a deep, healthy ego and release any power struggles or notion of duality. Thoughts that could get in the way of productive conversations might sound like, *Oh, it would be good to say how I feel here,* only to follow up that thought by thinking, *But this person does not deserve that,* or *But it won't go anywhere anyway.* Speaking from a place of compassion and reciprocity most often gets you the same in return.

This comes into play in any number of ways once we reach the throat energy center, but we can particularly see how important balanced lower energy centers are when it comes to speaking from a clear place, especially in parent-child relationships. Many parents of teenagers come in for readings and tell me that conversations with their teenagers can be difficult (and, if you're not a parent, you can probably remember how little you wanted to listen to your parents during those adolescent years). But all of this aside, parent-teen discussions are particularly fertile ground for imbalances in power and worth, wounded hearts, and holding back on speaking kind truths. If the parent is speaking from an imbalanced ego instead of from a centered or calm, balanced space, clashes can easily occur. Once we're consciously in the upper energy centers, we're thinking, doing, and being for the collective—the lower energy centers ruled by the self or earthly matters are still grounded. In parent-teen discussions that come from imbalanced lower energy centers on the part of the parent, projection or narcissism can come into play. The adult can project their fears or past experiences onto the child rather than treating the child as an individual or a soul with her or his own road, which results in scolding or lecturing, inherently becomes emotionally infused, and therefore often sparks mental sparring and protection that is unlikely to be effective. These same dynamics can come into play between mates, intimate friends, teams, coworkers, and adult relationships with our parents. It can happen between drivers at stoplights or between nations.

Another difficult scenario many experience is speaking out in a group. By nature, when we come together in a group setting, it can be difficult to maintain our own agency, remain clear about our intentions, and hold a strong belief in those intentions. A group can develop a mind of its own—the so-called hive mind—unless all of its members are free from hidden agendas and are able to act with clear intentions. Even when we do find the strength or self-worth to speak up in this sort of setting, it can often feel as though we are not really heard in a scenario where there are a lot of other voices and inner truths. When we do speak our truth, it's important that others are listening so we feel heard and seen. This is where a lot of communication breaks down. For mirroring what other people are saying and hearing in a pure way that allows more listening to occur, others must have an open heart and slow down, which inherently requires a balanced ego. When we are brief, honest, and to the point, our chances of being heard are more likely. Sure, honesty might not be received well when others are still working through the more self-interested aspects and focus of the lower, earthly energy centers. But it *will* work for you—and eventually for others—to always speak what is true and calm in your heart. This communication will keep you connected with your intuition, and with clearing and harmonizing your life experience. When we aren't communicating clearly and openly, we shut off our intuition and can't receive those intuitive signs to stop talking or slow our emotional thoughts.

Here's the thing, though: as scary as it is to communicate openly in a group setting, this is where our boundaries are so helpful. They help ensure that we will not get into a situation where we are left unprotected or unable to hear our intuition. When we are connected to our intuition, our connection with everything and everyone expands. For example, our intuition may tell us to continue engaging in conversation or that it's time to go home, thus removing us from a situation where we might become disengaged from our intuitive compass. Whatever the case may be, as long as we stay in that place of connectivity to our intuition, we can rest assured that both our needs and the needs of those we are with will be taken care of. Intuitive information that involves the heart and intuitive mind is information and action for the good of all. As I often tell clients, we can love everyone without inviting them all into our sacred breathing space, into our listening space. This is purifying our space. For the times you do not have complete say over your space, breathe. Ultimately, those who need to hear you will, even if it's not in an immediate way, and even if it's not outwardly acknowledged.

Not only does speaking the truth help others, but it also helps us. Our voice allows us to be honest and present, to be in the now, like very few other actions do. Our voice helps clear our past and those things that are painful, which means that the throat energy center is extremely purifying and directly assists with heart and chest health; it can even help our blood stay alkaline and keep our heartbeat even. At times it might feel like heavy lifting is taking place, especially when speaking about deeply personal experiences. It is. The more difficult you find it to discuss something, the more important it probably is to get it out. There are many situations in our culture that are difficult to talk about, especially when they deal with a situation in which we fear we will lose power or intimacy in a relationship because of what we might say. Some examples of this are things like discussing a raise or promotion at work or sharing with a family member a need that is not being met. This can also occur in breakups and makeups between significant others who are not listening to *both* their own needs and the needs of their love. Very understandably, not many people in our culture have an easy time stepping into the prospect of truthful conversation. Our mind has been trained to listen to its analytical, practical side even though our more feminine, nurturing side has a lot of wisdom to offer. There are so many reasons for this, including fear of great change, losing or possibly gaining social status, rocking family dynamics, or experiencing a shift out of an old, familiar dynamic of losing resources.

This fear of shifting familiar dynamics has felt very pertinent to many of the readings I have done since 2011. As my client Rita spoke, I began to understand that she was dealing with a combination of old pain, shame, and the inability to form a healthy ego because of mental and emotional abuse she'd suffered during her early years. In readings, abuse often shows up as a stifling of the voice because painful old situations have been buried; because family, friends, and at times the ego have been unable to honor the truth of the past; or because the person chose other outlets to try to release the emotion (overachieving, food, physical abuse of the self or others, or the mental or emotional abuse of those near to them). All of these factors led Rita to be in a lot of denial, to the point where she couldn't even find her voice.

Locating our voice and the voice of our intuition requires that we are out of our analytical, or fearful, part of the brain. Clarity in speech is not found in the rational, analytical side either. Ironically, Rita could talk for hours. I've done many readings with this same scenario, where people think or feel they are speaking their truth even though what they're really doing is speaking *around* it. This can look like a person who becomes overly abrasive because their food isn't prepared right, or who talks at length about celebrities or the news instead of addressing their own lives in conversation. It can appear in the form of a conversation between spouses in which projection and finger-pointing replace honest, heartfelt truth. All of these scenarios (even the ones that seem innocuous) can be quite detrimental when it comes to tapping into our intuition because we don't leave the space or time to receive what our intuition is trying to say or show, nor are we in touch with our inner voice enough for its graceful conversation to make its way to the surface. Talking too much or with too much force is often a sign of emotional disharmony and either an overdeveloped or underdeveloped ego. This ties to the confidence and worth of the third energy center and having an open, listening heart in the fourth center. For some, this can tie back to not being seen and heard as a child and then spending adulthood trying to get those now-old childhood needs met. These signs can also signal that we are acting from the fight-or-flight or warrior part of the brain, where the stronger listening, empathetic side of intuition does not reside. All of this goes back to fear, and fear masks intuition. If abuse is involved in this, our fear becomes extremely difficult to dig into, move through, and put voice to. Clearing out our body, mind, spirit, and soul to make way for the new—this is purification of space and of anything being held in the throat energy center. This clearing out can happen with more ease when we address why we are holding our voice back. We must release what we are afraid of, what holds us back, and ultimately, what's been facilitating stagnation or pain.

In Rita's case, the abuse was physical and emotional, and it occurred at the hands of a trusted adult. Rita, now a mother, was adamant about not talking about this abuse with her children. Our reading showed that as a result of holding on to all of this pain, Rita had become quite overweight, which was the manifestation of a lot of unfinished thoughts and emotions waiting to be cleared. She also had a lot of physical distress and disease from these mental and emotional bruises. It was time for Rita to bring her issues out from the throat to purify and clear the pain and old energy. This is the only way of lifting it up and out of the heart forever.

Rita did the work to address all the points in her life that arose during our reading to show her where she was holding back her truth and her voice. She faced her true thoughts about her father's quiet way of avoiding her feelings (which made her feel ignored) and his sharp tongue and hand. Rita also faced up to the anger and distress she felt toward her mother for projecting expectations of perfection and a certain body image upon her. In addition to her readings with me, Rita also spoke to a therapist to address all of the emotion that was coming up and out of her heart. Once Rita felt brave enough, she spoke her truth about her pain and feelings of being small to both her therapist and her mother. (I was so proud of her!) She was surprised by how relieved she felt. Upon speaking up, Rita came to find out that the same abuse had also happened to other family members and friends. Not only had she put voice to her pain and lifted it out of her, but she also no longer had to carry the pain alone. She now had support and was able to talk to her children about abuse to stop the cycle.

Many people come to me saying, "The past is the past." This can be true. But if things show up in readings, they're not actually in the past at all, no matter how much time has gone by. Through readings, I have learned that until we clear the past by speaking the truth of our stories and letting go, they stay in our aura, in our space. This old energy affects our current moment, denying us of the ability to feel light or free to speak our truth. It collects itself into a sort of energy that's kind of like a vibration, and that can eventually create disease or additional Groundhog Day cycles of the same scenario. Energy that is stale or old collects in the thyroid and glands, which serve the purpose of balancing our hormones and controlling calcium. This buildup collects even more of the stale and the old, and it gets harder for these glands to stay balanced and do their job until there is consistent release of energy. Clearing out this neck area is extremely powerful because it simultaneously clears out our heart and head as well. It is in the interest of our health that we speak up about what we feel and believe.

The other important part of this is not only putting voice to the truth of our past, but also moving through it by further activating the fifth energy center in the form of breath work, forgiveness, and allowing ourselves to complete full cycles of mourning losses, dissatisfactions, and expectations not met. In my many years of doing readings and receiving intuitive information, I have learned that the act of forgiving both ourselves and others is the most freeing action we can take. It *releases* emotional, physical, and, eventually, psychological pain. It gives us the opportunity and space in the body, heart, and brain to heal. Speaking our truth about both the present and the past is an opportunity to rebalance that is not to be missed. Forgiveness and moving through the hard stuff create miracles. I have watched the universe reward our hard work with blessings and gifts beyond measure. Some describe this act as clearing karma. I define *clearing karma* as "an act in the current moment that releases the past to create a better future." This clearing creates positive karma, which is the goal of a healthy intuition.

When we truly dive in and use our voice with an open heart, change happens, the old energy that stuffs us up is released, we move through our daily lives with more ease, and good karma ensues. Thus begins a cycle of new—a lighter and more enlightened now.

The Fifth Energy Center and the Spiritual Being: Let the Spirit Speak

When we clear out our throat energy center and find the bravery to speak truthfully and succinctly, what we are ultimately doing is manifesting more of the magic that comes with intuition. There is space for the new—new voices and new experiences. I believe that we are given the gift of intuition as a tool to use in our life—to make us happier and healthier, and to lead us down a well-lit path that provides both ourselves and the world at large with the most joy and fulfillment. If we are not able to use our voices to express the ultimate truth and clarity that our intuition provides us, ultimately that knowing will be for naught. We can never really put it to use.

When we are speaking from an open heart, we're letting spirit and intuition guide our words and, in fact, our very breath. We and everyone around us will naturally be enhanced by the wisdom and compassion that comes from this place of calm balance. We will put freedom rather than fear into the world—yes, through our words, but also through the vibration of our body and even the tone and cadence of our physical voice. Powerful stuff! Once you start using your intuition for the benefit of all—which is precisely what you're doing by putting a clear external voice to your inner voice—you'll find that your intuition becomes stronger and stronger. Just like a singer improves her sound, confidence, and ways of expressing herself with more practice, so too does our intuition when we use our voice. We become more connected and tapped into the seen and unseen world around us, which offers not only more confidence and knowledge but also more ease when it comes to speaking our truth. And, with this, you'll find that your life is increasingly infused with greater amounts of harmony, bravery, serendipity, and synchronicity.

Remember, especially in those moments when it feels difficult to speak up, that no matter how scary it may be or how alone you may feel, you are never alone when you speak your truth. Even if you feel briefly isolated in the moment, as long as you stay present in your truth, support will show up. Even in those cases where you're the only person speaking up, the universe has *always* got your back, and there simply is no greater support than that.

Throat Energy Center Sayings

Begin by reflecting on which of these sayings most resonates with you (or if you'd like, create one of your own beginning with the phrase *I am*).

> *I am letting go.*
> *I am balanced.*
> *I am truthful.*
> *I am liberated.*

Find a comfortable spot to sit or lie down on the floor. Lengthen your spine, and locate your breath as it enters your body through your nose and your throat. Exhale gently out of the mouth. Inhale more deeply through the nose on your next breath, and then exhale out the mouth saying, "Haaaaaaaa." Continue to breathe slowly and deeply, in through the nose and out of the mouth. Relax your shoulders and jaw, feeling your neck soften and drop down into your shoulder blades. If you are outside, become aware of the fresh air all around you, giving you oxygen. This will help connect you to the feeling of new life and new opportunity as you fill your throat and lungs. Let your throat and glands relax as you feel your shoulders and spine supporting and balancing you. Lean into the feeling of letting go.

Your eyes may be closed or slightly open, whatever feels more comfortable or natural to you. If eyes are closed, looking down at your nose can help keep you centered and balanced, like an arrowpoint moving through the sky.

Once your breath is slow and even, connect your purifying *I Am* saying with your intention for creating new room by letting go of old thoughts and old patterning, whether that patterning is the shallowness of your breath or your habit of withholding emotions. Create space and bravery in your life by taking ownership and action to release stalled or held energy.

Silently repeat the chosen saying to yourself until you feel your tongue and jaw completely relax. As your brain begins to calm and your mind becomes a blank slate, try to witness or take stock of this peaceful feeling. This is a form of freedom. Achieving it can take time, so be patient. The key is to engage in this mindful practice with a calm, clear intention for letting go of the old and creating a new life force—to feel brave enough to speak up when intuition arises.

After connecting your thoughts with your breath, it can help to simply notice your chest and stomach rising and falling. For the throat energy to feel open and connected, you may think of a favorite location or serene scene. This visualization and practice can help energy feel both surrounded in serenity and incredibly free. Visualize your breath reaching all the way to the bottom of your lungs or touching your diaphragm. Possibly say "La, la, laaaa" a few times out loud.

Continue breathing in new energy and life force, exhaling old thoughts or energy. Give yourself between three and five (or ten!) minutes per day for this energy center, perhaps increasing the time by thirty seconds to a minute per day. Repeat this practice of focusing on breath and truth as often as possible, at least every twelve hours to start.

The Throat Guide

What it governs:	Throat, voice, truth, liberation
Ages:	28–35
Color:	Blue
In balance:	Healthy glands and thyroid, ability to speak the truth, and to speak in a succinct manner. Brevity with warmth. Fresh ideas.
Imbalanced:	Gland and thyroid issues, askew hormonal regulation, inability to speak up, skirting around the truth.
Supportive foods:	Clear nutritional whole foods from the earth with air and water elements and, very important, listening to what your body needs at any time and giving it precisely that. Blueberries. Clear liquids or broths. Herbal teas. Alkaline or mineral water.
Beneficial practices:	Speaking truthfully and with brevity. Deep diaphragmatic breath, rest, meditation, getting things off of your chest. Being in or near the water. Walking outside under the big sky and breathing in fresh air. Visualizing speaking your truth to a loved one, friend, or authority figure. Being brave. Images or pictures of favorite bodies of water. Making sounds of soothing wind.

Sayings: *I am letting go.*
I am balanced.
I am truthful.
I am liberated.

7

THE SIXTH ENERGY CENTER: THE THIRD EYE

Intuition

Intuition is quite a mystery until it is not. So far we have discussed how much meditation and quiet time help our intuition. Our prefrontal cortex is mature and developed by our mid- to late twenties, we've got our healthy heart and brain capacity as tools, and we are equipped to implement intuition in our life. Now we will look at what we call our third, or wise, eye and locate its radiance.

In the topic of brain health today, it is important to realize that a balanced mind helps us have a balanced life (and intuition). We want to be open to the world but still keep our peace and sacred space. This is getting harder to do with more crowded environments and quicker communication. We want to keep regenerating the brain and heart with water, exercise or movement, good sleep, and clear and powerful food. This is very important for opening and using our intuition effectively. Some say the third eye is so high of an energy center, only stillness is needed for its use, but I have found that my love for swimming, walking, jogging, and yoga has had a profound strengthening, empowering, and clarifying effect on my intuition. Being in the zone is often viewed as being very skilled and intuitive with one's self and one's environment. Breath, movement, water, and practice are key for support and a feeling of centered peace in our mind.

Intuition in everyday language is becoming more and more accepted. We are seeing more articles written about intuition, as well as increased references to those things that are beyond our sight in television, music, and science. This is wonderful news. And like the brain, we cannot "see" intuition with our two eyes at first—we need something more like a scanner or a looking glass . . . this is our third, or higher, eye.

Before we launch into all the fun parts of what our intuition provides, it is important to understand that our actions cause reactions. We have learned to only notice exterior information, but intuition shows us what is beneath the surface. Just like a brain scan lets us know the health of our brain within our skull, intuition lets us, and sometimes others, know what is under the surface, within. This is often private and sensitive information. Intuition helps us follow others less, offering less attention to the outside view of things while ironically giving us an outside view *in, in the sense that our inner being is assimilating the outside world.* As these gentle shifts happen in our culture, it is good to be aware of how a powerful intuition can bring in great creativity, ideas, and alchemy. At the same time, what comes in intuitively is not always meant to be conversation fodder at the water cooler as gossip or against another. The magic of intuition will show you more than you might realize meets the eye. It is important to take the gift of intuition as a gift and not to scan for information that is not meant to be revealed. The third eye is a powerful gift, one that comes with kind responsibility. With the balancing of each energy center below the sixth, there is no worry that our intuition will be used unconstructively. Life is greatly enhanced with this eye open. Innovation, invention, and creation. Let's now have some fun with this gift!

Intuition is a word that is becoming more known (yay!), but what exactly is the *third eye* many are talking about, and where is it located? If you have done yoga or meditation for a while, you might know what this space looks and feels like. The shape of the almond, or an eye, is exactly what this energy center radiates. We can think of the round shape of the energy center (remember, another word for *energy center* is *chakra*, which means "a powerful spiritual wheel"), and the circle can be found within this eye or radiating around this eye, depending on your belief.

Our sixth energy center—known as the third eye location—is the home of intuition. Reaching it is like stepping into the Land of Oz. Once you reach this point, it's as if the world has gone from black and white to Technicolor.

Unlike Dorothy, though, you won't want to go back to Kansas after experiencing your third eye higher sight at work. You might want more sparkly shoes though. The gift of knowing our higher eye provides us with *so much:* the understanding that we are working with forces greater than ourselves, that we are never alone, that we are constantly taken care of, and that everything we need is already inside of us. And that life can be exciting. These ways of deeper connection to our brain, and therefore our body and life experience, create a stronger life force. This helps with each decision we make, how we communicate with the world, and how we take better care of ourselves *within.* We focus a lot on what we see on the outside. Our third eye helps us connect to that outside, and more importantly, to what our body and brain are saying on the inside.

This is the energy center we've been building up to, where all of our hard work and diligence pay off in magical and unimaginable ways. We begin to have a relationship with ourselves within, connecting ourselves with more of our soul knowing. The knowing is like a whisper at times, and this awareness might feel subtle at first. This will be an awareness of self, like our soul and our self are communicating in great partnership. It brings an awareness of what food and relationship are doing and feel like in our system (we become more fine-tuned in body awareness and brain functioning). We also now see we have an inner compass that is finely tuned to take us forward on our way, in evolvement and not stalemate thinking. We now see we have choices that impact a way of doing *everything.* It's no mistake that most of us come into the sixth energy center between our midthirties and early forties because it is at this point that we have accumulated the life experience that helps us to see a greater view of the world beyond ego and struggle for resource, and to use our intuition appropriately.

Our body, mind, and spirit are humming along like a well-oiled machine, which allows us to easily *feel* what our intuition is telling us. This adds the "soul" aspect. We are emotionally clear and calm, so churning thoughts or feelings do not cloud our intuitive knowledge. We are mentally even-keeled and do not overanalyze our intuitive knowledge. And we are spiritually attuned with the understanding that we are neither working alone nor are we working for only our own benefit. Everything in the universe and in heaven is one, and we are one with it.

It is in this sixth energy center, associated with a color ranging from violet to purple (which traditionally represents royalty—how perfect!), that we hold the extraordinary capacity to be guided far beyond our five senses. Once we open to the new intelligence provided by this higher knowledge, we can begin to use our third eye to work in harmony with everything we've learned so far. Here in the third eye, we find incredible powers like psychic ability, mediumship, clairaudience, and clairvoyance—all of the types of intelligence that go beyond schooling and logic. Soul intelligence. This is truly exciting, magical stuff! With an open third eye, not only is the world our oyster—the entire *universe* is our oyster, and its intuitive nuggets are the pearls. We receive information that helps us not only in practical ways, but we also learn that we are not alone in our life experience and that those we love are never completely gone. I can't even write about it without feeling my whole body bow to the incredible, beautiful magnitude of it all.

The sixth energy center is located in the lower or mid part of the forehead, near between the brows and above the eyes. Some consider the idea of intuition and the third eye to be New Agey, but it is actually an old concept shared by many cultures. The concept of the third eye dates back as far as the ancient Egyptians (if not further), who left behind hieroglyphs of the goddess Wadjet. The ancient Egyptians portrayed Wadjet with three eyes, the third of which was known as the Eye of Horus. The left eye symbolized the masculine, the right eye symbolized the feminine and intuition, and the third eye signified the union of feminine and masculine and high wisdom, or "seeing" all things and experiences in a heightened, balanced way.

I wholeheartedly feel intuition (and brain health) works exactly as the Egyptians believed—that it is housed in the heightened feminine side of our brain. Interestingly, their interpretation of the third eye shape closely matches the shape of our brain's pineal gland. Located in the center of our brain toward the back, this space is near the third eye center. When we understand how this region of the brain is linked to higher wisdom, we understand that a large part of the intuitive process is literally housed in our physical brain. This is why it's so important to relax our brains through practices like meditation and the release of stagnant emotions and thoughts. Sleep patterns are here as well. I often see using intuition makes us less tired, as we do not muddle over decisions, but it also helps us sleep soundly at night, a calming factor of the brain "knowing" and "connecting" knowledge with more ease (instead of racing). Modern science has shown that the pineal gland, as well as the prefrontal cortex, is most affected during meditation, visual yoga, and other forms of mind clearing. Seventeenth-century philosopher, mathematician, and scientist René Descartes, who believed the interaction of the mind and body occurred in the pineal gland, theorized that the pineal gland serves as the "seat of the soul." The concept of the third eye can also be found in Buddhism (where it is believed to be the eye of consciousness) and in the Hindu portrayal of Lord Shiva, who is depicted with a third eye in the middle of his forehead, which represents spiritual wisdom, knowledge, and seeing beyond the apparent. In Christianity this area of the forehead is often blessed with holy water or at the beginning of a prayer (such as the sign of the cross and certain blessings of saints, apostles, and biblical men). The third eye area has been both explicitly and implicitly celebrated across both Eastern and Western cultures by the placement of a jewel, dot, smudge, or touch of the fingers or prayer hand motioning across or on this area at the forehead.

So let's dig into the really fun stuff—what intuition is and the wonderful life experience it opens up!

Sixth and Seventh Senses

The sixth energy center is, appropriately, the home to our sixth sense, the ability to know that beyond which we can see, smell, hear, touch, and taste. In some cultures, the sixth sense is considered to be a given, no different from the five more tactile senses.

Despite the fact that Westerners have just as much of an innate sixth sense as anyone else, it is not as commonly recognized in our more empirically oriented culture. The sixth sense has not been nurtured, cultivated, or acknowledged in many conventional educational and religious systems. This means that although we Westerners all *have* a sixth sense, we have to learn to have a relationship with it, to trust it, and to use it. Since Western culture does not treat the sixth sense as real or valid, many people have difficulty giving it any credence. Even still, most of us have at least heard of the sixth sense. (Thank you, M. Night Shyamalan. But, don't fret. For the most part, the sixth sense is far less dramatic in real life than it is in Hollywood.) If you've ever had a feeling that something was going awry, that there was more to a situation than met the eye, or if you've ever simply had a hunch, then you've experienced your sixth sense at work.

The *seventh* sense, on the other hand, is far less commonly discussed in pop culture or elsewhere. In fact, many of us may have never even heard of it. The seventh sense is a more refined form of intuition than the sixth sense—I like to refer to it as higher intuition. Let's say you go out to have lunch with a coworker. Even though she doesn't come out and say something is wrong, you can tell it is. This is your sixth sense kicking in—that general extrasensory knowledge beyond that which is being said, heard, felt, smelled, or touched. You know that, *Hmmmm, something is off . . .* but you can't quite put your finger on exactly what it is. Your seventh sense, however, allows you to intuit the *specifics* of a situation. So, in this case, you would know exactly what is going on with that coworker to make her a little bit off—that she had an argument with her spouse or just received bad news from her doctor.

We can't force the seventh sense to kick in right away. It can take time. This honing of intuition comes when it comes, and it comes with focused attention on our inner voice, our healthy mind and body, and our openness to a new now. We *can* open the door for it by having very balanced energy centers and by being extremely calm, open, and clearheaded. This allows the seventh sense the space it needs to create its magical connection to our deeper sensory system.

Making sure the seventh sense begins to kick in is a lot like training a muscle in the body or mind, or using time and focused attention to master a subject or craft. (Yes, again, this is sounding a lot like *The Matrix* movie.) There are a few commitments to be made: 1) time, 2) breath, 3) choosing the feeling of calm versus chaos (adrenaline) in your day (or a few designated moments to start), and 4) brain and body health. Coincidentally (although not), all the things that need a bit more aligning to tap into your seventh sense are exactly what your body needs to stay fueled, avoid disease, and increase quality of life. This is not an accident. Intuition helps all of our senses heighten and center, and this in turn helps intuition grow and fine-tune. This occurrence is for all people to achieve; like in life, doing your best for your personal brain and body will reap rewards to the best of your capability. And everyone is capable of increasing the connection to both intuition and quality of life.

The Sixth Energy Center and the Physical Being: Knowing with Our Whole Being

By the time we reach the sixth energy center and are aware that we have a higher or third eye—whether we have opened it or have not yet done so—we are now offering space to the physical sense of intuition. We are inherently aware of how to help our brain and our human being (body) to be more open, wide-eyed, and balanced. When our intuition is online, it is a whole-body experience. We know that the third eye energy center is firing on all cylinders when we feel generally lighter, more synergized, alive, youthful, clear, and present. Because of the work we've already done in previous energy centers, everything—including our muscles, metabolism, brain waves, and heart rate—is in an increased state of healthy balance and full vitality. However, it's important to be aware that if we are unrooted and our intuition is nonetheless firing away, imbalances, which can feel like instability, may occur. Intuition will still show up, just more unmanaged.

Yes, as we get older and maturation or evolution has grown the space in our energy center for intuition (think post–age thirty-five), our intuition or third eye will still open even if we are not on stable footing. In readings, it shows up often that in leaving part of this area (or mind) dormant (and choosing more earthly or egocentric things to occupy or fret our mind with), a lot of mayhem can enter our brain and body health simply by the choices we make. Intuition will nag us to exercise or move more, and, if we don't, depression in the brain can set in. Intuition and the third eye will also see when you are not taking care of yourself or loved ones in your care, that you are letting old emotional wounds tire you out so you do not feel you have *time* to work out, move, and meditate (when really you are taking a lot of time browsing social media sites or grazing on too many foods laced with sugar). Yes, your intuition works with your body to save your physical life and your health. You may experience its signs physically as headaches, tension, spaciness, or fidgeting. You might even have the strong feeling that you need to take some sort of action. This is a form of your body and intuition talking, a way to get your body to take better care. No one else can take such good care of you or know what is best. Especially in adulthood.

As well, intuition tries to show us that we might be making decisions from habit or from what was ingrained in us in our youth . . . and this is not being in touch with our mature intuitive mind. Remember, we start to be more naturally in tune with our intuition around our midtwenties, but many habits are formed or introduced at a much younger age. These habits could include something we witnessed from a parent or loved one that we have logged in our DNA or memory, so they do not come into action or "doing" until later years. Habits witnessed can be habits we inherit without mindful, intuitive recognition. And from here, our mind and body will help us with the balance needed (as in energy centers or maturing) to create anew.

If you are experiencing any of these sensations or recognitions, a great way to balance things out, to root down and put everything into perspective, is by first honoring that re-grounding is needed. Again, this connects us to awareness. To then aid this awareness and foster letting go, visiting or visualizing a natural larger body, such as an ocean, forest, or mountain, can be very helpful.

Another excellent way to balance is to "root" bare feet in mud or sand at the edge of a body of water, and to literally pick up the earth at your feet and throw these ground materials into the body of water (be sure no people are nearby). Let your hands submerge in the water. This action of feet rooted and hands, arms, and shoulders clearing out emotion is quite powerful. If this feels too heavy, you can ground your feet accordingly and unabashedly scream, yell, or sing toward the sky or wind. If this feels too dramatic (and honestly, it does not have to be that intense), you can take a beautiful pause and release by standing, sitting, or lying down and looking up at the blue sky or the stars on a clear night while simultaneously remaining aware of your feet, seat, or back on the earth and connecting to deep breath to understand the vastness you are a part of and also what supports your *moment here now*. These are quick (or elongated) ways to help us understand that our place in all of this is both large and small, and to know that we and our life experiences are just a small part of something much bigger than our minimized perspective.

I really do feel that on some level—no matter how deep down—we all know that this intuition stuff is real. After all, it's a *part* of who we are and how we're made. But so many of us have the tendency to give our power, perception, or decision making to others. Dating back long before written work, including the Bible, people went to saints, visionaries, and shamans to obtain information. Today, some still go to see these great aides in healing, including going to visit psychics or mediums. But the truth is, we *all* have access to this information. And there is support to help us understand this when needed. That said, there is no need to only go to an outside source to tap into the intuition that we *all* have the ability to access. *Go* within. We can begin to get in touch with our intuition in small ways, in those simple moments when we are granted signs and synchronicity. Once we build up confidence and realize that we too have this ability, intuition starts to unfold in simple ways. You might walk into a store you've never visited before and navigate yourself to the product you were looking for. This might be that the layout of a store is somewhat familiar to you by shared industry principles of marketing (for example, magazines are near the front), but you might also have known that that was the store to stop at. Remember, intuition *is* working with your mind, and other parts of your mind are not excluded for their wisdom. This is just one more (exciting) piece of your brain to bring to the table, to the party . . . to life.

It can feel more fun or centering when your phone rings and you know who's on the other end of the line before looking at your caller ID (even a dreaded call you might answer confidently). This might even give you an extra minute to breathe or know what you want to say (or be ready for the energy at the other end) before picking up. You may think of someone you haven't spoken to in a long time only to find an email from them waiting in your inbox. And knowing this might offer you pause to think about how important it is to choose your words with whole intent before responding to an email. Intuition is a part of cultivating intention. You can become so clear that you know where a parking spot is going to be open on a busy street. (People call this the angel parker.) Or you have a sense that your child or a loved one needs you or is in some sort of distress. And you know to be more present to *help* that child with presence (meaning, you won't be in your distress or in your childhood triggers). All of this is intuition, and I'm willing to say that pretty much all of us have experienced it in action in subtle ways like these, and what can happen when we do or do not stay in a mindful, peaceful space.

Even for myself, when I step out of a present space, the consequences are the same (some would say mine are worse by "knowing better and not doing better") and I either feel mucky or the moment does not feel good at all. Listening to our intuition and then reading, understanding, and then acting (as in action) from the information our intuition brings, takes work and diligence. Having young children has definitely made my quiet time decrease, and I see the effects when I do not do my part to stay centered. I can read the signs, but I cannot stay clear and focused to see them all the way through and turn the nudges or larger clear signs into the action needed. I mention this because even as we begin to really tap in and understand our higher senses, just like getting too much sunshine or smelling a strong scent too long, we need balance, rest, and evenness.

Meditation, quiet time, walks, and stretching help us to open up to these types of moments, assist us in seeing the signs we are constantly presented with, and help us stay centered in what we see as well. Other simple movements like hiking, swimming, tai chi, walks in the hills, and the martial arts can greatly help us keep our third eye center vibrant. Getting a full wellness check can help us assimilate what we are experiencing and spark new ways of finding rest and new ways to care for our intuitive body. All of these work because they center the thinking side of our brain and open the being, creative side of the mind—offering balance and unity of both thinking and receiving. They calm our entire human being and open us up, making us more aware of the moment—they breed what we call *presence*. They get our *chi* or life force flowing. They clear all of the noise out of our head and allow us to be in the now—or, as I like to say, they allow us to be in the *know*. Educated, healthful know.

Stepping into the moment is like aligning your life with the universe. It's you being physically aligned so that your intuition can open and you can become aware of signs and next execution steps. How do we know when we're physically aligned with our intuition? We feel calm. Our stomach is settled. Our jaw is unlocked. We're not tensing up our face. Our bowel movements and urination come with ease. We feel our feet. We feel we have a way to clear our energy or let go. We may have the sensation of chills moving up our spine or moving down our legs or arms—and not as a result of cold weather, as this is an energy frequency and higher connection or sign to that connection. We feel balanced and light. We inherently have the feeling that something is watching over us or has our back—which it does. Then we can act.

The Sixth Energy Center and the Emotional Being: Intuition Speaks in a Balanced, Centered Tone

Being aligned with your intuition requires you to be in the now. This is precisely why we've focused so much on clearing the past up to this point. It's only when we're not dwelling in the past that we are able to fully *be* in the present moment and use newfound energy productively and precisely. Emotional and mental clearing allows us to see intuition for what it is— information. Information is not emotional, and therefore, neither is intuition. When intuition speaks, it's in an even tone, no high, no low. We add the high or low when we attach our ego's thought and emotion to it. This can be wearing. Think of a great person of deep wisdom. Maybe you know some wise, old professors who know their information deeply and are more cerebral thinkers, giving their students the choice on what to do with the information (no ego or voice raised), without excuse or falter. There is no emotionally charged feeling. There is just fact. And they were less apt to move with society's tides.

The more intuitive we become, the more important it is to keep our emotions in a check-and-balance awareness form. When we feel more emotional, as we will as humans, then it might be best not to share what we see intuitively and wait until we are more even and peace filled. This is particularly true when we are given information about loved ones or about someone experiencing pain. We must try to stay neutral no matter what knowledge we are given and remember that no matter how dramatic the information we receive may be, the information itself has no emotion. It just is. Yes, at times this is hard to do, but with understanding the energy centers and the mind-heart connection to intuition, along with offering ourselves stillness (meditation and quiet), it's easier to be neutral. Both opening our intuition and understanding what to do with our intuitive knowledge are key. Intuitive information fueled by a vibrant heart-mind connection is there to help us step out of pain. And to help those around us step out of pain (this might not be apparent to loved ones who still believe in the ego or outside imagery running the show and do not like intuitive assistance). Again, we do not go down the rabbit hole or be swept by the moving tide.

It is *we* and others who apply emotion (and drama) to the information with which we are provided. This is not the intuitive part of the brain, and it's not the mediumship "ghost" or "spirit" aspect either, to be honest. Intuition does not need to be scary or provoke high emotion (that is our culture and our fight-or-flight fear roaring) without comfort. Even with all my years of experience with intuition, I can still find it particularly difficult to navigate situations in which I am given information about someone I adore.

This is why the previous energy centers are so important. We must go back to the idea of brevity and discernment in our words and apply it to our intuitive experience. We may have an intuitive notion come in about someone we love, but does that always necessarily mean we should voice it to them? This answer varies from one situation to the next. As we become more and more intuitive, we understand that the knowledge coming in requires us to choose our actions carefully. Our heart and breath can help balance our nerves and throat while we make such decisions. We must be coming from an open heart and head for the person we are helping, coming from self-worth and the worthwhile healing that intuition and trusting our gut bring to all involved, and we must be grounded and believe that this information will bring ultimate joy and pleasure (now or down the road) to those we are sharing with. This part is tricky, as our culture or communal structure likes to strangle the messenger and fire the middleman. With time and emotional space, all becomes clearer one way or another. This has a lot to do with bravery, boundaries, and stepping into the ring; understanding who does or does not want to step into these aspects with you. Again . . . discernment; sometimes hindsight lends the key to this and we learn going forward. What is most important is we know we did our best, and in the end, we take responsibility for our action and try not to take anything personally.

Not understanding information we receive can happen. It can be because we are mentally exhausted or are not quite hearing our inner voice clearly yet. It took me the leap of being completely surrendered to the process that my intuition had room to grow. This means understanding we will be "wrong" and we will be "correct" and staying unattached to the outcome. We must be more focused on honing our intuition to receive clearer and stronger information. But we can be tired, or off, of course. When it happens to me, when I am tapping in a lower vibration or thought wave, I can now usually tell by the color or sound of the information, and I talk about my mistake. I make sure to get rest or move a reading prior to its scheduled date until I am more ready. If it is in a reading, I make sure to clarify how deeply I am clear, or I ask questions and show honestly what I am seeing and why. I am more prone to make simple mistakes when I'm extremely tired or emotionally drained. I do not do readings late at night, and when something comes in before bed, I ask to be shown again in the morning or I write it down. Remember, this is a conversation with something higher—in our brain or outside of us, or both—whatever we believe. I do my best not to get to that stage, and trust me, my intuition throws many flags, but at times being a wife and mother (and human), this state happens. Alternatively, this stage of my life and what is currently in my life have also created a wiser sense of intuition so all elements can play a more positive or more draining role if I let them (such is life).

This is what works for me in clarifying my third eye receptivity and deciding what to accept as true: 1) I do not share or give credence to anything I am not 99.1 percent sure of to the best of my knowledge or anything I'm feeling muddled or off about, even if only slightly. I *wait*, and I ask for more information from a clear, open heart (to attract more clear intuitive support). 2) If I do understand intuitive information that I think is coming in to the best of my ability and decide to share something and am found "wrong," I apologize right away. Then I share what intuition showed around it to offer help in dispelling confusion (remember, intuition is not wrong, but how we perceive it can be). I take the lesson if there is a lesson to be learned about understanding (or using) my intuition more clearly and more healthfully. 3) I offer to help see the situation through in all facets. This is not the time to drop the mic and run, or to avoid ownership of being "wrong." In readings, I make sure to be clear. If I have read information wrong, I send meditation and prayer that all involved found their right path, and I trust in the reason or lesson of why it happened this way.

As a professional I take several steps and prep to be ready for my readings. There is a fascinating psychic from the 1940s, Edgar Cayce, who only needed a name and physical address; I am the same, needing only a name and the invitation to come in to do a reading. I did not know until a year and a half after readings began that we were similar. Things would open up deeply and quickly for him as well, and the information went from simple to deeply expansive rather quickly. If this is a profession you would like to engage in, the layers of reading information correctly are a little different than using your intuition only for yourself or your loved ones.

The simple steps of understanding and being more of a humble witness and receiver have worked very well at helping people interested in understanding intuition to see to the best of their ability what intuition was showing. All of us will learn lessons all the way around about accuracy, depth, mistakes or pitfalls, and wisdom of intuitive support. Intuition can be complex and simple at the same time, and no matter what one might think, we are all human. So when you read information incorrectly for yourself or others and do not see the signs helping you address that (because signs will tell us, "No! Wrong!"), this is okay. We are still in a black-and-white, 0 percent or 100 percent accuracy culture. This is not human. So do your best to learn from mistakes and move forward.

A note here: I have never told someone they had cancer in a reading, nor when they were about to miscarry (two extreme examples for this point) even when it is shown. Intuitive information is not always for us to tell other people involved. It is coming to *us* as information on how we can *help*, not hinder, ourselves or eventually, another. When we receive information that turns out to truly be inaccurate (or close but not spot-on), these are signs to keep your energy centers aligned the best you're able, to have more quiet time, and to use meditation, yoga, or outdoor energy to support your third eye. In readings, much information will come in on how to prep the person for unwanted news, often giving remedies that will help them heal or subtle pieces of wisdom that they do not realize until later were referring to what they were about to experience (intuition is brilliant). I have never shared with a person that their spouse or loved one is cheating (and this shows in readings more often than I ever realized occurred), but I have supported when those come already knowing and we are moving on to answers of how to heal. In all my years of experience in professional readings, I have not let anything from a person's reading specifically leave my vault of knowing without the client's blessing or wish. This is an important factor for receiving information, as our intuitive connection can lessen with abuse or misuse, whether because of self-sabotage or because a gift has weakened or been taken away . . . or both. The takeaway here is to do your best to have a check-in and balance of your own to hurdle any factors that can derail your growing intuitive connection.

Try best to think of this as a higher gauge watching over and acting with you as you expand (and at times make mistakes). Just do not involve others negatively in your intuitive wake.

At times intuition will be simple, at times very complex (yet answers still simple), but we must learn to act on the side of caution with this valuable tool. This means that using our intuition might be slow and steady for a while, just using and gauging what we get right or know, until we become more confident (and are working in new forms of mastery). Questioning what we receive as being intuitive is a natural part of the process when we are learning the intuitive part of our being. A good way to gauge if our intuitive strength is growing is again by keeping a small journal, typed log, or voice memo of when we had a *hunch* or *strong knowing* and the information was true; or when we used our intuitive inner voice to help a friend, coworker, or loved one and how the results were different from when we were not fully listening (to our inner self and the other person) or were distracted. Lastly, receiving information that is intuitive will not give us indigestion or irritable bowels (but the fear of what we *know* or think to be true might if the fear is held within too long). Intuition will help us feel lighter and our day more fluid (deeper information coming in or not) when used with a sense of non-ownership.

There is a form of being too open, when the sixth energy center becomes too open or the energy centers around the wise or third eye are imbalanced. When this imbalanced or non-trusted connection occurs, for many the intuitive experience will feel more closed and intuition less accessible, but for a few reading this book, it will be so open that you can read strangers, images you see on TV, or what the gardener across the street is doing or thinking about. This has happened to me and, trust me, it is not that fun. Even if you doubt yourself or the information, visual proof will show itself quickly to show you your intuition is open. If this happens, going into better grounding practices and going to a healer or teacher who understands how to close down your intuition is important. For those who have a moment or day like this and are becoming uncomfortable with information that is streaming in, getting to a yoga or meditation center is helpful. Or you can do a self-scan over all energy centers' imbalances and take steps to balance, to feel more rested and grounded such as eating cleaner food, finding an acupuncturist, or even consulting a guide or medium that you trust to help you understand how to balance out energy. Remind yourself you are not alone, even if you feel a bit off center. Get help.

Receiving intuitive information will come in many forms, in many moments. I used to gamble with this gift until I officially knew it was a gift! And I used it once in my husband and my courtship to go dancing in Vegas, which got us on the dance floor faster by winning my husband's money back quickly plus a few extra at a blackjack table. (See why he married me?) Needless to say, intuition can help you alchemize or monetize many things, but your clean gut will know which information is which and when you've crossed over a line abusing the gift. The extended gambler mentality ends in trouble every time. I have not witnessed a gambler who does not pay the price in other ways; maybe the money comes but healthy relationships do not. Again, it is about balance and grace.

Intuition is a continuous stream, which can confuse or overwhelm people at first, but remember it's a stream always running, and it is our job to stay a clear, healthy, honest vessel of discerning its support. This helps our relationship with our intuitive voice, as, like any relationship, being a good listener and healthy partner is key. Balancing the energy centers will give us the tools we need to understand what to do when we misread or step over our comfort zone with our third eye growth in clarity and color.

This is yet another reason why it's so important to be emotionally clear—we want to ensure that we are never, ever using or disseminating intuitive information that is too close personally, or for negative reasons, or out of fear. This happens to me when I am worn out, should not be doing the reading, or have not gone to the healers I need to for making sure I am extremely clear and healthy in body, mind, spirit, and soul (aspects of being). A friend might ask me what sex her or his unborn baby is on the spot (at times I do this in readings and it is clear yet not as clear as I am coming out of the reading or coming out of a draining topic) or someone will ask the score of a game (yes, I get those sports gambling questions a lot). This is clearer with investment or the stock market. You can use intuition but the logical and historical patterns help greatly.

This might not seem to pertain to you, but it does. Like me, you must stay centered. For me, I do readings minimally each week, and I make sure I have close to centered emotion surrounding or tied to the subject (this work can take months at times). When I first tapped into my intuition, sometimes I would share what I saw in an effort to seek clarity for others, not realizing the clarity was within. I could have inadvertently hurt people because they weren't ready to hear the information I had intuited. I learned very early on that sometimes the purpose of knowing certain information is simply so that you can be aware enough to give a much-needed hug or answer an inquiry with pause, as opposed to sharing some piece of information. When I react to information from an emotional place, it becomes far more difficult to toe this line and much easier to act in a way that serves fear rather than the person the intuition is about.

Sometimes when you receive a bit of intuition, your heart might start to race and you may think, *I have to say this*. Remember, though, that this is just your heart (or adrenals) reacting to what your brain is telling you. Your brain is fearing danger, uncertainty, or potential pain. Remaining emotionally clear and acting from a place of emotional intelligence is always the most direct route to using your intuition in the best way possible—sometimes that means thoughtfully sharing information, and other times it means remaining silent.

When we are unbalanced, intuition can bring with it a sense of martyrdom or an onset of neurosis. This happens when we forget where the information came from. We begin to feel responsible for it, when this is simply not the case. The only thing we are asked to do is to connect with the energy out there that holds all of the information we need, as we need it. As light-filled as possible.

Keeping our emotions clear pays off when it comes to intuiting information about our own lives too. I once worked with a client, Veronika, who was desperately trying to get pregnant for the second time. Her first pregnancy had been easy, but for some reason, her and her husband's second attempt wasn't taking—she had suffered four miscarriages to date. It came through that she was deficient in folic acid, and that this was the single cause of her conception difficulties. "But my prenatal vitamin is full of folic acid," Veronika replied. Still, I kept hearing the same thing over and over again: that the solution to her problem was folic acid. Veronika remained calm and clear and allowed herself to absorb that information, despite the fact that it conflicted with what she logically felt to be true. Veronika had not asked me to tap into any specific distress in terms of her attempts to get pregnant or otherwise, so the information was even more poignant to her. Out of all the things we could have talked about that day, she knew this one sentence meant something. This is when I did ten-minute readings.

With this information in hand, Veronika visited her doctor who ran a list of tests . . . all of which came back normal. When she told me this, intuition kicked in again and showed that the doctor did not test for folic acid, "Yes, I think he did," Veronika replied. This is information that Veronika could easily have applied any number of emotions to, but she didn't. She calmly called her doctor's office to find that, yes, they had indeed forgotten the folic acid test. Veronika scheduled a follow-up appointment to take the folic acid test. Before her appointment rolled around, Veronika happened to read the fine print of the label for a medication she had been taking since the birth of her first son. "May block folic acid," it read in small print. All along, the answer Veronika needed had been right there in front of her on her kitchen counter, but she didn't see it. Because she remained clear and open throughout the process, she was able to allow intuition to do its work . . . through being open to intuition and herself. Immediately, Veronika switched when she took her medication and—sure enough!—she became pregnant on her next cycle and went on to give birth to a happy, healthy baby boy named Lukas.

While the sixth sense isn't magical in and of itself, the profound effect it has on our life once we begin to put it to use can certainly feel that way. Veronika and her family of four are a wonderful testament to this.

The Sixth Energy Center and the Intellectual Being: Finding the Zone

When it comes to intuited information and we understand how to read and interact with our inner voice, we will never have to make a choice on our own about what is right and what feels wrong, what is good and what is bad. Our intuition will truly show us what to do. Our body will get signs if we are on or off track. Our intuition creates win-win situations. There are no losers when we're tapped into this energy center because we've inherently already developed the heart energy center of acceptance and treating others as we want to be treated (by balancing lower energy centers, and now coming out of pure ego thinking or division of humans). Our heart center is *key* to our healthy, present experience with our intuition. *We need an open heart to hear intuition effectively and with unity to divine our higher wisdom.* We need the self and the soul active. If you feel yourself questioning the rightness and wrongness or goodness and darkness of a situation, you might be more guided by others' or your ego's actions or reactions than you are by intuition. Our intuitive mind does not look at things as "bad" or "good." Our analytical part of the brain does. This is a fraction of the mind, one that we have overtrained to take over in our culture—in school, in business, in capitalism, in Success with a capital *S*. Intuition working with the open, wise heart sees things incredibly differently. This is what many leaders, buddhas, lamas, Jesus, Mother Mary, and saints have come to show us, to represent.

Any living thing has strengths and weakness, but it is also loved. I know, this can sound crazy! But it's true. First, the intuitive part of the brain only sees the now, so honestly there is no judgment or pretense, even if someone is about to hurt another (this one took me a long time to understand—even I was in disbelief and fought this fact). This energy center is of high creativity or of the creator, so it knows little about the logic of right or wrong or hierarchal value judgment. But it does know healthy and unhealthy vibration, so it can stop streaming in, not because there is judgment but just due to a lack of life force energy or energy supporting creation, or forward flow.

We can think of this aspect like when we teach or do art in today's modern times. Valued, unlimiting creative programs know that we are meant to teach art without the good/bad concept, with no "better/worse" language, and most importantly, with the idea that there is no need for "redoes." This is a hard concept for adults, parents, and even for today's kids, to understand. Again, our society tries to apply linear thinking to a circular, rounded endeavor.

Intuition is the same. Remember, the sixth energy center is a feminine energy center. Think nest versus hunt. Nurture versus conquest.

Or perhaps life has not yet unfolded enough for you to see the good that will follow from a given situation or you do not trust the "obscurity" of intuition (or unlined art). Be brave. I'm sure we've all had plenty of experiences in which a situation seems to be difficult or not good in the moment it happens. "Creative" for some people may not be straight-lined, but it is methodical. This is lovely as long as we do not judge or analyze our intuitive third eye, or part of the calming, quiet mind. This is growth. It isn't until we move farther down the road sometimes that we can then see how our intuition led us to a new path that actually wasn't messy or unlined at all, or how it steered us in a better direction that has more of a well-lined feel to it than even what our analytics could muster. It's all about letting the story unfold and being surprised, being in the moment, which is sometimes easier said than done. It's about trusting your inner voice and instinct above all else to carry you *forward*.

Intention is everything. To step into intuition, it is wise to set an intention to help clear your mind. You can think of this mind clearing as being in the zone. If you are an artist, an athlete, or a successful businessperson, you've probably experienced this sensation before—when you're so in the moment and everything is churning along so smoothly and instinctually that you begin to act as a channel. And what feels like a symphony of steps comes together. You may be a channel for music, for words, for business strategizing, or for sports. *What* you're creating is unimportant—it's the creation in and of itself that matters (which is precisely why it's so important to nurture creativity, as discussed in the second energy center). During those moments in the zone, you are not being active so much as you're *allowing* something to flow through you, or merging with divine light-filled energy. You simultaneously feel incredibly rich and alive yet still calm.

Chances are, we've all had at least a brush with the zone before and, on the off chance you haven't, you've still witnessed it. Any time you've seen a professional athlete, actor, comedian, or singer perform to their highest potential; in a moment when you've felt the magic palpable and electric in the air; where all elements come together in one perfect moment, *that* is the zone. Whether you're watching it flow through someone else or it's happening to you, it's almost like witnessing a holy experience. When a basketball player effortlessly hits nothing but net from the three-point zone or a football player executes the perfect pass into the end zone, that's the zone. It's the culmination of a lot of physical practice, emotional stability (through the lack of emptiness filling our well), and the ability to balance the analytical brain's over-flexed muscle. When a person is able to do this, there is room for magic and possibility.

That is exactly what it feels like to experience in-the-moment balance in the body and mind, and it's *precisely* how we want our intuition to come into play. There is no thinking. There is no feeling. You *are* the moment. There is no better feeling than this, when all of the parts of us come together as one and simultaneously merge with those things outside of us. Once we are clear vessels, our intuitive muscle strengthens and becomes more vibrant and alive.

If you've experienced The Zone yourself, you've probably also noticed that as soon as you become aware of what's happening and your analytical brain snaps back into high motion, it's almost like *poof!* The magic of the zone disappears into thin air, and your emotions or nerves roll in. You come back into yourself and lose that effortless connection with everything around you.

The more we practice letting go of thought and letting it move through us, the more we can enjoy those ethereal moments of knowing. We can cease doing and trying in favor of simply being. Intuition also supports the zone in kind. Once we've stepped into some form of our intuition, we become more confident in what we're doing. We're a better performer, or we execute our work and home lives more efficiently. When our energy centers are balanced, we can use our intuition to its highest potential, which simultaneously benefits every other aspect of our life, creatively, pragmatically, emotionally, and mentally. When our intuition is really firing and moving through us, we may think that we are suddenly luckier in other aspects of our life. But that's not luck . . . it's simply *allowing*.

The Sixth Energy Center and the Spiritual Being: The Ultimate Connection

It has been an awe-inspiring pleasure in my life to see how intuition can guide us all to feel more centered, more capable, more confident, and calmer. Intuition may come through each of us as individuals, but it ultimately works for the good of all. Aside from the extraordinary magic that intuition is, in and of itself, perhaps the *most* magical part of it all is that as we apply it to our life, we can see how intuition ultimately works for the good of each soul and how all of our lives truly are intertwined. We learn that we are both one with the universe (which provides us with intuitive information) and that the universe takes care of us. The self and the soul aspects of "being."

By the time we make our way up to the sixth energy center, we have the potential to realize that we're part of something bigger than us, so we have more information and maturity, which allows us to move away from selfish motivations and incorporate a unified voice and value. Our roots are planted, our relationships are mutually beneficial, our ego is in check, and our heart is attuned to the space around us. We know how to put voice to all of this to bring good into the world and act with compassion. We know how to release what we don't need and what causes us pain and isolation. Intuition is like the icing on this cake. It provides us with wisdom that we can bring into the world from a grounded ego and heart-centered place.

Those who *do* try to use their intuition for selfish purposes will ultimately fail. Higher intuition utilizes universal energy, which is not something we can endlessly receive—it involves a collaboration. The way we give back is by working for the good or forward motion (evolution). When we fail to do this, our intuition simply shuts down. Intuition was not given to us so that we can pick out winning lotto numbers. It comes in for the purposes of evolving and forward movement, no matter how small that forward movement may seem on an individual basis. This is another reason why intention is so important. The more we set the intention to use our intuition for the greater good—and actually put it to use in that manner when it arrives—the stronger our intuition will become over time.

Since intuition serves us all, it is something we should all be encouraged to tap. That is yet another reason why there should be no hierarchy when it comes to intuition. Because accessing higher intuition without negative consequences requires that we treat people with compassion and that our energy centers be in balance, getting in touch with your intuition can lead those around you to do the same. Most of us treat others how we are treated, so the goodness we put into the world helps to create a cycle of increasing compassion and enlightened behavior. Once we become intuitive, we (consciously or not) give others the choice and the freedom to ignite their own intuition. This can cause a new wildfire of *hope* meeting intelligence. This can happen by chance, by intention, or as if by osmosis. And the more people who are aware of what a consciously whole heart-mind connection looks like, how valuable this whole living actually is, the better off we all are. Our world resource, our love for fellow living things, and seeing one another in straight, even connection to ourselves will exponentially grow back into balance.

In addition to providing us with important information, intuition can also serve as a stunningly precise higher compass for making each step and decision in our life. Another term for this might be *insight*, or *higher guidance*. Insight guides us forward, often on a clearer, easier path. Intuition helps us to make decisions from a wise place that benefits the most people possible. It also makes it easier for us to find solutions to difficult situations, which will help both others and ourselves. As your intuition grows, you might be surprised that clear and specific remedies to situations seem to materialize, no matter how muddled the situation may have seemed when you were acting from a place of earthly and ego-driven information.

And so, with that, here is the biggest indicator that you have come into balance in your sixth energy center and are truly tapped into your intuition: you will find more joy, a greater sense of worth and belonging, more support, and an assurance that all of the information you receive is not only good for you but is also good for others.

Third Eye Energy Center Saying

Meditation is extremely important to keep both (all of!) your eyes clear. This means that you not only "see" situations more clearly and evenly, but literally your eyes become clear visibly, as if a new updated vibrant window to your soul (and your higher wisdom or higher "eye"). You may also mirror back the truth to others more efficiently and without muddle (meaning seeing their light and soul without judgment or fog). This muddle is replaced by a clear, healthy brain, balanced in the quiet time of meditation, the silence of forgiveness, and the reaping of the benefits of better choices in more movement and more nutrient-rich foods. This all adds up to more opportunity and energy to make space for new, for an intuitive to sprout and grow like a field of fresh tall grass. To make space to truly see, we must clear the window, the air, or turn over the fertile ground we are rooted in. Again, our meditation does this to allow us to tap into that deepest, most centered, core part of ourselves.

In this meditation for the sixth energy center and third eye brightness, close your eyes and focus on the space of the mind or forehead where you think intuition physically resides. Let your two eyes focus and "look" (even with eyes closed) at this space. You might find your brain, mind, or space in the forehead begins to pulse a purple eye. This is normal and a wonderful sign that you are helping activate this spot of intuition and high creativity. You are also washing your prefrontal cortex in the brain, which greatly helps your intuition become more clear and strong, as well as your sleep to be more sound (both helping to enhance your joyous intuitive being).

Now bring in one of the *I Am* sayings or mantras, reflecting on which of these sayings most resonates with you (or, if you'd like, beginning using the phrase *I am* as a mantra or saying in itself). Do what feels most calming, relaxing, and deepening to you.

I am guided.
I am centered.
I am clear.
I am intuitive.

Find a comfortable seated position and allow your focus to come to your breath, using that focus to still the thoughts floating through your mind. Close your eyes gently, looking toward your third eye or centered part of your intuition at your forehead or center of brain. Keep your breath soft and quiet, inhaling and exhaling through your nose. If you need to exhale through your mouth for a few rounds to relieve tension or a clouded feeling, please do so. After you have found that inner quiet, if your inhale and exhale feel calm and balanced, begin to incorporate your saying into your breath. As you breathe in, silently recite your chosen saying. As you exhale, silently recite, "I am clear." Visualize the color purple or clear, fresh light.

Continue your soft breath, inhaling what you need and expunging all of the chatter and noise. Give yourself between three and ten minutes per day for this practice, perhaps increasing the time by thirty seconds to a minute per day. Repeat this practice for ten days in a row.

The Third Eye Guide

What it governs:	The third eye; intuition, mediumship, clairaudience, clairvoyance, higher wisdom, high creativity
Ages:	Generally, ages 35–42 and above
Color:	A range from violet to rich purple
In balance:	Being able to connect with information that comes from inside or outside of us; sense of oneness with both humankind and the universe; a feeling of the four aspects of being humming along in precision. Increased synchronicity and ease. Psychic ability. Hearing and seeing more than meets the eyes. Premonitions. Factual visions.
Imbalanced:	Using intuition for personal benefit at the detriment of others, neurosis, tension headaches, false god or martyr confusion. Neurosis.
Supportive foods:	Water; raw nuts especially walnuts; sprouted nuts especially almonds; metal detoxers from the ground, such as harvest grains and mushrooms; purple and purple-red fruits (in small amounts), such as goji berries and acai; plums; eggplant; cruciferous vegetables especially broccoli; clean organic meats; freshwater fish. Pineapple and papaya.

Beneficial practices:	Meditation; yoga or long stretches; simple repetitive movements such as hiking, swimming, or tai chi; visiting majestic landscapes that put the greater picture into perspective.
Sayings:	*I am guided.* *I am centered.* *I am clear.* *I am intuitive.*

8

THE SEVENTH ENERGY CENTER: THE CROWN

The Divine Connection

A crown in our culture is a holy grail, a sacred symbol in the history of being human or being superhuman. For figures from all civilizations, from Wonder Woman to the highest king or queen, from a priestess to the decorated graduate, the crown represents excelled knowledge, opportunity, and connective being. As well, the golden halo, jewel, or sparkle has also been placed on the likeness of many a saint and higher-minded individual as a decoration of unity and connection to aged lineage: of knowledge, hard work, brave attention to humanity, and the quest (or attainment) of higher wisdom. This is the same for the seventh energy center, what it offers to our intuition and to us moving forward in our higher intuitive mind and our quest of connective *being*.

Jumping in water, whether saltwater or freshwater, whether off a dock or boat, in our yard or at a club, does wonders for our psyche, our clarity, and our intuition. Have you ever felt how this act feels? And if you cannot get to a larger body of water, or the weather isn't right, have you felt the refreshing washing away of thoughts or energy that a shower or dunking in a bathtub (or sink) can offer? You are clearing and cleansing your crown energy center, and this center is worth its weight in gold. Alchemizing.

Intuition and our clarity of thought cannot be accomplished by too many things running through or around our head (including voices). The washing with water, cleansing of the space around the crown, is not only important but is also often seen as sacred. The third eye and the crown of our body can be forgotten but are quite important when taking care of ourselves and washing away our day or our old collected thoughts. Both our third eye and our head are sacred parts of our humanness, ones that offer great clearing and letting go.

Seeing as how this is a book about intuition, it might seem like the third eye energy center should be the big finale. But there is much value to be gained for our opened intuition by knowing this important space of our being above (and beyond) the third or higher eye. An entire universe of information is there for you (like a library and the reading glasses for the third eye), having your back, with loving guidance and distinctive leadership—a collective of supported guidance.

The seventh energy center, the crown, might be the most sacred and mystical of them all. And this energy center is not to be dismissed or untapped. This is the space where we feel that higher guidance and visual cues in real form helping us with our intuition every day. Helping us with our life experience every day. This energy center is different than the miraculous six energy centers that come previously because it is simultaneously *of* us and *outside of* us, connecting us to higher wisdom support, almost like having a walkie-talkie with the divine, our God, or our universal wisdom as a direct line. Whereas the previous energy centers are all seated in the body and mind, the crown energy center actually hovers just above the crown of our head. Some believe that this center lightly touches the head and extends upward from there. This is fine too—whatever helps you feel more connected and included in this supported wisdom.

What does *supported wisdom* mean? Well, you didn't think intuition is all controlled by our mind and body, did you?! What I have found—and this started long before knowing what an energy center or chakra was—is that the information is a discussion, that it is also coming from somewhere or being supported by something other than just the self, and this is what we have been calling the divine, God, or higher support. This is not only in the mind—in the same way that God, heaven, universal support or law, even new creative ideas are not just of the self or our own being making this stuff come to fruition. There is something more working with us, and our third eye is the translator into form or witnessing or opening the gate for the intel.

Feeling this higher support also helps clear the theory that this is only of the self or for the self. Or that we do things on our own. Nothing is ever done on our own or alone. It takes two or more to do anything, and this energy center shows this. This helps us understand intuitive information is for the good of the self/soul, the group, family, or community . . . and that this is not a brain malfunction or neurosis. This also helps us understand that heaven is not so far away. I have found that what we call heaven is within, without, in every breath if we let it be . . . all around . . . *everywhere* and in every *thing*. And it's free, like oxygen (and breath), for every human rain or shine, success or "failure." The collective of the crown shows unity of all things, interconnectedness of all action; our third eye explains this through the mind and through palpable, bite-size, high wisdom.

You may think of this energy center as the light, or as the oxygen mixed with the direct sunrays that shine down over a tree, interacting with the tree yet separate. This energy can be seen as the high wind on a bird's wings, helping that bird land efficiently in a chosen tree. The crown energy center is known for its gorgeous magenta fade or pure-white color, or for the alchemy color of gold. If we think of our rainbow of energy centers within us as more of a pyramid shape, with red at our foundation and purple at the tip where our third eye resides, then the shiny clear gem on top of the pyramid's tip would be the crown energy center. Many believe pyramids were built to house the true gem at the top tip. This visual (think of the album cover Pink Floyd with their music being at the top tip of the rainbow pyramid) is what this radiant, almost surreal experience of the crown energy center encompasses.

For those of you who are, or feel, overly grounded and cautious, the crown energy center may feel almost entirely closed, far away, lacking, or nonexistent. Don't worry too much about that right now. Chances are if you're reading this book, you'll soon makes its discovery; you will be tuned in enough to your other energy centers that you will not stop at your third eye and leave it unguarded . . . your crown energy center will become real and incredibly supportive to your intuitive experience.

The manner in which the crown energy center is seated perfectly represents what it is: our connection with the divine. You've probably seen this idea represented in images of religious and cultural figures throughout the ages, though the artist may not have been consciously aiming to depict the crown energy center. Or maybe they were. We see it in saints' halos and in portrayals of Jesus and Mary crowned by halos, in the crowns of high priestesses portrayed in Egyptian hieroglyphs, and today in princess depictions. Artists and creatives throughout time have depicted this glow or energy around many a saint and leader with the rays of light or circles of haloed energy right where a person unites with high spiritual or extraordinary support.

It is through the crown that we tap into the universal energy outside of us, which may be detected in our consciousness or higher intellect through the form of intuition or an open mind. It's as if our third eye is a wise, understanding witness or has understanding of energy not seen by the naked eye. Our third eye also interprets energy that is coming in from an outside source, and sometimes this energy is of an earthly matter and at times it will be coming from something bigger or beyond . . . whether it's around a person's head or mind, up over their shoulder, or from the "sky" or a different time, place, existence, or what we call realm or dimension. If the third eye is interpreting things from within, there is guidance hovering as well.

This energy is especially apparent in mediumship readings or readings where outside higher energy—almost a collective group of wise energy—is coming in around a person. This energy is understood and seen by the third eye, like a window or part of the collective *soul*. What I believe I'm doing through readings with clients is opening up my third eye—the sixth energy center—which acts as an antenna or key, a part of the mind with higher understanding, or like a nice, clean window to things sometimes unseen or ignored from the more rational side of our mind. This rational mind is more stimulated or trained in our culture, and connecting it with the crown energy center, which serves as sound waves or a bright light for the room, gives the third eye information and helps us "see." All of the other energy centers below the sixth energy center help to ensure that the signal is as clear and stable as possible.

There are many different names for this universal energy that the crown connects us to—spirit, the creator, source, the divine, heredity, the universe, and God, just to name a few. Whatever it is that you believe in, it is the crown energy center that gathers this energy, or *is this energy,* for us as individuals or as a whole.

There is a bit of a dichotomy at work here as well: the dichotomy being that we humans are different than the stars or that we are not in fact connected to anything outside our body . . . to what is around us. We feel that as humans, we are made of matter that is quite different from the sky or the stars. But readings, and now science, show to the contrary. Have you heard the saying, "We are all made of stardust"? This is more than just a beautiful bit of language. *Science tells us that 93 percent of our composition is the same as that of stars.* Those glimmering beacons of light in the night (and day) are both outside of us, in the sky, and inside of us, in our DNA. In much the same way, this higher power that is the source of intuitive information is both within us and outside of us. Another way of saying this might be that we are both the self we feel as an individual human being (which we are physically) and the soul, as in the connection to heaven or things around us being within us . . . the spiritual, mental aspects of our heart and mind. This makes us more than the physical sum of our parts. Within us, as well as around us, we begin to have a connection with a deeper understanding (and responsibility) of our soul code, a vibration and understanding inside our mind and radiating from our heart. The soul is within and without our body, and we govern our soul by the choices of the self. By *without* I mean not of our body—this can be thought of as the emotions or action/reaction we choose to bring into our inner life and how and what we exhale out. The crown energy center helps the soul and the self to be whole, clear, supported, and guided.

By the guidance and protection of the crown energy center, higher wisdom can assist our intuition in whole body healing, interpreting situations, and giving the body and mind rest and kindness, because we are guided to do so by something beyond the self. What we hear as intuition might be described as the merging of the soul and the self like a husband-wife or partner-partner team to assist our life in everything. If the third eye is the president, the crown is its senior council. This group effort can bring in higher knowledge that keeps us in unison with divine, or godlike, thought and action while still having one spokesperson, or one cook in the kitchen with many wise sous-chefs.

I love to think of the energy we receive through our crown energy center as being a clear, present, kind gateway to wisdom that is special to each one of us. We are sometimes receiving information that isn't in our language, like calculus, so we often have to translate when we first connect with outside or higher logic or wisdom. Our third eye is the window or interpreter, and trust me, you will use it at times when a lot of intuitive information comes in, or you will find yourself connecting with souls (most often loved ones) who have passed away.

This wisdom speaks very differently than our competitive, fight-or-retreat society. The reason is simple, as mentioned earlier—intuition does not come in clearly through your fight-or-retreat part of the mind. The parts of the brain we use for fight-or-retreat mode and for intuitive information are different. You are making decisions versus interpreting. As well, the competition-warrior part of the brain, developed in our evolutionary past (far past, I believe), is also not the same space in the brain. It is a choice we learn to make (or disable) about whether we take our intuitive information and add e-motion (energy in motion versus stillness in knowing), which vamps our analytical reaction state, or we keep our intuitive voice connected to our crown energy center (we can do this with age and wisdom!). The warrior still believes in number one. This is contradictory to wisdom. To create this movement of active mind, we add our calming breath techniques, through the fifth energy center, as backup. This way the mind will not bring an overdriven ego in, and the heart will keep the information neutral if the heart energy center is clear, open, balanced, and mature. Ego will often stomp on this information if given a chance. This is why our ability to understand our age in years and wisdom is very helpful; we should not need to act from such a younger self, stuck in a lower energy center. Translating the information that comes from our seventh energy center requires the balance of all of our energy centers. And you are ready to understand this.

Throughout these pages, we've talked a lot about how the information we receive from intuition ultimately works toward the good of all. This is because that information is coming through a source that is for all, connects us all, and is universal. Because this energy is collective, it inherently works for the forward movement of all. It also contains broader information than we could ever possess as individuals with our singular vantage point, therefore allowing us to be of service by guiding us in the direction that will ultimately serve greater wellness. The highest, most innovative ideas (songs, inventions, modalities, creations, and lessons) are housed here. When a musician or writer says that it was as though a fully formed song or story dropped into their head, they're talking about information that is derived from the crown energy center. From the crown energy center come infinite ideas. Infinite clarity. Always inclusive, and often quite humbling.

When important information does come in for me, I have a choice: Am I going to use the information for the good of all, or am I going to sway it to leverage my own wishes or situation? You have that same choice. The universe is wise. Those who use intuitive information solely for personal gain or to the detriment of others will, at some point, find that their connection with this universal knowing is lost. The ideas of the collective and wholeness are, in fact, the very basis of the crown energy center. We do not truly gain access to this energy center until we have done the work in the previous energy centers that allows us to understand that the gifts we are born with are not just for our own gain and that we must equally give and receive. Once we understand that giving and receiving are one fluid action and that we are ultimately here to help build up ourselves and our community, *then* we can begin to deeply tap into the crown energy center. We have an awareness that the information we are receiving is not ultimately ours, even if it is coming through us or to us. When intuitive information comes in, it's for everyone—there is no seg-regation, discrimination, or preferential treatment. It's a win-win for all, even when it feels new. Intuition steers us toward complete peace and harmony on both a personal and global level.

Most of us understand or have the wisdom necessary to tap into the crown energy center by our early forties. At this point in life, there can be a lot of things pulling at our attention—partners, spouses, kids, jobs, aging par-ents, and dreams yet to be realized, just to name a few. Because our own life is very connected to and invested in others by this point, we need to constantly check in with and balance the lower energy centers. By the time we are in our thirties and forties, we have had a good, strong love relationship or two (or more!). We often have brought children into the world or we are parents or aunties or father figures to those who are not next of kin. We might be taking care of aging parents by this phase of our life. Or we are taking on a senior space at work, within a group, or in business, and we are caring for or overseeing others. By the time we have reached forty plus, most all of us have others who look up to us, whom we mentor, or whom we provide for. We might have an ex-spouse or ex-lover, but they hold an almost permanent place in our heart.

By one or all of the above experiences, we have the life experience neces-sary to see the world outside our own selves and our own best interests, if we choose to take the wiser route and do not try to defy time or turn back the clock (acting more immature or without personal responsibility). We have practice working for the wealth and health of those around us and for ourselves. But, at the same time, we might be moving too quickly or with an intention to serve an imbalanced lower energy center. This is a reminder to just be or to be in our wise, whole state of being.

Just being is important for our age, as we age, and to keep us age-free. We need to make a point of establishing this quieter foundation so that we can use the divine energy we derive from the crown to help us compassionately, lovingly, and wisely guide ourselves as well as the people we love, interact with, and are in charge of.

You can think of the crown energy center as our well of blessing and knowledge showering over us, or a great access to wisdom and higher guidance. As we've discussed, intuition is simply information of a higher vibration. The crown and heart work together to offer our wise mind, in the prefrontal cortex or otherwise, the gifts, signals, and visions that help us see and know with clarity and pristine accuracy. It really does feel otherworldly when this connection of our intuition and crown work together.

Our crown energy center is helpful in understanding this information from a higher perspective, like the three wise men or visionary energy we covet and admire in history or stories, the energies and wise ones that just know things (think Obi-Wan Kenobi), which is what many people who receive readings compare this energy to. The third eye space lets us see clearly what the crown and higher light or guidance are trying to channel, access, show, or say to us. The third eye area offers an understanding or a seeing and hearing wisdom that is absolutely amazing, and the crown gives it more connectivity to a larger understanding and scale, like conferring an even higher collective degree (the interconnectedness of people relates to more than just how it pertains to us or the lives we physically see around us). This aspect of intuition or mediumship can seem strange at first.

Our inner voice is always with us. This comes at an early age. But the wisdom and understanding we attach to that voice grow through the phases of life. We instinctively feel things around our birth but are not cognitive, nor reflective, until later. When we are young, we begin to know things in our gut, and the connection to this gut—with an open, wise, connected heart—offers wisdom and maturity that helps us to use our instinct and at times intuition appropriately. Then as we mature from here, our third eye space can offer our life a deeper, richer understanding and witness that can then be shared with others as such (an instinct starts in the gut, but we have now added another step of information or higher knowledge to our gut's tug). By the time it reaches our third eye sight, or maturation of the brain, we can start to detect and connect to a higher working at hand. Our crown offers this connection and high guidance to what we see and know (its counsel).

This is how we come to know our crown. Because being psychic and deeply intuitive is in my Italian heredity and Aquarian nature, as well as in my birth chart and destiny, and I was physically active as a child and began yoga in my early twenties, my intuition opened to a greater degree or maturity than the average bear (and earlier than most people wish for!). This has also helped me connect to my crown and guides with some success (not intentional) at an earlier age. We can connect to our crown at any age . . . but the wholeness of the knowledge will come later. This is similar to our grandmother (or parent) imparting great wisdom to us when we are young. We may not understand it completely at the time the wisdom is received, but when we're older, with experience and growth under our belt, we are often ready to understand the wisdom more clearly.

This is the same with the crown energy center. I have talked with great musicians and actors who have taken mind-altering drugs to unlock or unleash this connection. This can come with high creativity, ideas, or energy but often at a physical cost not worth it in the end. This unlocking, when done in a balanced way through our energy centers, is a lot more fun and invigorating to wake up to (there's no hangover or price to pay when it's organic). Until we have gone through some growth, we might completely ignore what we hear and what comes to us—or we just might not be aware yet of this gift of the crown energy connection.

Our third eye is a window and channel to seeing and understanding information that might feel beyond our everyday reasoning (or analytics), and this might feel a bit odd at first, trusting this type of knowledge access. The access comes through meditation, breath technique, getting proper rest, movement (including exercise, especially outside), and trust. The stillness and peace of mind that come from being diligent to take care of the self, especially as we are in our forties and coming into our next decades—this stillness makes the room for us to access our intuition (or to be in touch with our crown collective radiance). With this connection comes a deeper and wiser collective backing to every decision we make . . . a richer counsel when we make decisions and cocreate our wishes and dreams into reality via insight. This helps our intuition to keep a clear charge or balanced clarity . . . to direct us toward our wishes or dreams.

Here we learn we have a counsel at hand. This also helps us expand to use our intuition to help both home and communities, to guide complex relationships and even help (if only in prayer or meditation) conflicts between neighborhoods and countries. We see more deeply, with insight and efficiency, into the interconnectedness of the human condition as a whole, including in our families (this goes for family of origin, my husband, and children). We know in the crown that there is no complete other (the belief that we are not connected to others in body, mind, spirit), so we learn and know to treat others, whether on the street or across countries and continents, as our fellow sisters or brothers of humanity. The crown puts our intuitive understanding to greater use not just for ourselves or our family, but also to share the wisdom exponentially if we are able. The crown fuels, helps clean, and offers dressing to our window. This puts what we see individually into a whole new purposeful light. It forms a mastery that can help spread and teach in great maturity and all one peace.

Even I am not always in this space, and I am a pretty giving, accountable person. When I think about the age when we are able to come into our crown effectively and efficiently, that is often the age we are able to become grandparents (or grandparents to teens in their power source if we had children young and they also had children young). It's interesting fitting in to this age. To be clear, I feel my crown chakra in place, and I believe we can feel higher guidance throughout our life. However, when we reach the age of forty heading to fifty, we are more able to *merge*, connect, or mature as one with this wisdom or state of being . . . at a miraculous, extraordinary rate, and I personally look forward to this day. For now, and for us all, the focus of understanding our third eye and intuition, at any age, is the goal. The crown will be the golden cherry on top. For all of you over fifty, salud and mazel tov.

Through the crown, heaven and earth are believed to be merged into an accessible wise unity (this first wisdom starts in the gut at an instinctive level in our teens), and in this merging, we can reach nirvana and blissful existence often in our lifetime. We can be in this state of being with balanced excellence and deserved respect. I feel many of us already intuitively, or unconsciously, respect those in their fifties. Or those in their fifties demand or quietly command this respect by their aura or way they act in a room or situation. Indeed, deep joy and peace can be found in this energy center if we have done the work to open, balance, and enliven the energy centers below this highest point of our main energy centers. It is here that we learn there is something higher guiding us and at play in our own evolution or maturation, again, if we have grown through our energy centers, cultivating vibration and radiant balance up the spine and through the head's height.

It is interesting to think of a guard watching our back (or our parents or a loved one), an energy and support keeping our highest interests in mind. If we are a caregiver (or a worrier), this can add great comfort to our tasks and current life circumstances. That we are not alone and we can call in help in whatever form the fates, the universe, or our God will give us. Many think of the crown energy center housing our angels, our earth angel, our guides, our saints, or our higher support in a savior (like Jesus Christ), or favorite leader, or even a grandparent. I have seen them all in the crown, but mostly they cascade down beside us to have our back (or help our heart). The collective can mean things (including things like larger energy sources like universes, heavens, or realms) that are human based or that are beyond our comprehension.

This crown is for all and yet no one has discovered indisputably what this crown is made of or contains. I am not sure what or if I would believe in the crown energy source if I had not seen it visually and auditorily wise for decades now. But this is still a question for scientists and doctors. What is the brain actually seeing, projecting, or picking up on? When I reach full maturity here, I will let you know what it seems to be showing in entirety!

Not only does the crown connect for those in the know, but the crown also helps us to guide the young, the unknowing, and the more rooted. Until we connect with the crown, many of us are missing this rich guidance that helps create synchronicity, that guides and offers clarity and wisdom to what our third eye sees and knows, and that leads this all in a forward direction. I have experienced that our crown energy center is explaining what creation is capable of as opposed to what man has chosen—meaning evolution and peace could be so much further along. That we can use our intuition to help all or to help only ourselves. That we have choice and free will as humans (hence a healthy ego helps us), that universal or "all one" energy makes the puzzle fit perfectly and magically moves or influences energy (yes, like *The Matrix* again, but this is true life). This gives us knowledge in our earthly life, especially if we've lost parents and believe there is not an elder or wise influence for us to gain knowledge from.

The crown energy center is also credited as where a lot of people have visionary experiences and see guides or an energy relating to a beacon that is leading a person through a particular experience or period. This can be a near-death experience for some, or sometimes it's seen in deep meditation. I use this in more practical ways. I visualize, or round up, the guides (or the force, as I like to call them) to help me through a tough or feared situation (although fear is diminishing as I age with wisdom and intuition as my guiding point, I have to admit). But during those moments when I am fearing something—whether it's the dentist's drill, or taking a step, or being in front of a live camera (I used to be scared to give a speech of any sort, mind you, and that was planned and written), or having a hard conversation—I call in support of my guides.

How? Similarly to all the training we have had in this book. I slow my breath down. I sometimes close my eyes (unless I'm driving or talking with a child). I breathe for one to three minutes, five if it is an extra hard experience I am about to step into. And I then visualize my guidance system surrounding me with love, with their light and highest wisdom on how to quell nerves. Sometimes I literally call them in by name. I swear I begin to feel them, or at times the essence of them. Sometimes for me they include Jesus or a passed grandparent to watch my back or to keep me feeling calm, centered, and in the present moment. Sometimes it is a happy Buddha or a wise, kind mentor. I've used this for the strength to birth my children and also when experiencing disagreements with a parent, sibling, or coworker. I walk or meditate longer when I can.

You can do the same. As stated above, remember your breath. Remember your meditations. Remember your *I am*s. You can do an energy-clearing rainbow meditation (on our website www.IMcommunity.com) to clear out all your energy centers so the crown center is flowing with good golden light. You can also remember to *literally* call in specific guides or brothers and sisters who are in the afterlife and will have your back, or at least keep you out of your worrying sector of the brain (because you'll be focusing on their peace and light, transcending you out of feeling the current situation too deeply or with stress and fear). The crown energy center taps us into who and what is watching over us, and it's our connection to that bridge of feeling more conscious of support. These guides support us through this earthly life, offering bravery, warmth, and help in finding our own agency. They do not have earthly matters (or ego) holding them down.

Just *talking* about the crown energy center and these guides may be enough to make your head spin. Let us remember, the crown is composed of very light, airy, and angel-like wise energy, which is precisely why we've put so much emphasis on rooting down and centering throughout this book thus far. If we manage to tap into the crown without being grounded, we are in danger of things like hallucinations, a false god complex—meaning we think we *are* a god or one of those guides coming in supporting us—and neurosis.

Of course, plenty of people have had experiences like the ones we're talking about without doing all of the work on the lower energy centers that we've discussed in this book. There *are* other ways of getting there, such as drinking and using recreational drugs, as we spoke of. This does lead to imbalance and, of course, a low will follow the high that gets you to that place of connection. Obviously, this is not how we want to go about tapping into information. Aside from the physical detriments, without connecting the lower energy centers, chances are that the recipient of this information won't translate it correctly, will not bring it into form, or will use it in ways that it is not meant to be used. There is also a high price in karma or future life experience for ourselves or our loved ones. Remember, we are not alone and our actions do affect others, both positively and negatively. The key is, when we know better, we must do better.

So what *do* you have to do to tap into the seventh energy center in a healthy manner that also recharges your chi or life force energy? Aside from balancing all of the energy centers that come before the crown, a great next step is simply to acknowledge the universal energy that exists both beyond and within us—whatever name you do or do not ascribe to it is honestly not as important. Once you do this, you will be amazed at how it opens and grows right before your very eyes. Essentially, you're allowing it to merge with you and into your life in the most beautiful and helpful of ways. The kind of connection with loving, whole wisdom that the seventh energy center offers can be a downright life-changing and joyful experience. The more we tap into this energy, the easier and more constant it will become, infusing our life with a level of security and protection that is not often found in earthly realms.

However, it's also important to understand that the connection can be turned off if you begin to feel overwhelmed or overloaded with information, whether that is in a general or in a situational sense. Turning it off is as simple as making the choice to do so. I've certainly done this myself, and I've seen my clients do the same. When it gets to be too much, many of them do this simply by blinking their eyes and diverting their attention to something in the physical world. Similar to getting too much unsolicited advice from well-meaning family members, you can leave the room or energy at any time. It can help to focus on the breath or heartbeat, which will support the upper and lower energy centers.

The Seventh Energy Center and the Physical Being: The Physicality of Energy

Once we get up to the crown energy center, it may seem difficult to understand how our physical body can be affected by this crown or "overhead" energy. But it is. When we are unable to connect with the higher universal energy around us, our life is more difficult. We think we have all the answers, or we feel we are alone as life gets harder and situations get more complex (including when our intuition comes in and shifts the course of our life). Life's questions and choices can become easily overwhelming. And understandably so.

As we move into our forties and reach a place in our life in which others rely on us financially, physically, and emotionally, and as we begin to realize that our parents are people, we might begin to feel we are an island, that we are not supported by a higher nurturer. Our body might feel like it needs a little extra TLC, as we are not tapped into our higher well of supported radiance and light, which in turn affects choices. When the responsibilities of daily life—which mount in our forties, though we experience that stress throughout our life, of course—weigh us down, it can begin to feel as though we're trying to breaststroke our way through mud and algae, with no solid ground in sight.

The crown energy center, and the connection to higher energies it provides, adds an extra little bit of fairy dust to our life, which can create more vitality during a time when our body is changing and our children and parents are getting older. This may seem like a little thing, but it's not. Perhaps you've noticed that as people grow older, there are more and more differences between the ways age expresses itself in individuals. While we're in our twenties, the vast majority of us are young and vibrant. As the years continue to advance, it seems as though there is more of a spread. Some forty-five-year-olds are nearly indistinguishable from a twenty-something. Others are tired and world-worn. Of course, some of this has to do with genetics, but a *lot* of it has to do with how we live and interpret our life, which influences our biology. Feeling supported and connected lifts so much of the weight off of our shoulders, allowing us to remain young at heart and quite vibrant. This difference from person to person becomes even more pronounced as age advances further. Have you ever met an octogenarian who has a youthful spark in his or her eyes despite advanced age? That's the magic this crown energy center offers.

The crown energy center allows us to tap into vitality and assists us in aging peacefully and gracefully. It brings us a virtual waterfall of blessings, part of which is this enhanced physicality. Many intuitives I know relate this energy center to a golden light or that glow that seems to emanate from some, those people you meet who have a certain indefinable "it" factor. That is greatly supported from the crown and comes from a source much bigger than any one person.

The other thing about being tapped into our crown energy center is that once we reach it, our other energy centers have had the time and opportunity to grow and mature healthfully and wholly. Mind, body, and spirit are holistically connected. Our soul sings light. And when all of our energy centers are balanced and operating in sync, we are truly healthy. Through many years of readings, I have come to believe that the Western world experiences such a significant rate of heart disease, breast cancer, and problems with our lungs because most of us are only activating the first two or three energy centers of the body. That fresh chi or life force energy cannot flow sufficiently through closed centers. I truly believe that if we lived in a world where all of our energy centers were cleared, balanced, and all the way open through the crown, we would see a lot less chronic disease.

Aside from lacking overall holistic health and vibrancy, there are some specific physical cues that may indicate your crown energy center is imbalanced. If you are overrelying on the crown energy center without being grounded enough in the lower energy centers, you may experience sharp headaches or mental confusion. If you are *too* grounded and not connected with your crown energy center, you may experience negative effects on posture, fascia (the connective tissue in the body), and joint health. All of this is the result of compression and lack of open chi or energy, which is an offshoot of our life force's inability to move freely and easily up and down the body. Another physical representation of being too grounded is that our body becomes acidic as a response to feeling helpless and choosing lackluster foods. Circulation can become poor in the legs and lower stomach, and elimination may become difficult.

Without balanced energy centers and an open crown, we begin to make life choices that are generally not healthful and can, therefore, lead to a range of physical ailments.

Now that we have made our way through the entire range of energy centers leading all the way up to the crown, when you experience physical issues, you can begin to identify them with the relevant energy center and make shifts from there. As we discussed at the very beginning of this book, maintaining balance within the energy centers is not a one-and-done process—it's ongoing. Throughout your life, as different stages and events occur, you will find yourself going back to certain areas to align and rebalance. This is all part of the process of attaining higher and higher levels of wisdom.

The Seventh Energy Center and the Emotional Being: All the Support We Need

For as much as we are independent creatures, we all need support and guidance. We are hardwired for community. This has nothing to do with personal strength or lack thereof; it's simply how we are made. The further along we get in life, the more difficult it can feel or be to find that sweet support. Just as our responsibilities and obligations multiply as the years go by, so too do those of our friends and family, sometimes making it impossible to offer each other the support we would like to. There can also be a toxic buildup of old, unresolved feelings and emotions.

There is a fine line between a healthy need for support and being emotionally reliant on others, however. When we depend entirely on others for our emotional well-being, we open up a whole host of problems, from codependence to becoming energy drains, depleting and otherwise adversely affecting others' emotional health and clarity. Narcissistic behaviors leave the upper energy centers with little room to breathe or thrive, both in the self that is exuding the behavior and those experiencing the behavior. This benefits no one!

The crown energy center, on the other hand, is an endless source of support we carry within ourselves. When our crown energy center is open and we are connected through it to that which is greater than ourselves, the higher energy above and around us is plentiful and infinite. We are never alone and never in danger of requiring too much support in a way that may be detrimental to ourselves or to others. Wisdom is infinite and beyond ego. The same cannot be said about human beings.

Not only do we receive the support that we need from the energy that surrounds us, but we also *add* to the oneness and expansiveness of that energy by utilizing it. When we open up our crown energy center, it helps everyone around us through osmosis, as those around us can feel the crown's light (and might credit you for the good feeling). As we become healthier, more supported, and act from a clearer place, so do those around us in a wonderful be-gifted kind of way.

As with everything else, moderation comes into practice here. Just as we cannot emotionally overtax others with our own situations and issues, we also cannot live so wholly in our crown energy center that we end up becoming emotionally burdened by the information of others or guidance of another voice. This is why it is so important to understand that we *can* turn off the information stream that comes from the crown energy center when need be. I learned this the hard way.

Several years ago, I took a break from readings to focus on being a mother and wife. Early one evening as I was hanging out with my kids, I felt a tap on my shoulder and heard a woman speaking very quickly. I continued playing, speaking to the voice as I was drawing with chalk with my child. I hoped that the voice would understand and quiet, as they usually do when I ask, as I have learned that we have more ability to lead in matters of this type of energy than we think. (When I have been asked to help children who see ghosts or energy, what often works is simply empowering the children to tell the energy to go away.) This particular time, though, she didn't just go away. I began to get the feeling that it was a mother talking to me, so I moved inside our house (not sure why, to feel "safer" and more grounded under a roof maybe?!) to listen. She showed me her two boys and that they were currently in a different state with their dad. She showed me the weather, land, and house where her kids were, but despite the visual, I still couldn't pick up on exactly where they were right away.

Feeling like I needed to focus on what this voice was trying to tell me, I sat down on my little one's bed, turned all of my attention to the spirit attempting to contact me, and said mentally, "Okay. Show me what you need to show me." She said that her name was Susan. I thought she said her last name was Cox, but I wasn't 100 percent sure. She then told me that her sons had a different last name than she did. She continued to speak, but I couldn't understand everything she was saying. I did my best to be open. I did understand enough of what Susan was saying to make out that her husband was going to hurt her two boys. She had passed away but was still a mother and a guardian of her children, even in the afterlife. Though her energy wasn't dark, she was trying to convey to me a horrible situation, one I simply didn't want to delve into with my own children so close.

I held on to the troubling information for a few days because I wasn't sure exactly who she was or the specifics of what she was trying to tell me. I spoke with my husband about the situation and then visited a great healer to see if she might be able to shed some light on it. Before I even had a chance to explain what was happening, the healer picked up the older of the two boys in my aura—the same one, physical details and all, that Susan had been trying to show me.

A couple of weeks later, Josh Powell was in the national news. It turned out that he had helped murder his wife, Susan Cox Powell, a few years earlier, and that he had just killed his sons and himself by setting their house on fire. I was devastated because I knew these were the boys Susan had been trying to get me to help, and I hadn't been able to pick up on what she was trying to tell me. Particularly as a mother, I struggled with the fact that I wasn't able to assist these two boys in any way. While logic, of course, says, "What would I have been able to do?" I had learned from many previous situations that the contact would not come in if there were not a reason or a chance to help or save someone. From this experience, I learned how important it is to completely close the crown energy center when we are in a place where we do not wish to receive information from more of a collective stance, as I was during this time. I knew that as soon as I heard this mother's story I would actively help, and I wanted to make sure I was in a time and space physically to do this. I later spoke to law enforcement about a few details Susan spoke of. A few details came out in the news (not by my help—they did their work stunningly). Personally, I had to strike a balance with helping others without leaving my own children for long.

The process of doing this involves vocally or silently setting the intention to hear these voices clearly and listening well objectively (to receive the information before becoming emotional after, which is understandable). It is important to take this step when we simply don't have the bandwidth to receive more information or when we feel caught between two worlds (which can happen in our everyday life at times). Then we can help in whatever way we can or wish to do so. This was, of course, an extreme situation that most people will never have to deal with, but it does illustrate an important point. Similar to having too many cooks in the kitchen, sometimes once we open the doors, more comes in than is technically invited. It is important to find healthy outlets when this happens. Mine are walks, yoga, forgiveness mantras or sayings, gratitude, and sometimes tears.

Most of the time, though, we do want to remain open to the flow of information and energy from the crown. When our crown energy center is in balance, we receive—and can give to others—the beautiful gift of knowing that we are protected, guided, and supported from a place that is above and beyond humanity. No matter what our human circumstances are, we will never feel alone, for we are not. We will rest easy in the knowledge that we can ask for those things we need and that our best interests will always be provided for, even in those moments when relief might seem impossible and when being provided for looks different than we expected it would. This is to say, we understand that we can cocreate our own destiny. We cocreate our health, happiness, joy, and wealth, and the cocreating of intuitive listening and receiving (it takes two, remember, like most all things) of many different kinds of higher connection becomes much, much easier because we are tapped into that universal energy.

I have used this force many times to finish a project, to get support for helping a friend or family member, or to assist my children in holding on to their joie de vivre. I do this by centering my breath, calming my mind into being more in my limbic system and less in my analytical thoughts, feeling my feet (visually or literally touching my feet more firmly to the ground or floor), and lastly, surrounding myself, my loved ones, and my space (with directed attention or prayerfully) with light or golden-like energy. This helps me feel like all intuitive information is coming in the name of healing and love. Like a trained muscle (or x-ray vision, just teasing) this will become easier with time, and also each situation will build onto itself with depth of information.

To understand connection to higher guidance in unique or new forms, it is helpful to understand that there is no such thing as empty space in our life or universe—there is only energy out of its unity with light or in another form. This is woman and man's free will or choices, as well as whatever (or wherever) we think souls and sages go when we "die." How we treat Mother Earth plays a role in this, as do the cycles of the tides and the planets. This is what many religious and sacred texts discuss—how to handle our human element and what happens after life on earth. Some forms of this energy of light (or not seeming of light), we cannot necessarily see. To think about this in visual terms, think of the space you see between two trees when you look up toward the sky. You may experience the space between them as nothing. But in fact, it's not really nothing at all. There is energy running between those two trees that is simply invisible to human (two) eyes. This is negative space or the unseen. Positive (the seen) and negative space are equally important. When we are working on manifesting an outcome or drawing on intuition, we are engaging with that invisible energy and negative space that, while we can't see it, nonetheless very much exists. We have the power to work with those forces or elements greater than ourselves to formulate that energy into something more tangible. Energy that is out of form still exists.

Recently, my friend Grace was feeling tired and burnt out. She has an incredible understanding of how to use intuition to create change yet, at the same time, she was worn out from a job she had just completed, and as a wife and mother, she found little time to shift some aspects of her life into a more balanced (and enjoyable) schedule. She knew she wanted to have the same zest for life and her work, and she could tell that her choices were literally causing her grief and pain. Her beloved family was supporting her, but she knew she needed to change a few things within for a better "through out" (her life). She was suffering through work, but still showing up, and her body was feeling the effects of being surrounded by unhappiness. Finally, Grace got out a piece of paper and wrote out, very specifically, what she wanted in a new job experience. On this piece of paper, she wrote down a couple powerful, fun-filled names of talented people in her industry with whom she wanted to work; the kind of hours she wanted to work; and where she wanted to work. Since Grace worked in television—an extremely competitive field—she knew logically that the odds of getting everything she wanted weren't on her side. But she ignored that part of her thinking, kept writing, and then put the list away.

It took less than two days for everything Grace wrote on that list to come to fruition. A phone call came offering Grace everything she had requested from the universe, including the salary and the ability to work only two days a week. It was blissful. Not only does Grace love the show and actors she is working with now, but also she is having a ball in the lighthearted environment she had always dreamed of.

Grace had known the power of healing through trusting her gut and had done readings with others and with myself, and she was connected to her powerful intuition. Grace had been doing her *I Am* mantras for almost a year by that time, even wearing her IM bracelet every day. She was becoming aware, through this process, that if she was to direct her life, taking the bull by the horn, her guides and higher intelligence would partner with her requests. And she could stay calm in the process, even as she had not seen her life clearly at times when overworked. Grace directed, and surrendered to, this act of trust, and it worked beautifully and in real time.

Like Grace, when we are tapped into the crown and working with powers beyond us, we have the profound ability to mold that energy into those things we need or wish for. Grace used her open third eye and gut in unison for physical change to execute, to see it was time to move on in her job, and she brought in higher help by making that list and letting her guides and angels go to work (they love direction). This showed all involved, including her family and coworkers (both old and new), the power of the infinite resource or what is within us and around us. Most importantly, Grace was able to show her "self" the great power she had within, unifying her gut instinct, her higher knowing, and help above and all around to manifest a new infinite pool of possibility.

There is an infinite well around us. All we have to do is to rest in the full and complete understanding that life is an ever-unfolding gift and all we have to do is be open to the blessings it offers. Those who do not experience or understand this gift may wish us or wish us not to help them unwrap it. It helps to understand that we are literally surrounded not only by an infinite well of possibilities but also by an infinite source that is ready, willing, and, in fact, *eager* to help us bring those possibilities to fruition. In record time!

The Seventh Energy Center and the Intellectual Being: Putting Intuitive Information into Play

There is a saying that goes, "The only thing we can control in life is our response." Although intuition can certainly help us better our life, the human experience will always include events that are difficult. This is often how we experience growth. During certain points in life, it can be far easier said than done to remain even-keeled, especially as our life is imploding around us. The crown energy center is extremely helpful in disseminating the negative energy that can sometimes settle around us during these difficult moments.

The seventh energy center helps us to better understand the information we are being given and guides us toward the best action, even when the waters are at their roughest. It also teaches us how to be less reactive by letting us witness more of our thoughts (and at times, actions) and create a new pattern or path. We become less reactive by understanding that the brain has different parts to use or draw from, giving us a guidance system we can hear and understand with a clear, present, centered experience. Remember, intuition and the crown energy center are connecting to action, not so much to reaction. Intuition wants to help in this current moment, even giving clarity to our irrational (or overly analytical or emotional) thoughts so we can let them go. We can assist in the process of centering our thoughts by taking quiet time and fostering positive feelings or affirmations (the simple *I Am* is an example), both of which allow us to connect to our centered intuitive being, including our higher guidance system, our third eye, our personal truth, and our heart. From here, we can act, pause, or reflect as needed. Meditation is a great way of accomplishing this, as is repeating an affirming thought or sentence to enforce positive thinking.

And of course, once we are up in the crown energy center, one of the greatest tasks we must all face is letting go of using only left-brain logic. To reap the full benefits of the crown, it helps to accept the fact that there is more to this world than our logical mind recognizes. Once we're open to it, we begin to realize that uncanny events and occurrences that seem to run counter to all probability are all around us. These things run the gamut from relatively subtle and mundane signs to extraordinary events or connections with those who have passed.

I did an intuitive reading with my client Kate during a darker-feeling time in her life when she was contemplating divorcing her husband. As we spoke, I kept seeing purple lilies. I told her to be on the lookout for these flowers as a way of knowing she was on the right path. A couple of weeks later, Kate and her husband officially decided to get a divorce. She walked out of her home *the next morning* to find purple lilies near her sidewalk line (she had planted none and had no knowledge they were already in some form in her yard). They were blooming, a sign of present movement, like spring and new beginnings (and it was spring figuratively but not literally). She took great solace in this, knowing that despite the fact that her marriage had ended, all would be well. That new life was in bloom. From this moment, the sky got clearer (in her mind and mind's eye) and signs came forward showing she had made the right decision.

Kate found out her husband was being quite dishonest (he claimed she was crazy, and "reading into things" . . . which she was!), and I was so proud of her finding her power. Kate trusted her gut and began to ask the universe for more signs. She was ready for her own and her family's more truthful existence. She was surprised when she began to see receipts in her dreams; this then connected to stories that began to surface of her partner's whereabouts instead of being home helping support her and raise the children. She was ready to honor the signs and align with the love she wished to model for her children.

Friends saw Kate's bravery, and this brought new acts of friendship (while also causing some needed letting go of friends who were not holding Kate's heart in mind and were caught gossiping hurtfully). This aspect of Kate's being present in the now (and aware of truth) gave a more honest connection to women around her. Kate also noticed their three children were happier almost instantly upon hearing the news. Although there were tears at times as they would go through the heartache of friends (and the friends' parents) talking about them, and the newness of two homes took some time for transition, they were energetically healthier instantly. It was like their aspects of being knew the health of creating room for a new now. Even I was surprised how quickly Kate and her children realigned their energy into more peaceful being. These incidents of profound peace and newfound joy instilled in Kate a confidence in the universe and propelled her to become more aware of the world around her and those little signs and synchronicities that pop up in *all* of our lives, despite the fact that, all too often, we fail to notice them.

Kate did exactly what readings recommend clients do, which is to take steps based on signs and synchronicity and turn those messages into a best-case–scenario reality. Then watch, stay present, and believe in the new: feel the deep support and love that follows (including with your gut or self-worth). By tuning in in this manner and trusting the information that is being provided to us through the seventh energy center, we get out of our fight-or-flight brain and allow higher wisdom to guide our actions . . . even if we don't know exactly where they're leading or why they're leading us there. It is so symbolic that the crown energy center hovers above our heads because what it is essentially doing is lifting us out of our brains and bodies and into something higher.

Subtle yet personally meaningful signs like Kate experienced are very common. In her case, the result of following those guideposts was profound. Much of the time, however, the results are subtler and simply make day-to-day life smoother. You can use the information conveyed to you by the seventh energy center for everything from determining what plane tickets to buy, to deciding what route to take to your destination, to knowing when it's time to conclude a relationship. You are adding higher wisdom and support, a counsel to what you see and feel that helps you turn your intuitive knowing into action. To do this, we have to be willing to let go of old patterning—the habits we fall back in or the fear we buy into (in Kate's case, being alone or damaging the kids)—the best we can and to go with the flow of the moment. We have to trust these signs and then *act* on them. We have to take that knowledge and turn it into form. The more we do this, the more signs will appear. So many people receive intuition but never act on it.

The Seventh Energy Center and the Spiritual Being: We Have All the Answers

We've spent a lot of time in this chapter talking about the divine, higher nature of the energy that filters into us through our crown energy center. Bear in mind, though, that the seventh energy center has nothing to do with religion—our relationship with religion emerges from the first energy center, where our needs for inclusive community, safety in numbers, security, and basic rules are formed. The source that we're talking about in the seventh energy center is completely separate from and has little bearing on religion. It does not involve judgment, boundaries, hierarchy, or guilt. Whatever faith you do or do not subscribe to, we all possess and have the potential to work with the information of the crown energy center. The separation between the higher energy of the crown and religion can be a difficult one for people to wrap their heads around—I frequently see both clients and friends struggle with the idea that the two can peacefully coexist.

It can feel uncomfortable to give credence to something beyond and greater than ourselves for those of us who have been brought up in a religion that puts limitations on the power of people and acts as though saints and figures like Jesus were not just a bit human, and taboos those things that exist beyond our ego self. I do believe, though, and have now seen in a cascade of readings and situations, that on some level, no matter how deep down, most of us know that the energy we're talking about in this chapter is real. It is good to bring this fact into consciousness. Honestly it can be quite comforting, joyful . . . and even at times humorous. We've all seen it at some point through an experience in which there's more than meets the eye. Acknowledging the presence of this energy is very important to receiving it wholly. The more we acknowledge that it's real and true, the more access we have to the information and positive energy that flow in through it. This, in turn, creates a lot more health, wealth, assistance, and comfort in the feeling of being part of something greater than us—something that deeply and genuinely cares for us. Intimacy. Or intimately.

Once we are tapped into our seventh energy center, we will understand that no borders exist. They do not exist between us as human beings, between us and the earth we walk upon, or between ourselves and the healthy energy that surrounds us. And when we come to this realization—when we really *feel* this with everything that we are—*everything* changes for the better. We know we don't need a middleman for our happiness—be that a partner, parent, religious figure, or psychic. Our joy spouts up from the well within, and we take more responsibility for our own actions. The crown energy center is expansive and all-inclusive. The biggest sign that your seventh energy center is open and activated is when you have that magnetic feeling of peace-filled unity and you understand that you are never, ever alone. You are ready to share your wealth—including all of the gifts you've received from your God, your world, or your universal law—with *everyone*, not just those who think, look, or behave like you do.

It is also critical to understand that information we receive is not a product of our own powers but comes from universal energy and is available to all of us who choose to tap into it. I've found that those with an imbalanced gut or gut health can confuse the information they receive as their own or for them exclusively. The crown energy center helps us even out our ego, helping us *mature* into an "all oneness" mindset. I have seen many people, whether socially or in readings, receive these amazing downloads and not realize that they are not the source of it nor are they solely responsible for it. This happens quite often with highly creative souls and those who are celebrated for an act, performance, discovery, or success. You can usually tell who believes in the "all one" and who believes in the success being theirs. These fine souls believe that they are the *root or source* of the information rather than simply serving as a transmitter or a receiver for it.

This high creativity, invention, and enlightened state can be too coveted, even for a person with an open third eye, and it's used without sharing all too often. If we are taking the information or creation received from a higher place and claiming it as our own, this can affect our life negatively, especially in today's age of transparency and more feminine (connective) support. The power is then misguided and can be misused. This can lead to delusions we do not want anyone to suffer through. This can be that a person feels overly godly or has incarnated as a great power figure. This holding of power will have a natural high or love. Remember, we wish to stay centered. To feel natural nirvana and to feel one with all there is, we must let go of ego.

Over the years I've worked as an intuitive, the thousands of clients I've met with have asked questions about a wide variety of situations. A favorite question is always: *How do I tap into my own intuition?* I tell each and every one the same thing: begin to understand you have it within, and doors will open. This book is a product of the many questions they ask after I say this! And understandably so—this road to opening our intuition can feel wild and klutzy. Or scary. And who wants to feel or get stuck in these spaces? In the end, you do not need me, but you do need guidance and trust in something bigger than yourself, more positive and higher than human thought, to navigate and utilize your intuition. That guidance will never come solely from a teacher, guru, psychic, guide, leader, or religious group. A lot comes from the connective aspects to these voices. Activation and support of intuition is a part of the conscious collective—and you are *already* an important part of that collective. If you keep your radar up, strong support will come through from what appears a magical, higher place to give you what you need, no matter how big or small.

Crown Energy Center Saying

For this final meditation, let's open and connect to everything and everyone. Begin by reflecting on which of these sayings or mantras most resonates with you (or, if you'd like, create one of your own, beginning with the phrase *I am*).

If you feel ready, simply using *I am* is very powerful, like the waves coming in and the waves going out, like the inhale (*I*) and the exhale (*am*) as one full act; oneness. This is the beginning of a balanced, more whole feeling of present *anew*.

I am present.
I am here.

JILL WILLARD

I am connected.

I am being.

As you sit or lie down quietly, gently stretch and scan your body for tight or congested areas. Visualize fresh, clear air flowing into each tight or congested spot as you breathe, with the intention of opening up your body's energy to help open the crown center. While you gently stretch, begin to come into your body and your present moment.

Now let's visualize the body as a clear vessel of light or power. Notice where your shine comes from. Is it in the gut, the heart, or your third eye? All of these centers work positively.

If you are lying down, disturbing yourself as little as possible, sit up, remaining connected to your breath as you move. See the light around and within you radiating and growing, pushing out all of your thoughts until there is just light.

Begin to incorporate your saying or mantra into your mind, centering your thoughts with each breath. Connect a ray or multiple rays of light, and watch them enliven above your head and then go down into each energy center (or only the crown if doing more feels too scary or strange). Have the rays of light radiate and shine inside the center of each energy center and radiate outward like the spokes of a wheel. Then go down the spine, through the third eye, down into the throat, through the heart, down into the gut, the pleasure organs, down through the hips, legs, and feet . . . and visualize this light traveling back up . . . all the way up again through the third eye, continuing up through the soft spot on your head, that spot or opening that you have located since birth. Send the light up above this spot, up through your crown. Send it all the way up until it connects to the guides or light (or halo) you visualize above you. After a few moments (or minutes here), bring the radiant energy back down into the heart. Here, let this warm glow *grow*.

The color gold might surround you, or you might see a white fog or a clear white light. Take a moment to surround your entire self in this feeling and space. Shower yourself with this light and balanced, peaceful feeling. When you're ready, connect back to your breath (intently focus on breathing in and out) and wiggle your fingers and toes gently. Open your eyes if they are closed.

Once you are back in your centered space in the heart or roots, notice if you have opened up a new space above you or around you. See if you feel lighter.

Now it is time for your simple *I Am* meditation that you have learned to do in each chapter of this book. If you have the time, try a five-minute *I Am* meditation after the above visualization (or guided meditation) with one of the *I am* suggestions above. You can also sit quietly if you feel your mind is calm and just radiate your simple *I am* again. Inhaling *I,* exhaling *am.* This act is about presence, joy, and grace—feeling connected to the higher wisdom and anew waiting for you. A new *now.*

Open your eyes.

Give thanks.

Notice you are here.

And you are supported.

You have now learned how to begin accessing your deep intuition in a clear, balanced way. You are an *intuitive being.* Enjoy all the blessings ~ grace be!

The Crown Guide

What it governs:	Connection with the whole self, divine, all oneness, universal law, complete guidance
Ages:	Early 40s onward!
Color:	White, gold. Some see plum fading into magenta.

In balance:	Vibrant and smoothly running physical form; the "it" factor; calm, centered thoughts and heart rate; a glow; feeling of support; ability to tap into a higher intelligence and to more easily manifest those things we need in life.
Imbalanced:	Spacy thoughts or neuroses, migraines, numbing in nerves and stiff joints, feeling of being alone and unsupported in the world, delusions of grandeur.
Supportive foods:	Water, purified or salt, absorbed through the skin or top of head/scalp; cleansing herbs; aloe vera; various seeds like chia and sesame; bone and vegetable broths; essential oils (topical) for balance or unity.
Beneficial practices:	Meditation and positive thought; asking for help from guides above and all around, including loved ones passed; gratitude practices; awareness of breath.
Sayings:	*I am present.* *I am here.* *I am connected.* *I am being.*

FINAL THOUGHTS

Being intuitive brings a love and clarity that can only be explained as presence or the now. It provides us with eyes that can see life radiantly and intently. With intuition, love becomes more vivid and real.

No, being intuitive does not make us perfect. But it *does* allow us to catch our unawareness and our reactions more quickly, and to act from a place of grounded, loving wisdom rather than from a place of misinformation. Our mind and heart become lighter in this process. Aging becomes a lot more fun and enlightening.

Listening to our gut can make life much richer and more meaningful. Using our intuition makes everything better, especially our connection to one another. Since the founding days of our U.S. culture, we have been taught to focus less on intimacy; it's time we bring back connection and focus on what's real versus what is perceived or projected. Most projections come from fear or lack of information. This type of information is more binding than freeing. It is time to honor the chaos of only focusing outward and, instead, enjoy the realignment inward that being intuitive brings. This brings life. This brings love. This brings the new.

Be brave and be intuitive. Bring joy and understanding to what intuition reveals. You are already here and ready. Allow yourself to be here. Carry on in your quest.

Energy centers are incredible spiritual, powerful wheels or circles of energy, an energy system that comes into full use or synthesis when we support its radiant subtlety. This is with healthful choices to support our strength and balance. This offers us a lighter, happier, more peaceful experience on earth. It lets us hear and act in new innovative ways . . . constantly and consistently.

As you have read in this book, every energy center matters, and each part of us bring in our life experience, including many years of living. And our experiences have brought us here now. I would like to add life force energy as the final concept of an open, balanced intuition, and a life of an *intuitive being*.

This book has been written with great joy that it was gifted to us all by the combination of focused work and a mightier source. It was a pleasure to be one of the vessels passing on this information to you. Above all, stay open to this information . . . continue your quest toward the freedom and great love that intuition can bring into your life. It's quite a force. May this force be with you!

We have learned that by giving ourselves good, clean food and enough water as well as adequate rest, movement, and meditation, we can keep our energy centers, and human body, in optimal and wise health and harmony. We have also learned techniques of letting go of old emotion or old thought patterns, past memories, or old, stale relationships that are holding us back rather than enlivening our spirit and soul experience.

Each *I Am* meditation brings in chi or life force. Getting outside supports this life force or vital energy. What is most important is that we bring *in* (*inhale*) and send *out* (*exhale*) life force energy to keep our energy systems and the connective space between them alive, vital, and richly *supported*.

Prioritize your life to include yourself in the magic and power of repeating your *I Am* sayings or mantras. May these be a gateway or golden path to your higher self and your happier living being. Presence creates many presents and gifts. Dreams realized. Living dreams.

As I was editing the final pages of this writing, Steven Spielberg gave a speech on living our dream: that the hardest thing to listen to is your instincts, your intuition, because it never shouts and always whispers. . . . just as we shared throughout this writing. May it now be easier to listen and follow this whispering voice within, which connects us with every dream unimaginable.

I have faith that you have now found new ways to address, and connect, to your intuition. Remember, this a relationship, one that can add great pleasure, magic, and support to your every breath. Do not forget to water your garden, your seeds of intention, with mindful, clear breath and fresh chi energy.

Meditate. Meditate. Meditate.

We created this site to help you with the visuals, to present the technique in color, and to give you tools: www.IMcommunity.com.

Every meditation will increase chi. Every act of quiet and stillness will do it. Prayer, mindfulness, and pranayama breathing will help. Yoga, walking, dancing, playing. Loving and forgiving. Breath techniques and anything that enhances your increased oxygen consumption and release of carbon dioxide. Importantly, it is the will and the belief in your great life force, combining with the greater union of life force (air, sky, God, universe, creator, source) that will help enliven this act; the *knowing* that you are meant to be *here* . . . and you matter.

Visualize Our Life Force

Chi is what creates movement in us as living beings. Anything that is living (whether plant, animal, human being, or angel) has chi or life force energy.

So now let's move energy through our third eye and our newfound energy centers to feed our force within, and all around, to its fullest potential. Let's activate and use what we have learned. Let the four aspects of being—the physical body, emotions, intellect, and spirit—unify and soar. Let e-motion, energy in motion, out. Let it flow. Release the rocks. Alkalinize and be free of old discomforts, DNA, and disease.

Life force energy enlivens our energy centers, clears out (like a good rain or wind), and helps us hear that inner *whisper* . . . our intuition will continue to grow and flourish with vital new energy entering us every day. I cannot state this enough: intuition likes the new and the now. It helps remove old blockages for newfound energy, grace, and forgiveness—for *feeling alive and thriving*.

Use this new energy to journal or write down your feelings and what you have learned. Take the time to have clearing and helpful conversations. No longer avoid conflict, or the truth. Dedicate time to the energy centers that feel weakest to you or are just beginning to open. Make a commitment to letting go, or cleaning house, until you feel light and free.

Energy Centers and Life Force Energy in Union

We know what energy centers are. It is important that we revisit life force energy.

In many cultures this is known as chi (vital energy) brought in by breath or mindfulness techniques. For many, by bringing the five supports of our higher health (clear food, water, rest, meditation, and movement), we are able to breathe deeply and with clarity, with more intention, and with respect to the gift of oxygen and *life*.

This life force is what will enliven, support, and clear our energy systems that are open to receive this life force energy. This clear force is like a shot of caffeine or a drink of water from the clearest spring—it enlivens our soul and ignites our intuition, giving us the power, energy, and grace to carry on into the new.

Happy anew, Intuitive Beings.

WITH GRATITUDE

This writing would not be here now without the gifts and powers of these many women and men below:

Nikki Van Noy, for . . . all.

Coleen O'Shea, for holding space for the new.

Libby Edelson at HarperElixir—your trust got us all here.

Erin Branning Keogh, for her brilliance and bravery. You make this world much better. Thank you for your edits of the heart, and the rooting of soul anew.

Carol, the alchemist, for originally getting this to New York and back again, and for her ageless, glowing wisdom.

Shell, for always being a believer, for the music through the ages, and the great achiever of power in supporting family.

My mom, for teaching me attention to detail and to show up on time.

My dad, for showing me how far kindness can go.

Jess, for teaching me the importance of letting go and for raising the next generation of lady sisters.

Jennifer Freed, for explaining this path in color. For always having a direct line to peace and harmony.

Dharam Dev Kaur Khalsa, for teaching me forgiveness and what eye contact and love encompass.

Rosie Mac for her long, glowing table.

Erika (aka "Mother Teresa"), whose offerings are never small or lacking in taste.

Julie Rader, for female power, heart, light, friendship, and that first Mukti meditation evening, when everything changed.

Nicole Stoddard, for the walks and serendipity. Many years, my friend.

T Jackson, for her amazing open-door policy.

Cherish, for infinity and beyond.

"Miss" (Mrs.) Diane O'Brien, for being a pillar with each birth, death, and rebirth of all things meaningful and important. Thank you for your care and for being a cornerstone.

Luisa, Judy (and Uncle Joe)—this book would still be in the heart without your support, meals, and conversations. For Ilventos (.com) feeding us all.

Gigi—you are a bridge for our family and a woman who gives like no one else. You are a true artist.

Wendy, for all your prayers and faith. To all the children that give us such purpose and who make sure we show up for holy growth.

Katherine, for UW, and for being a gift of strength and voice beyond measure.

Mon, for being the first spiritual female warrior within walking distance who supported this dearly. For your chair to hang my tired head. You fed me on every level.

Lo Roxburgh, for standing up, for aligning growth and celebration, for smiling through lessons, and for supporting everyone else in theirs.

Elise, for giving me my first monster edit for *goop*, and for forward change.

All the outlaws, you know who you are.

All the angels, you know who you are.

All the mamas who held my hand and our children with laughter at the big wooden gate.

My next ring of family, deep tree roots, Twin Lakes dearest, you made me a cougar.

Julie Hayashida, your partnership at the end of every line is irreplaceable. You've made me who I am by listening and standing tall. Your insights are for the ages.

Megs, for your constant bravery and pure intent, and for making this world more even.

Jake and Nikki, for *all* the salted toasts. For the strength and beginnings of www.IMcommunity.com.

Lydia, for holding my left hand, my right hand, and always bringing so much light.

For JJ—you are the biggest shot of love, strength, and womanhood. You are the Goddess of Good, Mama.

To Vimma and Vimmia.com for the lovely radiance while meditating.

Kat/the other K Wigg, for her sistahood and equipping us with pretty, calming tools.

Amy Stanton—you are the magical. May the land unfold before your power and grace. Being all you already are.

Ellen Padnos, for your ear and eyes. Your ability to see and hear extend beyond human measurements. You are beyond a gift to this planet. Thank you.

To the Joy Full-givers' First Fridays (and Tuesday evenings)—may all forces of love be your guides. You are all visionaries.

Grace, amazing peaceful warrior. Thank you.

Kristen and Melis, stars and star striking you are. Thank you for being.

Willard family, thank you for the power of the family gathering and your hands-on help whenever needed. To Amber, Court, and Blake, three cherished dancing elves . . . keep being you.

Joe and Rose, for my first understanding of love and angels.

Ms. Gwyneth P, for her enriching, inquisitive conversation, her inspiration toward wonder and the feminine . . . and her guidance to this generation. *Grazie mille.*

To Marky, the rock, pillar, and biggest champion for the cause of kindness, caring, and fearlessness. Although fear is good, you always held mine. I love you.

To our warm, wonderful children: Abe, Ella, and Juju the bear. Thank you for supporting us in making this world a better place for you.